Duration, Convexity, and Other Bond Risk Measures

Frank J. Fabozzi, Ph.D., CFA
Adjunct Professor of Finance
School of Management
Yale University

WILEY

To my wife Donna, and my children, Francesco and Patricia.

Editorial consultant: Megan Orem
Cover designer: Scott C. Riether
Cover color selector: Francesco Fabozzi

ISBN: 1-883249-63-5

Table of Contents

Chapter 1

Overview

A major risk faced by bond investors is interest rate risk. This is the risk that the value of a position in a bond or the value of a bond portfolio will decline due to an adverse interest rate movement. Managers must be capable of controlling this risk. But, controlling this risk does not mean eliminating it. Rather, it means adjusting a bond position or a bond portfolio to capitalize on the manager's expectations. However, a manager is typically not given total freedom in selecting a portfolio's interest rate risk exposure. There are constraints that are often imposed by clients and, for regulated entities, there are constraints imposed by regulators.

To effectively control interest rate risk, a portfolio manager must be able to quantify the portfolio's interest rate risk exposure. This means that the manager must be capable of quantifying the interest rate exposure of all the positions in a portfolio — the individual bonds and any derivative instruments (e.g., futures/forward contracts, swaps, and options). If a manager cannot quantify the exposure, he or she cannot control it.

There are two approaches that can be used to assess the interest rate risk exposure of a bond or a portfolio. The first is *scenario analysis*. This involves selecting likely scenarios for how interest rates and yield spreads may change and revaluing the bond position or portfolio for each scenario. The outcomes are then assessed. A special case of scenario analysis is *stress testing*. In this case, extreme adverse scenarios are analyzed in order to assess how a bond or a bond portfolio will be affected. The problem with scenario analysis is that it involves revaluing every position in a portfolio for each scenario. This is not a simple task for a portfolio with complex bond positions and interest rate derivatives.

The second approach is to compute measures for a bond or a bond portfolio that *approximate* how the price of a bond or the value of a portfolio will change when interest rates change. These approximation measures are called *risk parameters*. We will discuss several risk parameters throughout this book. This approach to measuring interest rate risk exposure is called *parametric analysis*.

The two risk parameters that we focus a good deal of attention on in this book are *duration* and *convexity*. The advantage of risk parameters is that it is not necessary to revalue a bond or a portfolio to obtain an estimate of the change in a bond's price or a portfolio's value when interest rates change. For example, as will be explained in this book, if the duration of a $500 million bond portfolio is 4, the portfolio manager will have a pretty good idea about how the portfolio's value will change in percentage terms and dollar amount when rates change by 20 basis points, 50 basis points, 75 basis points, or 100 basis points without having to revalue the portfolio in each case.

The disadvantage of using risk parameters relative to using scenario analysis is that risk parameters are summary measures that are based on certain assumptions. Throughout this book we will discuss the assumptions underlying the risk parameters duration and convexity. The relaxing of some of these assumptions leads to other risk parameters. For example, we will see that *key rate durations* are risk parameters that overcome one important assumption regarding duration. Also, as we stress throughout this book, in order to get good estimates of risk parameters it is necessary to have good valuation models — models that value bonds and derivative instruments. Without good valuation models, the risk parameters are not useful for assessing interest rate risk exposure. But, as we will see, valuation models are built on assumptions. The risk that these assumptions are wrong is called *modeling risk*. Measures have been developed to determine how sensitive risk parameters are to the underlying assumptions of a valuation model.

The purpose of this book is to describe the various risk parameters used in bond portfolio management, focusing on duration and convexity. We will describe variants of these measures. Where appropriate we explain how dealers and vendors of analytical systems compute certain measures and why there may be differences in reported values for some risk parameters. We will also see that there are differences in the terminology used to describe some risk parameters.

The emphasis throughout this book is on the practical application to managing portfolio risk. There is no attempt to derive the results using mathematical proofs. Instead, important results and their implications are presented using illustrations. A discussion of the topics covered in each chapter of this book is provided in the remainder of this chapter.

CHAPTER 2: THE REASONS WHY A BOND'S PRICE CHANGES

To be able to quantify a bond or a bond portfolio's exposure to changes in interest rates, it is necessary to understand the reasons why a bond's price changes. We do this in Chapter 2 by explaining the basic principles for valuing a bond. The value or price of a bond is the present value of the expected cash flows. Sounds simple: estimate a bond's expected cash flows (coupon interest payments and principal repayments) and then discount the expected cash flows at an appropriate interest rate.

What we will see is that this process is complicated for certain types of bonds. These are many bonds in which either the issuer or the investor have the option to change the cash flows. Such bonds are referred to as *bonds with an embedded option* and include callable bonds, prepayable bonds (such as mortgage-backed securities and certain asset-backed securities), and putable bonds. Given the expected cash flows, the appropriate interest rate at which to discount the cash flows is the sum of the yield on a comparable U.S. Treasury security plus a spread that reflects the perceived risks associated with realizing the cash flows. We'll see that there is not one interest rate at which all cash flows are discounted but rather a term structure of interest rates. The *term structure of interest rates* shows the relationship between the yield on zero-coupon Treasury bonds and maturity. The term structure of interest rates is sometimes referred to as the *yield curve*, although technically there is a difference between the two relationships.

Once we know the factors that determine the price of a bond, we can identify the reasons why the price of an individual bond changes and why the value of a bond portfolio changes. The price of a bond will change if the required yield sought by the market changes and/or the expected cash flows change. The price of an option-free bond changes in the opposite direction to the change in the required yield. With the exception of some unusual types of bonds, the price of a bond with an embedded option will also change in the opposite direction to the change in the required yield. Since a bond portfolio typically consists of bonds with different maturities, a bond portfolio's value will change when the term structure of interest rates change. A change in the spread required by the market will also change the price of a bond.

For bonds with embedded options, the expected cash flows may change because the cash flows may be related to the level of interest rates. The best example is a bond that is callable. When interest rates decline below the issue's coupon rate, there is an incentive for the issuer to refund the issue and therefore an investor may expect the cash flows to change.

For a floating-rate security the coupon rate is reset periodically based on a coupon formula. The formula specifies that the coupon rate is the sum of a reference rate plus a "spread," the latter being a fixed number of basis points over the life of the security. While the coupon rate for a floating-rate security, or floater, does reset periodically to close to the prevailing market rate, its price will change. In Chapter 2 we give three reasons why a floater's price will change.

CHAPTER 3: PRICE VOLATILITY CHARACTERISTICS OF BONDS

In Chapter 3 we turn to the price volatility characteristics of bonds and the features of a bond (i.e., coupon, maturity, and embedded options) that affect its price volatility when interest rates change. First we look at option-free bonds (i.e., bonds that do not have any embedded options). While we know that the price of an option-free bond will decline as the required yield increases, the relationship is not linear. That is, the relationship between price and yield (i.e., the price/yield relationship) is not a straight line. Rather, the price/yield relationship for an option-free bond has a shape that is bowed to the origin and is referred to as *convex*.

There are several properties of an option-free bond that are demonstrated in Chapter 3. One is that for small changes in yield, the magnitude of the percentage price change of a bond will be the same whether the yield increases or decreases. However, because of the convex price/yield relationship, this is not the case for a large change in yield. Specifically, the price of a bond will appreciate by more when interest rates decline by a large number of basis points than the price will decline for an increase in interest rates of the same number of basis points.

We will see that a bond's coupon rate and maturity affect its convexity (i.e., the shape of the price/yield relationship). The level of interest rates also affects a bond's price volatility when rates change. Specifically, the lower the level of interest rates, the greater the price volatility when interest rates change.

A bond with an embedded option can be viewed as a package that consists of an option-free bond and an option. Thus, the value of a bond with an embedded option is equal to the value of an option-free bond plus the value of the embedded option (or options). In turn, the price of a bond with an embedded option will change for the same reasons that the price of an option-free bond will change plus the reasons that cause the embedded option to change.

For a callable or prepayable bond, the price/yield relationship exhibits both positive and negative convexity. *Positive convexity* is the property described earlier for an option-free bond that for a large change in interest rates, the price appreciation will be greater than the price decline. *Negative convexity* means that the price appreciation when interest rates decline by a large number of basis points will be *less* than the price decline when interest rates increase by the same number of basis points. At low levels of interest rates (relative to the bond's coupon rate), a callable or prepayable bond exhibits negative convexity. At high interest rate levels, a callable or prepayable bond exhibits positive convexity.

CHAPTER 4: THE BASICS OF DURATION AND CONVEXITY

Knowing the price volatility properties of a bond and the characteristics of a bond that affect its price volatility is not enough to manage the interest rate risk of a portfolio. The key in controlling and altering the risk of a portfolio is the ability to quantify a portfolio's exposure to rate changes. In Chapter 4 we provide the two basic risk parameters that can be used to quantify this exposure — duration and convexity.

Duration is a measure of the sensitivity of the price of a bond or the value of a portfolio to changes in interest rates. A useful working definition is that duration is the approximate percentage change in the price of a bond (or value of a portfolio) for a 100 basis point change in rates. In contrast to duration which is related to percentage price change, *dollar duration* is a measure of how the dollar price of a bond or the dollar value of a portfolio changes when interest rates change. With the working definition for duration and dollar duration provided in the chapter, a manager can determine, for example, how much the value of a portfolio of, say, $500 million will change if rates change by 25 basis points. And, a manager can determine the amount of a position in an interest rate derivative needed to reduce a portfolio's current duration of 6 to a target duration of 5.

Duration is estimated by changing (shocking) interest rates up and down and determining how the price changes. The duration estimate is dependent on a good valuation model for estimating what the price will be when interest rates are changed. In estimating these prices when rates are shocked, one can assume either (1) that there is no change in the expected cash flows when interest rates change or (2) that there will be changes in the expected cash flows resulting from the change in interest rates. In the first case, the duration computed is called *modified duration*. In the second case, the resulting duration is called *effective duration*. It is effective duration that is the appropriate measure to use for bonds with embedded options.

The duration of a portfolio is just the weighted average of the duration of the bonds in the portfolio. A leveraged portfolio is one in which the manager has borrowed funds to acquire one or more bond positions. To compute the duration of a leveraged portfolio it is necessary to first determine the sensitivity of the bonds in the portfolio to rate changes and then relate that change to the amount of the equity investment (i.e., the amount without borrowing). For portfolios that include derivative instruments, it is necessary to determine the sensitivity of each derivative instrument to rate changes, a subject covered in Chapter 8.

In Chapter 4, we explain that duration is the first approximation as to how the price of a bond or value of a portfolio will change when rates change. A second approximation can be used to improve the estimate of the price change obtained from duration. The second approximation is sometimes called "convexity," not a very good word to use to describe the second approximation since too often market participants confuse this term with the shape of the price/yield relationship. More specifically, to adjust the estimate of the price change based on duration, a convexity measure can be computed and then a convexity adjustment to the estimated percentage price change based on duration can be made. We will see that the convexity adjustment formula depends on the how the convexity measure is defined. Thus, dealers and vendors may report different convexity measures for an option-free bond but come up with the same convexity adjustment for a given change in yield. As with duration, a modified convexity and effective convexity measure can be computed. The latter is the more appropriate measure for bonds with embedded options.

Chapter 4 provides a discussion of the interpretation of duration. Unfortunately, duration is often referred to as the "first derivative" of the price/yield function or given some temporal meaning. In the chapter it is argued that these interpretations are operationally meaningless and should be discarded. Such interpretations provide absolutely no insight into how to control the exposure of a portfolio to rate changes.

There is also a discussion of the relationship between modified duration and another duration measure called *Macaulay duration*. One of the recommendations in Chapter 4 is that if a manager has the standard formulas for these two duration measures programmed on a spreadsheet, he or she should delete them and use the formula for duration provided in the chapter. A major reason is that the standard formulas mask the fact that for bonds with embedded options it is necessary to evaluate how the expected cash flows may change when rates change.

There are two applications provided in Chapter 4. One is how to do a duration-weighted swap trade. The second is how to control a portfolio's duration.

CHAPTER 5: DURATION MEASURES FOR BONDS WITH EMBEDDED OPTIONS AND FOREIGN BONDS

When a bond has an embedded option, the appropriate duration and convexity measures are effective duration and effective convexity. In Chapter 5, we explain how to compute the effective duration and effective convexity of a bond portfolio. The calculation of a bond's effective duration and convexity requires that a valuation model be used to determine the price of a bond when rates are shocked, allowing for the cash flows to change. For valuing agency debentures, corporate bonds, and municipal bonds with embedded options, as well as certain types of structured notes and floating-rate notes with a cap, the valuation model commonly used is the binomial model. In Chapter 5, we provide a description of this model and then demonstrate how it can be used to compute a bond's effective duration and effective convexity.

Other duration measures are introduced in this chapter. For a fixed-rate bond a *spread duration* can be computed. This is the approximate percentage change in the price of a bond if the Treasury yield is constant but the spread changes by 100 basis points. The problem with interpreting this measure when it is reported by dealers or vendors is that the spread of a bond can be measured in several ways: *nominal spread*, *zero-volatility spread*, and *option-adjusted spread*. A spread duration for each can be computed. The manager must check with the dealer or vendor as to which spread measure is being computed or reported. Moreover, the term option-adjusted spread duration is ambiguous because it can be a spread duration measure or it can mean the effective duration since many market participants use it in that way.

In the description of the binomial model, we explain that an input into the model for valuing bonds with embedded options is the expected yield volatility. This input is an assumption about the volatility of interest rates over the life of the security. The sensitivity of the bond's price to changes in the expected yield volatility can be estimated. This sensitivity is called *volatility duration*.

For a floating-rate note an index duration and a spread duration can be computed. An *index duration* measures the price sensitivity of a floater to changes in the reference rate holding the spread constant. A *spread duration* can also be computed for a floater. It is the price sensitivity of a floater to changes in the spread holding the reference rate constant.

An inverse floating-rate security or inverse floater is a security whose coupon rate moves inversely with the change in the reference rate. In Chapter 5 we explain that an inverse floater is effectively a leveraged position in a fixed-rate bond that is financed on a floating-rate basis. We then show that the duration of an inverse floater is a multiple of the duration of the fixed-rate bond. We also explain that the duration of an inverse floater may exceed the number of years to maturity of the fixed-rate bond that is effectively owned, something that is puzzling to a manager who interprets duration in terms of years, but is clear to someone who interprets duration as a measure of potential price volatility to rate changes.

For a foreign bond added to a U.S. portfolio, the duration of the foreign bond in terms of foreign rates must be adjusted to determine its contribution to the U.S. portfolio's duration. This is because a foreign bond's duration is the sensitivity of the bond to changes in the yield in that foreign country. Of concern to a U.S. manager that is considering the addition of a foreign bond to a U.S. portfolio is the sensitivity of the bond's price to changes in U.S. interest rates. In Chapter 5, we show how the adjustment of the foreign bond's duration can be made based on an empirically estimated *country beta*. This measure is estimated from a regression showing the relationship between changes in U.S. rates and foreign rates.

CHAPTER 6: DURATION AND CONVEXITY MEASURES FOR MORTGAGE-BACKED SECURITIES

Mortgage-backed securities (i.e., mortgage passthrough securities, stripped mortgage-backed securities, and collateralized mortgage obligations) are securities with embedded options. The embedded option is due to the option granted to the homeowner to prepay a mortgage loan prior to the scheduled principal repayment date. Because of the complexity of this prepayment option, a good deal of research has been done by dealers in these securities and vendors of analytical services to estimate duration and convexity.

There are various approaches to estimating the duration of mortgage-backed securities — *effective duration* (also called *option-adjusted duration*), *cash flow duration*, *empirical duration* (including *hedging duration*), *coupon curve duration*, and *option-implied duration*. The last three measures use market data to estimate duration. In Chapter 6 we discuss these measures, explain the advantages and disadvantages of each, and present some empirical evidence on their relative performance in explaining price changes.

The effective duration and convexity of a mortgage-backed security are generated using a Monte Carlo simulation model. This model is explained in the chapter, emphasizing the assumptions that are made in constructing this model. Evidence is presented that shows that the effective durations reported by dealers and vendors may vary widely. This is due to the assumptions made in constructing the Monte Carlo simulation model. The factors that cause differences in effective duration estimates include differences in prepayment models and yield volatility assumptions.

Also discussed in Chapter 6 are various risk measures for assessing prepayment uncertainty. These measures include an *overall prepayment uncertainty sensitivity measure*, a *refinancing partial prepayment uncertainty measure*, and a *relocation partial prepayment uncertainty measure*.

CHAPTER 7: YIELD CURVE RISK MEASURES

In the earlier chapters of the book, it is explained that when using a portfolio's duration and convexity to measure the exposure to interest rate changes, it is assumed that the yield curve shifts in a parallel fashion. For a nonparallel shift in the yield curve, duration and convexity may not provide adequate information about interest rate risk exposure. This is demonstrated with an illustration at the outset of Chapter 7.

Exposure of a portfolio to a shift in the yield curve is called *yield curve risk*. Several approaches have been suggested for measuring a portfolio's yield curve risk. One approach is to calculate a portfolio's *yield curve reshaping duration*. This duration measure decomposes the yield curve into a short end and a long end. The sensitivity of a portfolio to changes in the short end of the yield curve is called *short-end duration* and to changes in the long end of the yield curve is called *long-end duration*.

An alternative approach to measuring yield curve risk is to change the yield for a particular maturity of the yield curve and determine the sensitivity of a security or portfolio to this change holding the yield for all other maturities constant. *Rate duration* is the sensitivity of the change in a portfolio's value to the rate change for a particular maturity. A rate duration can be computed for every maturity. In practice, however, dealers and vendors compute a set of *key rate durations*. These are the rate durations for key maturities. The most popular version of key rate duration uses 11 key maturities of the spot rate curve (3 months, 1, 2, 3, 5, 7, 10, 15, 20, 25, and 30 years).

A third approach to measuring a portfolio's yield curve risk is by estimating the yield curve by a mathematical function that describes the yield curve in terms of level, slope, curvature, and location of the yield curve hump (i.e., the maximum point of curvature). From the mathematical function, the exposure to a change in level, slope, curvature, and location of the hump of a yield curve can be determined, thereby summarizing the total price change of a bond. This approach is applied to foreign bonds to show how these measures can be used to determine the contribution that a foreign bond adds to the riskiness of a U.S. bond portfolio.

CHAPTER 8: RISK MEASURES FOR INTEREST RATE DERIVATIVES

Futures/forward contracts in which the underlying is a bond, interest rate swaps, and options on bonds and bond futures are examples of interest rate derivatives. Derivatives play a key role in controlling the interest rate risk of a portfolio. Derivatives do this by adjusting a portfolio's dollar duration and thereby a portfolio's duration to the target exposure sought by the manager. Effectively, derivatives are leveraged instruments that permit the manager to quickly adjust interest rate risk at low transaction costs (i.e., low commissions and minimal market impact cost).

In Chapter 8, we show how to calculate the dollar duration of futures/forwards, swaps, and options. The economic interpretation of each derivative is explained to make it easier to understand how a particular position in a derivative instrument alters a portfolio's dollar duration. For example, a long futures position (i.e., buying a futures contract) is equivalent to buying bonds on a leveraged basis and therefore when added to a portfolio increases the portfolio's dollar duration. A short futures position is equivalent to shorting a bond and the addition of this position to a portfolio reduces the portfolio's dollar duration.

In the case of an interest rate swap, we show that it is economically equivalent to a package of forward contracts or a position in a package of cash market instruments. For the party in a swap that pays a floating rate and receives a fixed rate, it is shown that this position is equivalent to purchasing a fixed-rate bond and financing the purchase with a floating-rate loan. The dollar duration of a swap for the floating-rate payer is then approximately equal to the dollar duration of the underlying bond that is financed. For the party to a swap that pays a fixed rate and receives a floating rate, the position is equivalent to buying a floating-rate bond and financing it on a fixed-rate basis. So, the dollar duration of a swap for the fixed-rate payer has a negative dollar duration equal to roughly the dollar duration of the underlying bond. Thus, adding a swap to a portfolio in which the manager pays a fixed rate and receives a floating rate decreases the dollar duration of the portfolio.

There are options on bonds and options on bond futures contracts. The values of these contracts are affected by several factors. One key factor is how changes in interest rates change the value of the underlying bond for the option and the underlying bond futures contract for a futures option. Option pricing models have been used to determine the fair value of an option and these models are briefly reviewed in Chapter 8. From an option pricing model, the sensitivity of the option to changes in the price of the underlying bond (the *delta* and *gamma of an option*), changes in expected yield volatility (the *kappa* or *vega of an option*), and changes in time remaining to the option's expiration date (the *theta of an option*) can be computed. It is also shown that the duration of an option is determined by the delta of an option, the duration of the underlying bond, and the leverage embedded in the option.

CHAPTER 9: OTHER RISK MEASURES

The focus up to Chapter 9 is on quantifying the potential change in a bond's price or a portfolio's value to changes in interest rates. In Chapter 9, other risk measures for individual bonds and bond portfolios are introduced.

The chapter begins with a review of basic concepts in probability theory. The focus then turns to the *variance* of a probability distribution. This is a measure of the dispersion of the outcomes of a random variable around its expected value. The *standard deviation* is the square root of the variance. The standard deviation of the return of a bond is commonly used as a measure of a bond's risk.

The standard deviation is a misleading measure of risk if the probability distribution for bond returns is not symmetric. That is, by using the standard deviation to measure risk it is assumed that the probability distribution is not skewed. When using standard deviation as a measure of the risk for bond returns it is assumed that the underlying probability distribution is a *normal distribution*. A normal probability distribution is a symmetric distribution around the expected value and the only information needed to make probability statements about outcomes is the expected value and the standard deviation.

Downside risk measures look at only that portion of the return from a bond or bond portfolio that is below a specified level. Downside risk measures include *target semivariance* and *shortfall probability*. For the different downside risk measures, the manager must define the target return so that returns less than the target return represent adverse consequences. The target semivariance is a measure of the dispersion of the outcomes below the target return specified by the portfolio manager. The *semivariance* is a special case of the target semivariance where the target return is the expected value.

When a probability distribution is symmetric around the expected value, using the semivariance as a risk measure will give the same ranking of risk as using the variance or standard deviation.

While theoretically the target semivariance is superior to the variance (standard deviation) as a risk measure, the reasons why it is not used in bond portfolio management to any significant extent are explained in Chapter 9.

We also introduce the *value-at-risk measure* in this chapter. With this measure, the manager specifies a target probability and then computes the return that the outcomes will not fall below that return that percentage of times. When applied to a bond position, value-at-risk uses the duration of the bond to measure the potential change in value when interest rates change.

Shortfall risk is the probability that the outcome will have a value less than the target return. A special case of shortfall risk is the *risk of loss* which is based on a target return of zero.

When we move from an individual bond to a bond portfolio, we find that a portfolio's variance is not simply the weighted average of the variance of the return of the component bonds. A portfolio's variance depends not only on the variance of the return of the component bonds but also the covariance (correlation) between each pair of bonds. The lower the covariance (correlation) between the returns of bonds in the portfolio, the greater the reduction in the portfolio's variance.

In practice, the two major problems in computing a portfolio's variance are (1) that the number of estimated inputs increases dramatically as the number of bonds in the portfolio or the number of bonds being considered for inclusion in the portfolio increases and (2) the absence of meaningful historical return data for many bonds. Factor models can be used to overcome the problems associated with using historical standard deviations to compute the risk of a bond portfolio. Studies of historical returns suggest that there are three factors that drive bond returns. These factors are (1) changes in the level of interest rates (the most important factor explaining historical returns), (2) changes in the slope of the yield curve, and (3) changes in the curvature of the yield curve (the least important of the three factors in explaining historical returns). The results of this empirical analysis explain why it is important to have good estimates of duration and measures of yield curve risk to control the risk of a portfolio.

CHAPTER 10: MEASURING YIELD VOLATILITY

Yield (interest rate) volatility is used in earlier chapters in the book in two ways. First, yield volatility is a critical input into a bond valuation model. We explained this in Chapters 5 and 6. Second, in Chapter 9 it is shown how the duration estimate and yield volatility estimate combine to determine the value-at-risk of a bond position. Duration simply indicates how a bond's price will change if interest rates change. Yield volatility indicates the extent to which interest rates may change.

In Chapter 10 we review *historical yield volatility*, how it is calculated, and the issues associated with its estimation. The standard deviation is commonly used as a measure of volatility. Yield volatility can be estimated from daily yield observations. The issues associated with calculating yield volatility using historical data include the number of observations, the time period that should be used, and the number of days used to annualize the daily standard deviation. *Implied volatility* can also be used to estimate yield volatility.

The first part of the chapter explains how historical yield volatility is calculated. The second part looks at the different approaches and issues associated with forecasting future yield volatility. State-of-the-art statistical techniques for forecasting yield volatility such as *generalized autoregressive conditional heteroskedasticity* (GARCH) models are briefly reviewed. These models are used to capture the time series characteristic of yield volatility in which a period of high volatility is followed by a period of high volatility and a period of relative stability appears to be followed by a period that can be characterized in the same way.

Chapter 2

The Reasons Why a Bond's Price Changes

In order to understand how duration and convexity can be used to measure the exposure of an individual bond or a bond portfolio to changes in interest rates, it is necessary to understand how the value of bond is determined. Once this is understood, the reasons why the value of a bond will change will be clear. In this chapter we introduce a basic model for valuing or pricing a bond and then discuss the reasons why a bond's value will change.

VALUING A BOND

The price or value of a bond is equal to the present value of the expected cash flows. Thus, valuing a bond involves two steps. First, determining the expected cash flows, and second, discounting those cash flows at an appropriate interest rate to obtain the present value.

The cash flow for a bond is equal to the coupon and principal that will be received each period. For a typical bond, the cash flow prior to the maturity date is the periodic coupon payment and the cash flow at the maturity date is the par value plus the final coupon payment. For example, consider a 6% coupon bond with 5 years to maturity that pays interest semiannually. The cash flows per $100 of par value are as follows. For the first 4.5 years the cash flow is the semiannual coupon payment of $3 (6% times $100 divided by 2). The last cash flow is the sum of the final coupon payment of $3 plus the par value of $100. So the last cash flow is $103.

For amortizing securities, the periodic cash flows are the periodic coupon interest and the regularly scheduled principal amount. The latter is referred to as the *scheduled amortization*. For example, consider a 6% coupon amortizing security that matures in 10 years and makes semiannual payments. The cash flow for this security is $6.7216 every six months to fully amortize $100 of par value over 10 years. Thus, assuming that the issuer of this security does not accelerate payments or defaults, the cash flow is 20 semiannual payments of $6.7216.

Given the expected cash flows, the next step is to discount them at an appropriate interest rate. This means calculating the present value of the cash flows using a suitable interest rate. The interest rate or discount rate is referred to as the *required yield*. For example, consider the 6% coupon 5-year bond whose cash flows were described above and are shown in Exhibit 1. If the required yield is 6.5%, this means each cash flow will be discounted using an interest rate of 3.25% (one half the 6.5% required yield). Column (3) shows the present value of each cash flow and the last row shows that the total present value is $97.8944. Thus, $97.8944 is the value of the bond.

As a second example, consider again the amortizing security with a coupon rate of 6% and 10 years to maturity that pays semiannually. Assuming that the required yield is 6.5%, the present value of each cash flow is shown in Exhibit 2. The last row indicates that the total present value is $97.7272 and this is therefore the security's value.

Exhibit 1: Computation of the Value of a 6% Coupon 5-Year Bond Based on a Required Yield of 6.5%

(1) Period	(2) Cash flow	(3) Present value at 3.25%*
1	$3	$2.9056
2	3	2.8141
3	3	2.7255
4	3	2.6397
5	3	2.5566
6	3	2.4762
7	3	2.3982
8	3	2.3227
9	3	2.2496
10	103	74.8060
	Total	$97.8944

* The 3.25% interest rate is one half the required yield of 6.5%.

Exhibit 2: Computing the Value of a 6% 10-Year Amortizing Security Assuming a Required Yield of 6.5%

(1) Period	(2) Cash flow	(3) Present value at 3.25%*
1	$6.7216	$6.5100
2	6.7216	6.3051
3	6.7216	6.1066
4	6.7216	5.9144
5	6.7216	5.7282
6	6.7216	5.5479
7	6.7216	5.3733
8	6.7216	5.2042
9	6.7216	5.0403
10	6.7216	4.8817
11	6.7216	4.7280
12	6.7216	4.5792
13	6.7216	4.4351
14	6.7216	4.2955
15	6.7216	4.1603
16	6.7216	4.0293
17	6.7216	3.9025
18	6.7216	3.7796
19	6.7216	3.6607
20	6.7216	3.5454
	Total	$97.7272

* A discount rate of 3.25% is used because the annual rate is 6.5%.

Complications in Estimating the Cash Flows

We've made this all sound so simple. While for all bonds the process described above for valuation is the same, for the majority of bonds the process is complicated because of the uncertainty about the cash flows. For an option-free bond there is no uncertainty about the cash flows. For other bonds the cash flows are uncertain due to defaults and embedded options. The effect of defaults on cash flows is captured through an adjustment of the required yield.

Embedded options such as call or prepayment options require a projection of cash flows that recognize how the embedded options impact the cash flows. The valuation of bonds with embedded options becomes complicated because there is a relationship between the expected cash flows and the required yield. For example, if a bond is callable, the required yield is close to the yield at which the issuer can refinance. Thus, the required yield is related to the likelihood that the issuer will call the issue in order to refinance which, in turn, affects the expected cash flows. For a mortgage-backed security and certain types of asset-backed securities, the borrowers in the underlying loan pool are given the option to prepay all or part of their loan prior to the scheduled repayment date. The required yield for the security is related to the refinancing rate available to borrowers. Thus, the required yield affects the expected cash flows.

Determinants of the Required Yield

Now let's look at the required yield. The required yield is composed of two parts: (1) a minimum yield and (2) a risk premium. The minimum yield is the yield on a comparable Treasury security. The reason why Treasury securities provide the benchmark for the minimum yield is that they are viewed as default-free and have no embedded options.[1]

The hard part is determining the second component of the required yield, the risk premium. Investors commonly refer to this risk premium as the *yield spread* or simply *spread*. The risk premium or spread reflects the risks associated with a bond's expected cash flows. These risks include default risk, liquidity risk, and the uncertainty about the cash flows due to any embedded options. This last risk is called *option risk*. More specifically, for callable bonds it is referred to as *call risk* and for mortgage-backed and asset-backed securities it is called *prepayment risk*.

The Term Structure of Interest Rates and the Required Yield

There is another aspect regarding the appropriate interest rate used to discount the cash flows that is critical to understand. In principle, there is no reason why the same interest rate must be used to compute the present value of every cash flow. In fact, not only is there no reason that this must be the case, financial theory tells us that there is no reason why the interest rate should be the same. Financial theory says that each cash flow of a security should be treated as if it is a stand alone financial instrument. More specifically, each cash flow should be viewed as a zero-coupon instrument. So, for

[1] There are a few outstanding callable Treasury bonds. The Treasury no longer issues callable bonds.

example, the 6% 5-year bond should be viewed as 10 zero-coupon instruments with maturity dates corresponding to the time when the cash flow will be received. The 6% 10-year amortizing security that pays semiannually should be viewed as 20 zero-coupon instruments each with a maturity value of $6.7216.

That is what financial theory tells us. But how do we know that the market will value a security in that manner? The reason is that dealers have the ability to "strip" securities. Stripping a security means that the dealer can separate all the coupon payments and principal payments and sell them as separate securities — specifically, zero-coupon instruments. If a security sells in the market for less than its strippable value — that is the value at which all the zero-coupon instruments that are created from stripping the security are worth — then a dealer will strip the security and sell the package of zero-coupon instruments at a higher price. That is, the dealer will realize an arbitrage profit. This action will push the price of the security towards its value as a package of zero-coupon instruments.

If the security is trading at a price that is more than its strippable value, dealers can recombine zero-coupon instruments to synthetically create a coupon security. This process is called "reconstitution." The synthetic security can be created at a lower price than a security with the same coupon rate can be purchased for in the market. The dealer will again realize an arbitrage profit and it will force the price of the security not to deviate significantly from its value as a package of zero-coupon instruments.

The relationship between the yield on zero-coupon Treasury instruments and maturity is referred to as the *term structure of interest rates*. The relationship between Treasury securities (coupon securities and bills) and maturity when graphically depicted is called the *yield curve*. Technically, the yield curve does not depict the term structure of interest rates because the yields on coupon securities are depicted in the relationship. However, using arbitrage arguments, a theoretical zero-coupon Treasury curve that represents the term structure of interest rates can be created.[2] These theoretical zero-coupon rates are referred to as *spot rates*.

---

[2] For an explanation of how this is done, see Chapter 2 in Frank J. Fabozzi, *Valuation of Fixed Income Securities and Derivatives* (New Hope, PA: Frank J. Fabozzi Associates, 1997).

Exhibit 3: Computing the Value of a 6% 10-Year Amortizing Security Using Spot Rates

(1) Period	(2) Cash flow	(3) Spot rate (%)	(4) Present value
1	$6.7216	6.1	$6.5226
2	6.7216	6.1	6.3296
3	6.7216	6.1	6.1422
4	6.7216	6.1	5.9604
5	6.7216	6.1	5.7840
6	6.7216	6.1	5.6128
7	6.7216	6.1	5.4467
8	6.7216	6.5	5.2042
9	6.7216	6.5	5.0403
10	6.7216	6.5	4.8817
11	6.7216	6.5	4.7280
12	6.7216	6.5	4.5792
13	6.7216	6.5	4.4351
14	6.7216	6.5	4.2955
15	6.7216	6.5	4.1603
16	6.7216	6.5	4.0293
17	6.7216	6.7	3.8388
18	6.7216	6.7	3.7143
19	6.7216	6.7	3.5939
20	6.7216	6.7	3.4775
		Total	$97.7765

Note: The interest rate used to discount the cash flow in Column (2) is one-half the rate in Column (3).

Given the theoretical spot rates, the procedure for valuing a bond is the same as discussed earlier. The difference is that each cash flow is discounted by the corresponding spot rate. For example, consider the 6% 10-year amortizing security. Suppose that the theoretical spot rates are those shown in Column (3) of Exhibit 3. Then each cash flow is discounted using one-half the interest rate shown in that column. Column (4) shows the present value for each semiannual period. The value of this security is $97.7765.

WHY THE PRICE CHANGES

Now that we understand the fundamentals of valuing a bond, let's look at why the price of a bond can change. The key is to see what can cause either the required yield to change, the expected cash flows to change, or both.

Change in the Required Yield

The price of a bond will change when the required yield changes. First, let's understand why. The coupon rate for an option-free bond is fixed for its life. Typically, when a coupon bond is issued it will be offered to investors so that its price will be par value (or near par). This means the issuer will set the coupon rate at issuance so that the coupon rate is equal to the yield required by investors. Over time, interest rates in the market change. Yet, in the case of a bond with a fixed coupon rate, the issuer does not change the coupon rate nor the maturity date of the bond. The price of the bond is the only thing that can change in order for the price of the bond to offer a potential buyer a competitive market yield (i.e., a yield that is the same as comparable bonds).

For example, suppose that a 6% coupon 5-year bond is purchased by an investor today at 10 a.m. and assume that the yield available on comparable 5-year bonds at 10 a.m. is 6%. The price of this bond will be par value when discounted at the required yield of 6%. Now suppose at 2 p.m. of the same day the investor who purchased this bond wants to sell it. Suppose that the Federal Reserve between 10 a.m. and 2 p.m. announced an increase in interest rates such that the market at 2 p.m. now wants a 6.5% yield in order to purchase a 5-year bond. This means that the bond the investor purchased at 10 a.m. is no longer competitive at a price of $100 since it is a 6% coupon 5-year bond. At 2 p.m. if some investor is willing to invest $100 in a comparable 5-year bond, that investor can get a 6.5% coupon rate. For this bond to be competitive, the price must decline. By how much? It must decline in price until it offers a yield of 6.5%. What is the price? This price is found by computing the present value of the cash flows at 6.5%. We already demonstrated in Exhibit 1 that this price is $97.8944.

This illustration also explains why a bond trades below its par value — the coupon rate is less than the required yield. A bond that trades below its par value is said to be trading at a "discount." The amount of the discount (i.e., difference between par value and the price) is compensation to the investor who purchases this bond at a below market interest rate offered by the bond's coupon rate.

The explanation for why a bond may sell above its par value can also be explained with the same bond. Suppose that the Federal Reserve between 10 a.m. and 2 p.m. announced a cut in interest rates and that the market now required a 5.5% yield for comparable 5-year bonds. Certainly, if an investor is willing to pay $100 to acquire this bond, this bond offers a better coupon rate than available in the market (6% versus 5.5%) for an investment of $100. The price of the bond will increase above par value in order to bring the yield on the bond in line with the required yield of 5.5%. When the cash flows for the 6% coupon bond are discounted at 5.5%, the price of the bond is $102.16. Thus, when the required yield declines, the price of a bond increases.

This illustration demonstrates why a bond trades above its par value. Bonds that trade in the market above par value are said to be selling at a "premium." The amount of the premium (i.e., the difference between the price and par value) translates into a reduction of the yield due to the higher coupon rate offered by the bond relative to that available in the market for comparable bonds.

For option-free bonds, there is an inverse relationship between a bond's price and the required yield. For bonds with embedded options, in general the same relationship between bond price and required yield holds. The reason why the statement is qualified by "in general" for bonds with embedded options is because there are some unusual types of bonds that have been created, particularly in the mortgage-backed securities market, where this may not be the case for all interest rate levels.

Reasons for Yield Changes

As explained earlier, the required yield is composed of the minimum yield, as measured by the yield on a comparable Treasury security, plus a spread. When the required yield changes it could be the result of any of the following: (1) a change in the Treasury yield, (2) a change in the spread, or (3) a change in both the Treasury yield and the spread.

In turn, the spread changes because of the perceived change in the risks associated with investing in the bond. For example, if the credit rating of a bond is downgraded or expected to be downgraded by the market, the default risk increases and the spread increases. If the number of dealers in an issue declines, liquidity risk increases and the spread increases. If the interest rate at which the issuer of a callable bond can refinance the issue declines, the risk that the issue will be called increases and therefore call risk increases. This leads to an increase in the spread.

Changes in the Term Structure of Interest Rates

We explained earlier when discussing the valuation of a bond that while market participants talk about an "interest rate," there is not one rate but a term structure of interest rates as represented by the spot rates. When yields change in the market, there is no reason why the spot rate for every maturity must change by the same number of basis points. If the spot rate for each maturity does change by the same number of basis points, this is referred to as a *parallel shift in the term structure of interest rates*. Typically, the spot rate will not change in a parallel manner. That is, there will be a nonparallel shift in the term structure of interest rates.

To see the implications of shifts in the term structure, consider a 6% amortizing security that matures in 10 years and pays semiannually. The cash flows for this security are 20 semiannual payments of $6.7216. Suppose the current term structure of interest rates is as shown in Column (3) of Exhibit 3. The value of this security is then $97.7765. Suppose that the term structure changes as shown in Column (3) in Exhibit 4. Notice that this is a parallel shift in the term structure since all spot rates increased by 50 basis points. The value of this security declines from $97.7765 to $95.5867.

Consider instead of a parallel shift in the term structure a nonparallel shift. We'll consider three different nonparallel shifts. Assume that the term structure of interest rates shifts up in the manner shown in Exhibit 5 (Scenario 1). Notice that the term structure has flattened. Parts of the term structure shifted up by 50 basis points but the short end increased by 70 basis points and the long end increased by only 40 basis points. The bond's value would then be $95.5571. Notice that this decline is greater than in the parallel shift scenario of 50 basis points. The difference is about 3 cents per $100 par value.

Exhibit 4: Computation of the Value of a 6% 10-Year Amortizing Security for a +50 Basis Point Parallel Shift in the Term Structure

(1) Period	(2) Cash flow	(3) Spot rate (%)	(4) Present value
1	$6.7216	6.6	$6.5068
2	6.7216	6.6	6.2990
3	6.7216	6.6	6.0978
4	6.7216	6.6	5.9030
5	6.7216	6.6	5.7144
6	6.7216	6.6	5.5318
7	6.7216	6.6	5.3551
8	6.7216	7.0	5.1044
9	6.7216	7.0	4.9318
10	6.7216	7.0	4.7650
11	6.7216	7.0	4.6039
12	6.7216	7.0	4.4482
13	6.7216	7.0	4.2978
14	6.7216	7.0	4.1525
15	6.7216	7.0	4.0120
16	6.7216	7.0	3.8764
17	6.7216	7.2	3.6843
18	6.7216	7.2	3.5563
19	6.7216	7.2	3.4327
20	6.7216	7.2	3.3134
		Total	$95.5867

Note: The interest rate used to discount the cash flow in Column (2) is one-half the rate in Column (3).

Suppose the upward nonparallel shift in the term structure is the one shown in Exhibit 6 (Scenario 2). Notice again that most of the middle part of the term structure shifted up by 50 basis points. However, the short end only increased by 10 basis points while the long end increased by 60 basis points. In this case the value of the security decreased to $95.7747, a smaller decline than in Scenario 1.

Finally, suppose that the term structure shifted in the nonparallel fashion shown in Exhibit 7 (Scenario 3). Here the term structure became inverted. At the short end, interest rates increased such that the short-term rates exceeded most of the other rates. All the other rates increased by 50 basis points. In this scenario, the security's value declines to $95.1252, a greater decline than in Scenarios 1 and 2.

Exhibit 5: Computation of the Value of a 6% 10-Year Amortizing Security for a Nonparallel Shift in the Term Structure: Scenario 1

(1) Period	(2) Cash flow	(3) Spot rate (%)	(4) Present value
1	$6.7216	6.8	$6.5006
2	6.7216	6.8	6.2868
3	6.7216	6.8	6.0801
4	6.7216	6.8	5.8802
5	6.7216	6.8	5.6868
6	6.7216	6.8	5.4998
7	6.7216	6.8	5.3190
8	6.7216	7.0	5.1044
9	6.7216	7.0	4.9318
10	6.7216	7.0	4.7650
11	6.7216	7.0	4.6039
12	6.7216	7.0	4.4482
13	6.7216	7.0	4.2978
14	6.7216	7.0	4.1525
15	6.7216	7.0	4.0120
16	6.7216	7.0	3.8764
17	6.7216	7.1	3.7147
18	6.7216	7.1	3.5873
19	6.7216	7.1	3.4643
20	6.7216	7.1	3.3456
		Total	$95.5571

Note: The interest rate used to discount the cash flow in Column (2) is one-half the rate in Column (3).

The purpose of these scenarios is to demonstrate how the change in a security's value can be sensitive to how the term structure of interest changes. Notice that in the illustrations we used an amortizing bond. For nonamortizing bonds, the impact of a change in the term structure is much less. However, for a portfolio of bonds a shift in the term structure of interest rates may dramatically impact how the portfolio's value will change.

Changes in the Expected Cash Flows

The price of a bond can change because of changes in the expected cash flows. For all bonds the cash flows change as a bond moves closer to maturity. For bonds with an embedded option, the cash flows may change due to changes in the yield.

Exhibit 6: Computation of the Value of a 6% 10-Year Amortizing Security for a Nonparallel Shift in the Term Structure: Scenario 2

(1) Period	(2) Cash flow	(3) Spot rate (%)	(4) Present value
1	$6.7216	6.2	$6.5195
2	6.7216	6.2	6.3234
3	6.7216	6.2	6.1333
4	6.7216	6.2	5.9489
5	6.7216	6.2	5.7700
6	6.7216	6.2	5.5965
7	6.7216	6.2	5.4283
8	6.7216	7.0	5.1044
9	6.7216	7.0	4.9318
10	6.7216	7.0	4.7650
11	6.7216	7.0	4.6039
12	6.7216	7.0	4.4482
13	6.7216	7.0	4.2978
14	6.7216	7.0	4.1525
15	6.7216	7.0	4.0120
16	6.7216	7.0	3.8764
17	6.7216	7.3	3.6542
18	6.7216	7.3	3.5255
19	6.7216	7.3	3.4014
20	6.7216	7.3	3.2816
		Total	$95.7747

Note: The interest rate used to discount the cash flow in Column (2) is one-half the rate in Column (3).

Changes in Expected Cash Flows Due to Changes in Yields

For bonds with embedded options, the difficulty is that changes in market interest rates affect the cash flows. Thus, in valuing bonds with embedded options when yields change, it is necessary to include in the modeling process how changes in yield affect the expected cash flows.

This will be explained further in later chapters when we review models for valuing bonds with embedded options. What will be seen is that these models adjust for how the cash flows will change when interest rates change.

For now, let's illustrate this with a simple example. Consider once again our 6% coupon 10-year amortizing security. Suppose that the current price of this security is $97.7272 as shown in Exhibit 2 based on a required yield of 6.5%. If interest rates decline to 5%, it can be shown that the value of this security will increase to $104.7837. However, this assumes that this security is not callable or prepayable. Suppose that the borrower can prepay. Exhibit 8 shows the amortization schedule for this security. Column (5) shows the scheduled amortization for each period. Let's assume that if the required yield declines to 5% then investors expect that the borrower will accelerate the repayment of principal as shown in Column (3) of Exhibit 9. How investors project that the principal will be repaid as shown in the exhibit is not important for us here. What is important is that if the borrower has the right to prepay and interest rates decline by a sufficient amount below the borrowing rate, there is an incentive to prepay.

Exhibit 7: Computation of the Value of a 6% 10-Year Amortizing Security for a Nonparallel Shift in the Term Structure: Scenario 3

(1) Period	(2) Cash flow	(3) Spot rate (%)	(4) PV
1	$6.7216	7.2	$6.4880
2	6.7216	7.2	6.2626
3	6.7216	7.2	6.0449
4	6.7216	7.2	5.8349
5	6.7216	7.2	5.6321
6	6.7216	7.2	5.4364
7	6.7216	7.2	5.2475
8	6.7216	7.0	5.1044
9	6.7216	7.0	4.9318
10	6.7216	7.0	4.7650
11	6.7216	7.0	4.6039
12	6.7216	7.0	4.4482
13	6.7216	7.0	4.2978
14	6.7216	7.0	4.1525
15	6.7216	7.0	4.0120
16	6.7216	7.0	3.8764
17	6.7216	7.2	3.6843
18	6.7216	7.2	3.5563
19	6.7216	7.2	3.4327
20	6.7216	7.2	3.3134
		Total	$95.1252

Note: The interest rate used to discount the cash flow in Column (2) is one-half the rate in Column (3).

Exhibit 8: Amortization Schedule for a 6% 10-Year Amortizing Security Assuming No Prepayments

(1) Period	(2) Beginning balance	(3) Payment	(4) Interest	(5) Scheduled repayment	(6) Ending balance
1	$100.0000	$6.7216	$3.0000	$3.7216	$96.2784
2	96.2784	6.7216	2.8884	3.8332	92.4452
3	92.4452	6.7216	2.7734	3.9482	88.4969
4	88.4969	6.7216	2.6549	4.0667	84.4302
5	84.4302	6.7216	2.5329	4.1887	80.2415
6	80.2415	6.7216	2.4072	4.3144	75.9272
7	75.9272	6.7216	2.2778	4.4438	71.4834
8	71.4834	6.7216	2.1445	4.5771	66.9063
9	66.9063	6.7216	2.0072	4.7144	62.1919
10	62.1919	6.7216	1.8658	4.8558	57.3360
11	57.3360	6.7216	1.7201	5.0015	52.3345
12	52.3345	6.7216	1.5700	5.1516	47.1829
13	47.1829	6.7216	1.4155	5.3061	41.8768
14	41.8768	6.7216	1.2563	5.4653	36.4115
15	36.4115	6.7216	1.0923	5.6293	30.7823
16	30.7823	6.7216	0.9235	5.7981	24.9842
17	24.9842	6.7216	0.7495	5.9721	19.0121
18	19.0121	6.7216	0.5704	6.1512	12.8608
19	12.8608	6.7216	0.3858	6.3358	6.5251
20	6.5251	6.7216	0.1958	6.5258	0.0000

Exhibit 9: Value of a 6% 10-Year Amortizing Security Based on Assumed Prepayments and a Required Yield of 5%

(1) Period	(2) Beginning balance	(3) Scheduled repayment	(4) Assumed prepayment	(5) Total principal repayment	(6) Interest	(7) Cash flow	(8) Present value at 5%
1	$100.0000	$3.7216	$9.0000	$12.7216	$3.0000	$15.7216	$15.3381
2	87.2784	3.8332	11.0000	14.8332	2.6184	17.4516	16.6107
3	72.4452	3.9482	10.0000	13.9482	2.1734	16.1216	14.9705
4	58.4969	4.0667	9.5000	13.5667	1.7549	15.3216	13.8806
5	44.9302	4.1887	8.0000	12.1887	1.3479	13.5366	11.9644
6	32.7415	4.3144	8.0000	12.3144	0.9822	13.2966	11.4656
7	20.4272	4.4438	4.0000	8.4438	0.6128	9.0566	7.6190
8	11.9834	4.5771	2.0000	6.5771	0.3595	6.9366	5.6932
9	5.4063	4.7144	0.6919	5.4063	0.1622	5.5685	4.4588
			Total	$100.0000			$102.0010

Exhibit 9 shows this security's value assuming the required yield declines to 5% and the principal repayment schedule is accelerated as shown in the exhibit. Any amount of principal repayment in excess of the regularly scheduled amount (i.e., the amount in Column (5) in Exhibit 8) is called a *prepayment*. Based on the assumed prepayment, the security will be completely paid off at the end of 4.5 years (9 periods). As can be seen from Exhibit 9, this security's value would increase to $102 if the required yield is 5%. This increase is less than in the case where the borrower does not have the option to prepay ($104.7837). Thus, while a decline in interest rates has increased this security's value, because of the prepayment option the value has not appreciated as much as it would have had it been option free.

Changes in Expected Interest Rate Volatility

The value of a bond with an embedded option can be thought of as a combination of an option-free bond and a package of options on the bond. For example, a callable bond can be viewed as an option-free bond plus a call option allowing the issuer to call the bond at the dates set forth in the call schedule and at a price equal to the price set forth in the call schedule. Therefore, the value of a bond depends on the value of the embedded options.

Now, it is well known from option pricing theory that the value of an option depends on expected volatility. Expected volatility in the case of an option on a stock is the stock's expected price volatility. In the case of an option on a bond, the value of the option depends on expected interest rate volatility. The relationship is as follows: the greater the expected interest rate volatility, the greater the value of an option.

Consequently, since the value of a bond with an embedded option depends on the value of the embedded options and the value of the embedded options depends on expected interest rate volatility, then the value of a bond with an embedded option depends on expected interest rate volatility. This means that even if the required yield does not change, the price of a bond can change if expected interest rate volatility changes.

When we describe the valuation models for bonds with embedded options in later chapters, we'll see the role expected interest rate volatility plays. In Chapter 10 of the book we'll look at how interest rate or yield volatility is measured.

Time Path of a Bond

In discussing the relationship between price and the required yield, the statement should have been qualified by saying it holds for an instant in time. Notice that in the illustration of buying a bond and selling the same bond when the required yield changed, we assumed that the bond was bought and sold on the same day. The reason for this is that the price of a bond can change as the bond moves toward maturity even if the required yield is unchanged.

This is because the cash flows change as a result of a bond moving towards its maturity date. In the case of an option-free bond, the amount of each semiannual cash flow does not change. What changes is the number of cash flows. For example, consider an option-free bond with a 6% coupon and 20 years to maturity selling to yield 8%. The cash flow for this bond is 39 coupon payments of $3 and a final payment 20 years from now of $103. The price of this bond is $80.2072. That is, this bond is selling at a discount. In 15 years, this bond has 5 years remaining to maturity. The cash flow is now 9 payments of coupon interest of $3 and a final payment at the maturity date of $103. So, the cash flows have changed. If the required yield remains at 8%, the price of this bond will be $91.8891.

Notice that the price of the bond has increased from $80.2072 to $91.8891. This will always occur with a bond selling at a discount. The reason for this is that as the bond moves toward maturity, there are fewer coupon payments. Thus, the present value of the coupon payments decreases. However, the maturity value is received sooner, thereby increasing the present value of the maturity value. The increase in the present value of the maturity value is greater than the decline in the present value of the coupon payments, resulting in an increase in the price. At the maturity date, the price of the bond is the maturity value.

Let's look at a bond selling at a premium. Consider the same 6% 20-year bond selling to yield 5%. The cash flows are the same as when this bond was selling to yield 8%. The price is $112.5514. Moving forward 15 years, the bond is a 5-year bond with a 6% coupon. If the required yield does not change, that is, it is still 5%, the price of this bond will decline to $104.3760. Thus, the price declines as the bond marches toward its maturity date even if the required yield is unchanged. At the maturity date, the price is the maturity value.

WHY THE PRICE OF A FLOATING-RATE SECURITY CHANGES

Our discussion thus far has focused on bonds with a fixed coupon rate (i.e., a fixed-rate bond). Now let's look at floating-rate securities (floaters). For a floater, the coupon rate is reset periodically based on a formula. In general the formula is as follows:

Reference rate + Spread

The spread is fixed over the floater's life. A floater will typically have a cap (i.e., a maximum coupon rate). Some floaters have a minimum coupon rate in addition to a cap. The minimum coupon rate is called a *floor.*

As explained in this chapter, the change in the price of a fixed-rate bond when market rates change is due to the fact that the bond's coupon rate differs from the prevailing market rate. By contrast, for a floater, the coupon rate is reset periodically, reducing a floater's price sensitivity to changes in rates. A floater's price will change depending on three factors:

1. time remaining to the next coupon reset date.
2. whether or not the cap is reached.
3. whether the spread that the market wants changes.

The longer the time to the next coupon reset date, the greater a floater's potential price fluctuation. Conversely, the less time to the next coupon reset date, the smaller the floater's potential price fluctuation. To understand why, consider a floater that resets once a year. Suppose that the coupon rate is reset today at 5% and suppose that 5% is the market rate for a 1-year security. The floater will then trade at par. One month from now, the floater is an 11-month security. Suppose that market rates have changed such that the rate for similar 11-month securities is 5.4%. Then, our floater with 11 months until the coupon rate resets is offering a below market rate (5.4% market rate versus 5% coupon rate set the month prior). This floater will then trade below par. As the floater approaches its coupon reset date, the floater will approach par value. At the coupon reset date the floater will trade at par value (assuming neither of the situations described below occurs).

With respect to the cap, once the coupon rate as specified by the coupon reset formula rises above the cap, the floater then offers a below market coupon rate, and its price will decline. Turning to the spread, at the initial offering of a floater, the spread is set such that the security will trade near par. If after the initial offering the market requires a higher spread, the floater's price will decline to reflect the higher spread. For example, consider a floater whose coupon reset formula is 1-month LIBOR plus a spread of 40 basis points. If market rates change such that investors want a spread of 50 basis points rather than 40 basis points, this floater would be offering a coupon rate that is 10 basis points below the market. As a result, the floater's price will decline.

SUMMARY

In this chapter we have presented the basic principles for valuing a bond. The value or price of a bond is the present value of the expected cash flows. The complication arises for bonds with embedded options because of the difficulty of estimating the cash flows. The appropriate interest rate at which to discount the cash flows is equal to the yield on a comparable Treasury security plus a spread. The spread is a risk premium that depends on the perceived risks associated with investing in the bond. Actually, there is not one interest rate at which all cash flows are discounted but rather a term structure of interest rates.

A bond's price will change if the required yield changes (or the term structure of interest rates changes) or the expected cash flows change. The price of an option-free bond changes in the opposite direction to the change in the required yield. With the exception of some unusual types of bonds, the price of a bond with an embedded option will also change in the opposite direction to the change in the required yield. A change in the spread required by the market will also cause the price of a bond to change.

For bonds with embedded options, the expected cash flows may change because the cash flows may be related to the required yield. The best example is a bond that is callable or prepayable. When interest rates decline below the borrowing rate, there is an incentive for the borrower to accelerate the scheduled principal repayment in order to refinance the issue. Also, expected interest rate volatility will affect the expected cash flows for bonds with embedded options.

The price of a bond may change over time even if there is no change in the required yield. For a bond trading at a discount, its price increases as it moves toward the maturity date even if the required yield does not change. For a bond trading at a premium, its price decreases as it approaches the maturity date even if the required yield does not change.

A floater's coupon rate is reset periodically based on a reference rate plus a spread. The spread is fixed over the floater's life and there is typically a cap. A floater's price will change depending on three factors: time remaining to the next coupon reset date, whether or not the cap is reached, and whether the spread that the market wants changes. The longer the time to the next coupon reset date, the greater a floater's potential price fluctuation. When the coupon rate is below the market rate because the cap is reached, the price declines below par value. Once the coupon rate as specified by the coupon reset formula rises above the cap, the floater then offers a below market coupon rate, and its price will decline. If the spread required by the market changes, the floater's price will change.

Chapter 3

Price Volatility Characteristics of Bonds

In the previous chapter we saw how a bond's price (value) is determined, the factors affecting a bond's price, and how a change in these factors will cause a bond's price to change. In this chapter, we look at the price volatility characteristics for both option-free bonds and bonds with an embedded option. Specifically, we will examine the relationship between price and required yield and explain how a bond's price will change when the required yield changes. We will also look at how the features of a bond (i.e., coupon, maturity, and embedded options) affect the sensitivity of the bond's price to changes in interest rates.

PRICE VOLATILITY CHARACTERISTICS OF OPTION-FREE BONDS

Let's begin by focusing on option-free bonds (i.e., a bond that does not have any embedded options). As explained in the previous chapter, a fundamental characteristic of an option-free bond is that the price of the bond changes in the opposite direction from a change in the bond's required yield. Exhibit 1 illustrates this property for four hypothetical bonds assuming a par value of $100.

When the price/yield relationship for any option-free bond is graphed, it exhibits the shape shown in Exhibit 2. Notice that as the required yield increases, the price of an option-free bond declines. However, this relationship is not linear (i.e., it is not a straight line). The shape of the price/yield relationship for any option-free bond is referred to as *convex*. As we mentioned in the previous chapter, this price/yield relationship is for an instantaneous change in the required yield.

Exhibit 1: Price/Yield Relationship for Four Hypothetical Option-Free Bonds

	Price ($)			
Yield (%)	6%/5 year	6%/20 year	9%/5 year	9%/20 year
4.00	108.9826	127.3555	122.4565	168.3887
5.00	104.3760	112.5514	117.5041	150.2056
5.50	102.1600	106.0195	115.1201	142.1367
5.90	100.4276	101.1651	113.2556	136.1193
5.99	100.0427	100.1157	112.8412	134.8159
6.00	100.0000	100.0000	112.7953	134.6722
6.01	99.9574	99.8845	112.7494	134.5287
6.10	99.5746	98.8535	112.3373	133.2472
6.50	97.8944	94.4479	110.5280	127.7605
7.00	95.8417	89.3225	108.3166	121.3551
8.00	91.8891	80.2072	104.0554	109.8964

Exhibit 2: Price/Yield Relationship for an Option-Free Bond

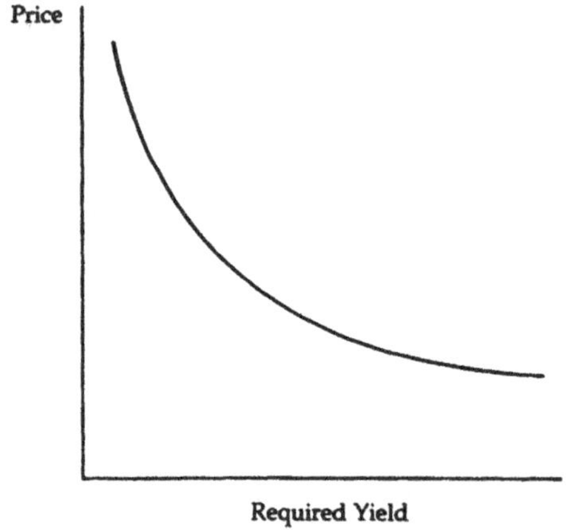

Properties of Option-Free Bonds

The price sensitivity of a bond to changes in the required yield can be measured in terms of the dollar price change or the percentage price change. Exhibit 3 uses the four hypothetical bonds in Exhibit 1 to show the percentage price change in each bond's price for various changes in the yield, assuming that the initial yield for all four bonds is 6%. An examination of Exhibit 3 reveals the following properties concerning the price volatility of an option-free bond:

Exhibit 3: Instantaneous Percentage Price Change for Four Hypothetical Bonds
(Initial yield for all four bonds is 6%)

	Percent Price Change			
New Yield (%)	6%/5 year	6%/20 year	9%/5 year	9%/20 year
4.00	8.98	27.36	8.57	25.04
5.00	4.38	12.55	4.17	11.53
5.50	2.16	6.02	2.06	5.54
5.90	0.43	1.17	0.41	1.07
5.99	0.04	0.12	0.04	0.11
6.01	−0.04	−0.12	−0.04	−0.11
6.10	−0.43	−1.15	−0.41	−1.06
6.50	−2.11	−5.55	−2.01	−5.13
7.00	−4.16	−10.68	−3.97	−9.89
8.00	−8.11	−19.79	−7.75	−18.40

Property 1: Although the price moves in the opposite direction from the change in required yield, the percentage price change is not the same for all bonds.

Property 2: For small changes in required yield, the percentage price change for a given bond is roughly the same, whether the required yield increases or decreases.

Property 3: For large changes in required yield, the percentage price change is not the same for an increase in required yield as it is for a decrease in required yield.

Property 4: For a given large change in basis points in the required yield, the percentage price increase is greater than the percentage price decrease.

While the properties are expressed in terms of percentage price change, they also hold for dollar price changes.

An explanation for the last two properties of bond price volatility lies in the convex shape of the price/yield relationship. Exhibit 4 illustrates this. The initial yield in the exhibit is denoted by Y. The corresponding initial price is denoted by P. In the exhibit, the initial required yield is decreased to Y_1 and is increased to Y_2. The change in the required yield is the same. That is $Y_2 - Y$ is equal to $Y - Y_1$. The corresponding prices are denoted by P_1 and P_2. The vertical distance from the required yield axis to the price/yield relationship represents the price. The distance between P_1 and P measures the price change if the yield decreases; the distance between P and P_2 measures the price change if the yield increases. Exhibit 4 clearly shows that for a large change in the required yield of a given number of basis points, the price change is not equal for an up and down movement in the required yield. It can also be seen that the price gain will exceed the price decline.

The implication of Property 4 is that if an investor is long a bond, the price appreciation that will be realized if the required yield decreases is greater than the capital loss that will be realized if the required yield increases by the same number of basis points. For an investor who is short a bond, the reverse is true: the potential capital loss is greater than the potential capital gain if the yield changes by a given number of basis points.

To see how the convexity of the price/yield relationship impacts Property 4, look at Exhibits 5 and 6. Exhibit 5 shows a less convex price/yield relationship than Exhibit 4. Notice that while the price gain when the required yield decreases is greater than the price decline when the required yield increases, the gain is not much greater than the loss. In contrast, Exhibit 6 has much greater convexity than the bonds in Exhibits 4 and 5 and the price gain is significantly greater than the loss for the bonds depicted in Exhibits 4 and 5.

Exhibit 4: Graphical Illustration of Properties 3 and 4 for an Option-Free Bond

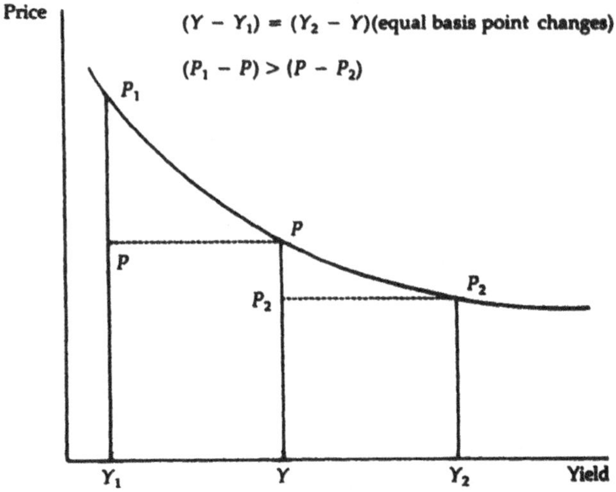

Exhibit 5: Impact of Convexity on Property 4: Less Convex Bond

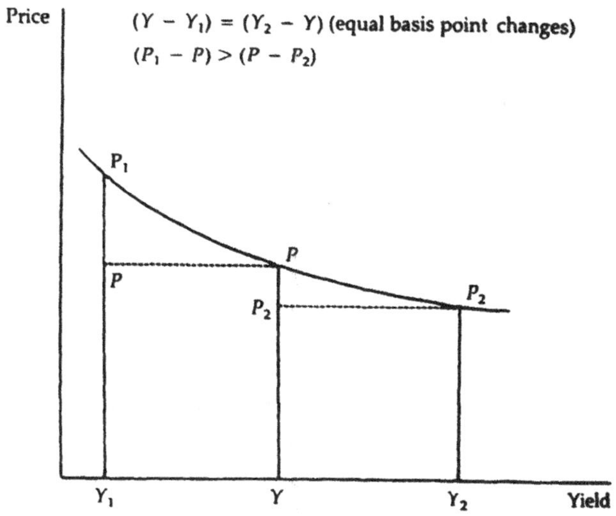

Exhibit 6: Impact of Convexity on Property 4: Highly Convex Bond

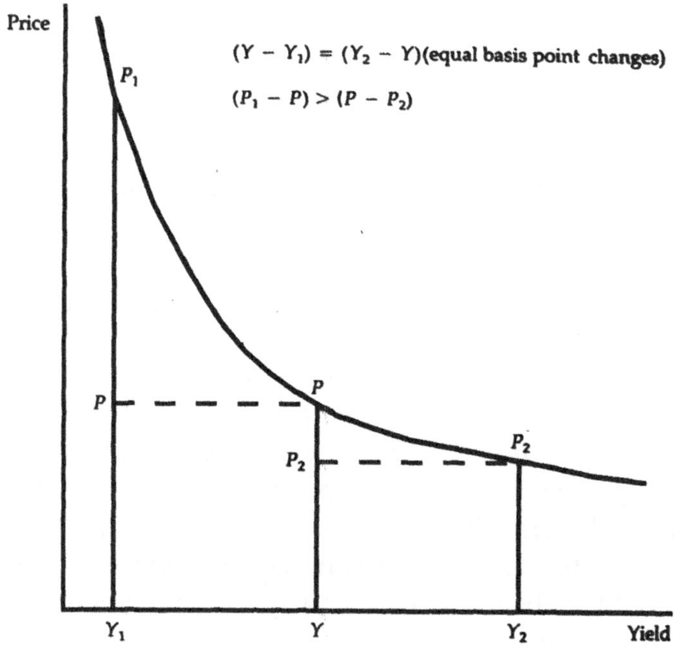

Characteristics of a Bond that Affect its Price Volatility

There are two characteristics of an option-free bond that determine the magnitude of its price volatility when the required yield changes: (1) coupon and (2) term to maturity. Equivalently, this is saying that the coupon and term to maturity determine the degree of convexity of the price/yield relationship — that is, whether the price/yield would have the degree of convexity shown in Exhibits 4, 5, or 6. How these characteristics affect price volatility as measured by the *percentage price change* are summarized below and can be verified by looking at Exhibit 3.

> *Characteristic 1:* For a given term to maturity and initial required yield, the lower the coupon rate the greater the percentage price change of a bond.
>
> *Characteristic 2:* For a given coupon rate and initial required yield, the longer the term to maturity the greater the *percentage price change.*

An implication of Characteristic 1 is that bonds selling at a deep discount will realize a greater percentage price change than bonds selling near or above par for a given change in the required yield. Zero-coupon bonds will have the greatest percentage price change for a given maturity.

An implication of Characteristic 2 is that investors who want to increase a portfolio's price volatility because they expect interest rates to fall, all other factors being constant, should hold bonds with long maturities in the portfolio. To reduce a portfolio's price volatility in anticipation of a rise in interest rates, bonds with shorter-term maturities should be held in the portfolio.

Do the same bond characteristics hold if volatility is measured in terms of dollar price change rather than percentage price change? The problem lies with deep discount long-term bonds because they trade at lower dollar prices. Look at the first characteristic that deals with the coupon rate. Consider the two 20-year bonds in Exhibit 1. If the initial required yield is 8% and the required yield declined instantaneously for both bonds to 6%, from Exhibit 1 we see that:

	6% 20-year bond	9% 20-year bond
Price at 8% yield	$80.2072	$109.8964
Price at 6% yield	$100.0000	$134.6722
Dollar price change	$19.7928	$24.7758
Percentage price change	24.7%	22.5%

Thus, the lower coupon bond has a smaller dollar price change but a larger percentage price change.

For Characteristic 2 that deals with maturity, we can use zero-coupon bonds to demonstrate what happens to deep discount bonds. Exhibit 7 has three panels with each panel showing prices for zero-coupon bonds with different maturities. In each panel there is an initial yield and a yield 50 basis points lower and then the corresponding prices. As can be seen in each panel, at first both the dollar price change and the percentage price change increase as maturity increases. At some maturity, the dollar price change decreases as maturity increases even though the percentage price change increases. Notice that at the higher yield level, the maturity at which Characteristic 2 does not hold is shorter. This is because at a higher yield the discount for a bond decreases much faster than at a lower yield.

The Effects of Yield to Maturity

We cannot ignore the fact that credit considerations cause different bonds to trade at different yields, even if they have the same coupon and maturity. How, then, holding other factors constant, does the yield affect a bond's price volatility? As it turns out, the higher the required yield that a bond trades at, the lower the price volatility.

To see this, we can compare a 6% 20-year bond initially selling to yield 6% and a 6% 20-year bond initially selling to yield 10%. The price of the first bond is $100 and the second is $65.68. Now, if the yield on both bonds increases by 100 basis points, the change in the price for the two bonds is as follows:

	Initial yield	
	6%	10%
Initial price	$100.00	$65.68
New price if 100 bp increase	$89.32	$59.88
Dollar price change	$10.68	$5.80
Percentage price change	10.68%	8.83%

Exhibit 7: Demonstration that Characteristic 2 May Not Hold for Deep-Discount Long-Term Bonds: Dollar Price and Percentage Price Changes for Zero-Coupon Bonds

Panel A

Years to maturity	Price at 3.5% ($)	Price at 3% ($)	Dollar price change ($)	Percent price change (%)
1	96.6184	97.0874	0.4690	0.49
5	84.1973	86.2609	2.0636	2.45
10	70.8919	74.4094	3.5175	4.96
15	59.6891	64.1862	4.4971	7.53
20	50.2566	55.3676	5.1110	10.17
25	42.3147	47.7606	5.4459	12.87
30	35.6278	41.1987	5.5708	15.64
35	29.9977	35.5383	5.5407	18.47
40	25.2572	30.6557	5.3984	21.37

Panel B

Years to maturity	Price at 9% ($)	Price at 8.5% ($)	Dollar price change ($)	Percent price change (%)
1	91.7431	92.1659	0.4228	0.46
5	64.9931	66.5045	1.5114	2.33
10	42.2411	44.2285	1.9875	4.71
15	27.4538	29.4140	1.9602	7.14
20	17.8431	19.5616	1.7185	9.63
25	11.5968	13.0094	1.4126	12.18
30	7.5371	8.6518	1.1147	14.79
35	4.8986	5.7539	0.8553	17.46
40	3.1838	3.8266	0.6428	20.19

Panel C

Year to maturity	Price at 14% ($)	Price at 13.5% ($)	Dollar price change ($)	Percent price change (%)
1	87.7193	88.1057	0.3864	0.44
5	51.9369	53.0910	1.1541	2.22
10	26.9744	28.1865	1.2121	4.49
15	14.0096	14.9645	0.9548	6.82
20	7.2762	7.9448	0.6686	9.19
25	3.7790	4.2180	0.4390	11.62
30	1.9627	2.2394	0.2767	14.10
35	1.0194	1.1889	0.1695	16.63
40	0.5294	0.6312	0.1018	19.22

Exhibit 8: Impact of Yield Level on Price Volatility

$(Y_H' - Y_H) = (Y_H - Y_H'') = (Y_L' - Y_L) = (Y_L - Y_L'')$
$(P_H - P_H') < (P_L - P_L')$ and
$(P_H - P_H'') < (P_L - P_L'')$

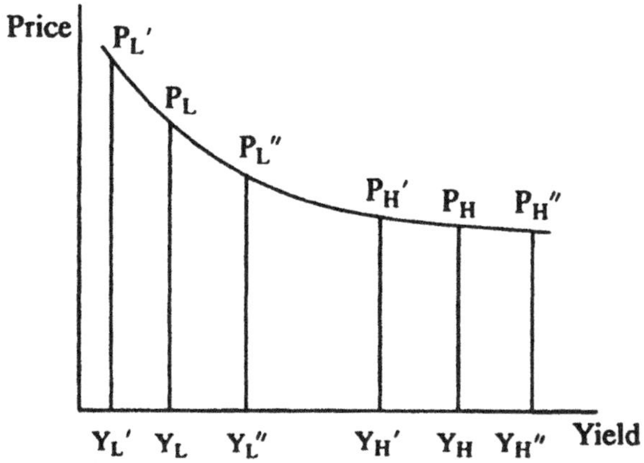

Thus, we see that the bond that trades at a lower yield is more volatile both in terms of dollar price change and percentage price change, holding the other features of a bond the same (i.e., coupon and maturity).

This is also demonstrated in Exhibit 8. When the yield level is high (represented by Y_H in the exhibit), a given change in the required yield will not produce as large a change in price as when the yield level is low (represented by Y_L in the exhibit).

An implication of this is that, for a given change in yields, price volatility is lower when the yield level in the market is high, and price volatility is higher when the yield level is low. For example, when the yield on the 30-year Treasury bond was 15.25% in October 1981, a yield change of 10 basis points produced a much smaller price change than in October 1998 when the 30-year Treasury bond traded at a yield of 4.7%.

PRICE VOLATILITY CHARACTERISTICS OF BONDS WITH EMBEDDED OPTIONS

Now let's turn to the price volatility characteristics of bonds with embedded options. As explained in the previous chapter, the price of a bond with an embedded option is comprised of two components. The first is the value of the same bond if it had no embedded option. That is, the price if the bond is option free. The second component is the value of the embedded option.

The two most common types of embedded options are call (or prepay) options and put options. We discussed these two features in the previous chapter. As interest rates in the market decline, the issuer may call or prepay the debt obligation prior to the scheduled principal repayment date. The other type of option is a put option. This option gives the investor the right to require the issuer to purchase the bond at a specified price. Below we'll look at the price/yield relationship and its implications for price volatility for bonds with both types of embedded options.

Bonds with Call and Prepay Options

In the discussion below, we will refer to a bond that may be called or is prepayable as a callable bond. From the issuer's perspective, the advantage of a callable bond is that the issuer has the opportunity to refinance the debt with lower cost debt should interest rates in the future decline below the issue's coupon rate. There are two disadvantages to the investor. First, the proceeds received when a bond is called or when prepayments are received because interest rates have declined must be reinvested at a lower interest rate. Second, the appreciation potential of a bond when interest rates decline is reduced. This is because the issuer will only pay the call price if the bond is called. We'll examine this disadvantage more closely later because of the significant impact it will have on the price volatility of a bond when interest rates decline. These two disadvantages are referred to as *call risk* or *prepayment risk*.

Exhibit 9 shows the price/yield relationship for an option-free bond and a callable bond. The convex curve given by *a-a′* is the price/yield relationship for an option-free bond. The unusual shaped curve denoted by *a-b* in the exhibit is the price/yield relationship for the callable bond.

The reason for the price/yield relationship for a callable bond is as follows. When the prevailing market yield for comparable bonds is higher than the coupon rate on the callable bond, it is unlikely that the issuer will call the issue. For example, if the coupon rate on a bond is 7% and the prevailing market yield on comparable bonds is 12%, it is highly unlikely that the issuer will call a 7% coupon bond so that it can issue a 12% coupon bond. Since the bond is unlikely to be called, the callable bond will have a similar price/yield relationship as an otherwise option-free bond. Another way of saying this is that the call option is deep out-of-the-money and that the value of the embedded call option granted to the issuer is close to zero. Consequently, the callable bond is going to be valued as if it is an option-free bond. Since there is still some value to the call option, the bond won't trade exactly like an option-free bond.

As yields in the market decline, the concern is that the issuer will call the bond. The issuer won't necessarily exercise the call option as soon as the market yield drops below the coupon rate. Yet, the value of the embedded call option increases as yields approach the coupon rate from higher yield levels. For example, if the coupon rate on a bond is 7% and the market yield declines to 7.5%, the issuer will not call the issue. However, market yields are then at a level at which the investor is concerned that the issue may eventually be called if the market yield declines further. Cast in terms of the value of the embedded call option, that option becomes more valuable to the issuer and therefore it reduces the price relative to an otherwise comparable option-free bond. In Exhibit 9, the value of the embedded call option at a given yield can be measured by the difference between the price of an option-free bond (the price shown on the curve *a-a´*) and the price on the curve *a-b*. Notice that at low yield levels, the value of the embedded call option is high.

Let's look at the difference in the price volatility properties relative to an option-free bond given the price/yield relationship for a callable bond shown in Exhibit 9. Exhibit 10 blows up the portion of the price/yield relationship for the callable bond where the two curves in Exhibit 9 depart. We know from our discussion of the price/yield relationship that for a large change in yield of a given number of basis points, the price of an option-free bond increases by more than it decreases (Property 4 above). Is that what happens for a callable bond in the region of the price/yield relationship shown in Exhibit 10? No it is not. In fact, as can be seen in the exhibit, the opposite is true. That is, for a given large change in yield, the price appreciation is less than the price decline.

Exhibit 9: Price/Yield Relationship for a Callable Bond and an Option-Free Bond

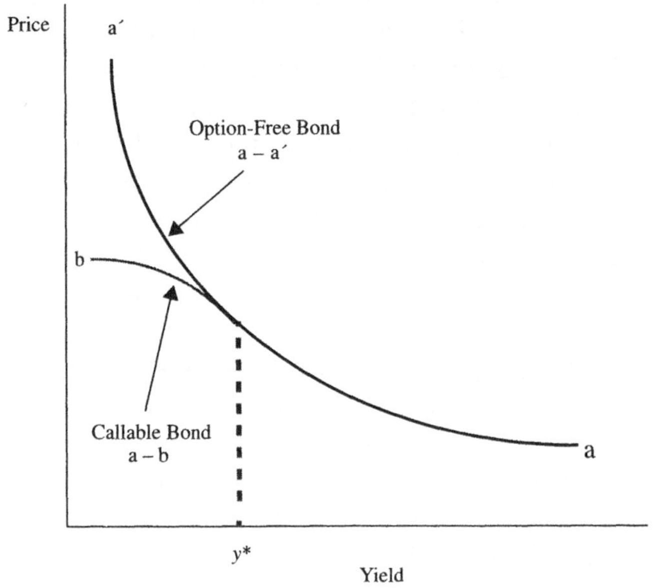

Exhibit 10: Negative Convexity Region of the Price/Yield Relationship for a Callable Bond

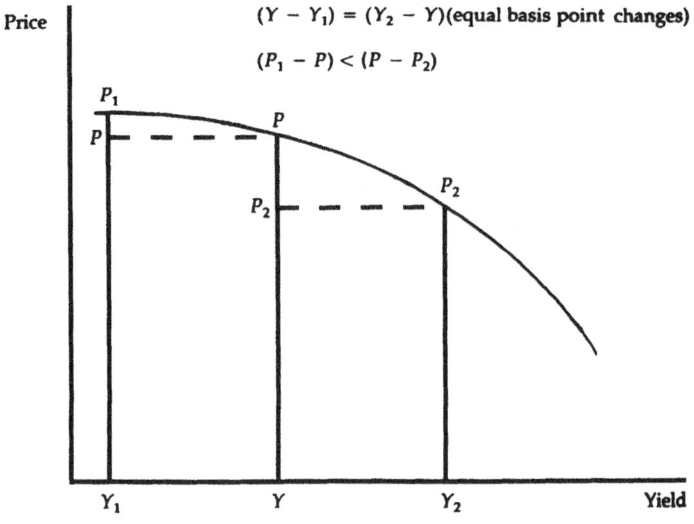

Exhibit 11: Negative and Positive Convexity Exhibited by a Callable Bond

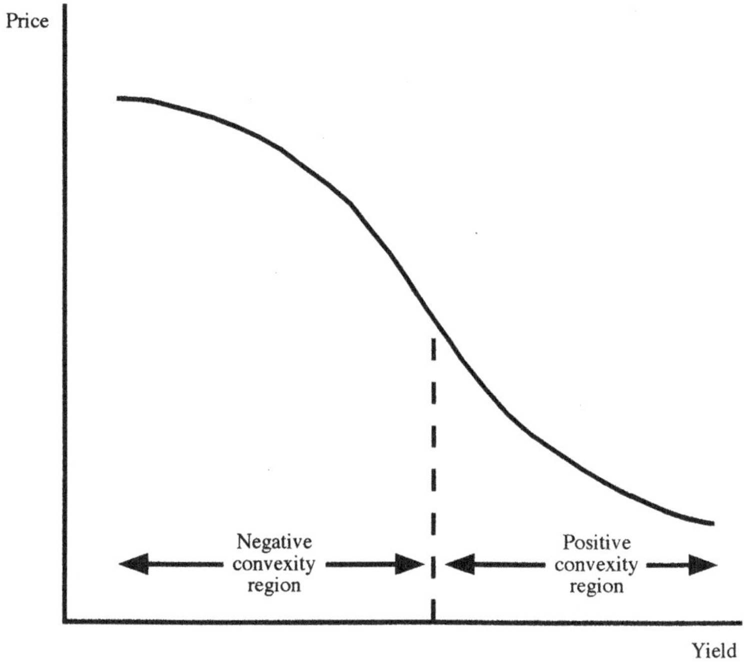

The price volatility characteristic of a callable bond is important to understand. The characteristic of a callable bond that its price appreciation is less than its price decline when rates change by a large number of basis points is referred to as *negative convexity.* But notice from Exhibit 10 that callable bonds don't exhibit this characteristic at every yield level. When yields are high (relative to the issue's coupon rate), the bond exhibits the same price/yield relationship as an option-free bond and therefore at high yield levels also has the characteristic that the gain is greater than the loss. Because market participants have referred to the shape of the price/yield relationship shown in Exhibit 10 as negative convexity, market participants refer to the relationship for an option-free bond as *positive convexity.* Consequently, a callable bond exhibits negative convexity at low yield levels and positive convexity at high yield levels. This is depicted in Exhibit 11.

As can be seen from the exhibits, when a bond exhibits negative convexity, as rates decline the bond compresses in price. That is, at a certain yield level there is very little price appreciation when rates decline. When a bond enters this region, the bond is referred to as a "cushion bond."

In the previous chapter we presented an illustration that showed how the price of a callable bond is less than an otherwise option-free bond when yields are low relative to the issue's coupon rate. Recall the 6% 10-year amortizing security we used in the previous chapter. When the required yield was 5%, the value of this bond was $104.7837 if it was option free. However, if the security is prepayable and the prepayments are those assumed in Exhibit 9 in Chapter 2 when the yield level is 5%, the value of this security is $102.0010, which is $2.7827 less than if the security is option free.

Bonds with Embedded Put Options

Putable bonds may be redeemed by the bondholder at the dates and at the put price specified in the indenture. Typically, the put price is par value. The advantage to the investor is that if yields rise such that the bond's value falls below the put price, the investor will exercise the put option. If the put price is par value, this means that if market yields rise above the coupon rate, the bond's value will fall below par and the investor will then exercise the put option.

The value of a putable bond is equal to the value of an option-free bond plus the value of the put option. Thus, the difference between the value of a putable bond and the value of an otherwise comparable option-free bond is the value of the embedded put option. This can be seen in Exhibit 12 which shows the price/yield relationship for a putable bond (the curve *a-b*) and an option-free bond (the curve *a-b´*).

At low yield levels (low relative to the issue's coupon rate), the price of the putable bond is basically the same as the price of the option-free bond because the value of the put option is small. As rates rise, the price of the putable bond declines, but the price decline is less than that for an option-free bond. The divergence in the price of the putable bond and an otherwise comparable option-free bond at a given yield level is the value of the put option. When yields rise to a level where the bond's price would fall below the put price, the price at these levels is the put price.

Exhibit 12: Price/Yield Relationship for a Putable Bond and an Option-Free Bond

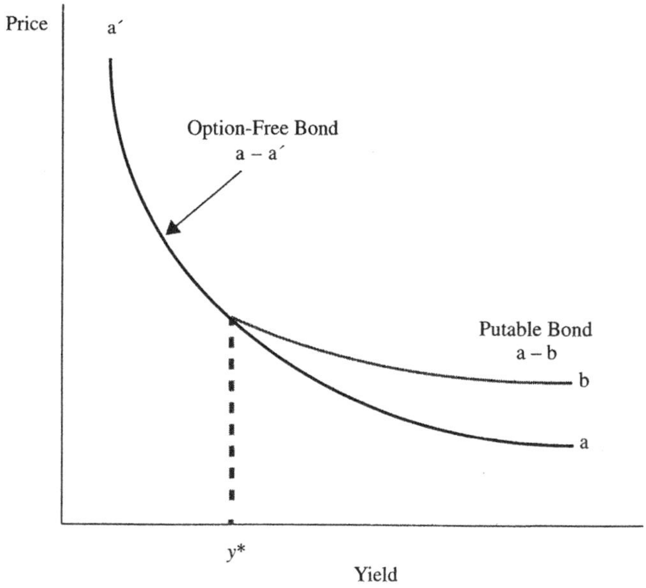

SUMMARY

The price/yield relationship for an option-free bond is convex. Because of this convex relationship, the price of a bond will appreciate by more when interest rates decline by a large number of basis points than the price will decline for an increase in interest rates of the same number of basis points. Two characteristics of a bond affect its convexity (i.e., the shape of the price/yield relationship): the bond's coupon rate and maturity. For two bonds with the same maturity, the lower the coupon rate the greater the percentage price change when interest rates change. For two bonds with the same coupon rate, the longer the maturity the greater the percentage price change when interest rates change. The level of interest rates also affects a bond's price volatility when rates change. Specifically, the lower the level of interest rates, the greater the price volatility when interest rates change.

The change in the value of a bond with an embedded option will reflect how the value of the embedded option changes when interest rates change. For a callable bond, the price/yield relationship exhibits both positive and negative convexity. Negative convexity means that the price appreciation when interest rates decline by a large number of basis points will be less than the price decline when interest rates increase by the same number of basis points. This is a property exhibited at lower yield levels when the embedded call option has value. When interest rates are at a high level relative to the issue's coupon rate, the value of the embedded option is close to zero and a callable bond exhibits positive convexity.

For a putable bond, the bond's price/yield relationship exhibits positive convexity up to a point where the yield would result in the price falling below the put price. At that point the price/yield relationship is flat as interest rates rise further.

Chapter 4

The Basics of Duration and Convexity

We now know the properties of the price/yield relationship for option-free bonds and bonds with embedded options. We also know the characteristics of bonds that affect their price volatility when interest rates change. That is not enough. To be able to implement portfolio strategies and control the risk exposure of a position or portfolio to changes in interest rates, it is necessary to understand how to quantify a bond and a portfolio's exposure to changes in interest rates. In this chapter we will show how this is done by using two risk parameters, *duration* and *convexity.* As we move along in this book, we will see the problems with using these two measures of interest rate risk. In this chapter, we'll introduce the basics of duration and convexity and in the next two chapters we will look at the duration and convexity of bonds with embedded options.

DURATION

The most obvious way to measure a bond's percentage price sensitivity to changes in interest rates is to change rates and calculate how its price will change. To do this, we introduce the following notation. Let

Δy = change in the yield of the bond (in decimal form)
V_+ = the estimated value of the bond per $100 of par value if the yield is increased by Δy
V_- = the estimated value of the bond per $100 of par value if the yield is decreased by Δy
V_0 = initial price of the bond (per $100 of par value)

There are two key points to keep in mind in the foregoing discussion. First, the change in yield referred to above is the same change in yield for all maturities. As we explained in Chapter 2, this assumption is referred to as the *parallel shift in the term structure* or *parallel yield curve shift assumption*. Thus, the foregoing discussion about the price sensitivity of a security to interest rate changes is limited to parallel shifts in the yield curve. In Chapter 7, we will discuss measures that identify the exposure of a bond or portfolio to nonparallel shifts in the yield curve.

Second, the notation refers to the estimated value of the bond. This value is obtained from a valuation model. Consequently, *the resulting measure of the price sensitivity of a security to interest rate changes is only as good as the valuation model employed to obtain the estimated value of the bond.*

Now let's focus on the measure of interest. We are interested in the percentage change in the price of a security when interest rates change. The percentage change in price per basis point decrease in interest rates is found by dividing the percentage price change by the number of basis points (Δy times 100). That is:

$$\frac{V_{-} - V_0}{V_0(\Delta y)100}$$

Similarly, the percentage change in price per basis point change for an increase in yield (Δy times 100) is:

$$\frac{V_0 - V_{+}}{V_0(\Delta y)100}$$

As explained in Chapter 3, the percentage price change for an increase and decrease in interest rates may not be the same. Consequently, the average percentage price change per basis point change in yield can be calculated. This is done as follows:

$$\frac{1}{2}\left[\frac{V_{-} - V_0}{V_0(\Delta y)100} + \frac{V_0 - V_{+}}{V_0(\Delta y)100}\right]$$

or equivalently,

$$\frac{V_{-} - V_{+}}{2V_0(\Delta y)100}$$

The approximate percentage price change for a 100 basis point change in yield is found by multiplying the previous formula by 100. The name popularly used to refer to the approximate percentage price change is *duration.* Thus,

$$\text{Duration} = \frac{V_{-} - V_{+}}{2V_0(\Delta y)} \tag{1}$$

To illustrate the calculation of duration using equation (1), consider the following option-free bond: a 9% 20-year bond trading to yield 6%. The initial price or value (V_0) is 134.6722. Suppose the yield is changed by 20 basis points. If the yield is decreased to 5.8%, the value of this bond (V_-) would be 137.5888. If the yield is increased to 6.2%, the value of this bond (V_+) would be 131.8439. Thus,

$$\begin{aligned} \Delta y &= 0.0020 \\ V_+ &= 131.8439 \\ V_- &= 137.5888 \\ V_0 &= 134.6722 \end{aligned}$$

Substituting these values into the duration formula given by equation (1) we get:

$$\text{Duration} = \frac{137.5888 - 131.8439}{2(134.6722)(0.002)} = 10.66$$

Interpreting and Using Duration

The duration of a security can be interpreted as the approximate percentage change in a bond's price for a 100 basis point change in interest rates. Thus a bond with a duration of 4.8 will change by approximately 4.8% for a 100 basis point change in interest rates. For a 50 basis point change in interest rates, the bond's price will change by approximately 2.4%; for a 25 basis point change by about 1.2%, etc.

A manager who anticipates a decline in interest rates may decide to extend (i.e., increase) the portfolio's duration. Suppose that the manager increases the present portfolio duration of 4 to 6. This means that for a 100 basis point change in interest rates, the portfolio will change by about 2% more than if the portfolio duration was left unchanged.

The approximate percentage price change of a bond using duration is found as follows:

$$\text{Approximate percentage price change} = -\text{Duration} \times (\Delta y) \times 100 \qquad (2)$$

The reason for the negative sign on the right-hand side of equation (2) is due to the inverse relationship between price change and yield change.

For example, consider the 9% 20-year bond trading at 134.6722 whose duration we just showed is 10.66. The approximate percentage price change for a 10 basis point increase in yield (i.e., $\Delta y = +0.001$) is:

$$\text{Approximate percentage price change} = -10.66 \times (+0.001) \times 100 = -1.066\%$$

How good is this approximation? The actual percentage price change is −1.06% (as shown in Exhibit 3 in Chapter 3 when yield increases to 6.10%). Duration, in this case, did an excellent job in estimating the percentage price change. We would come to the same conclusion if we used duration to estimate the percentage price change if the yield declined by 10 basis points (i.e., $\Delta y = -0.001$). In this case, the approximate percentage price change would be +1.066% (i.e., the direction of the price change is the reverse but the magnitude of the change is the same). Exhibit 3 in Chapter 3 shows that the actual percentage price change is +1.07%.

Let's look at how well duration does in estimating the percentage price change if the yield increases by 200 basis points instead of 10 basis points. In this case, Δy is equal to +0.02. Substituting into equation (2) we have

$$\text{Approximate percentage price change} = -10.66 \times (+0.02) \times 100 = -21.32\%$$

How good is this estimate? From Exhibit 3 in Chapter 3 we see that the actual percentage price change when the yield increases by 200 basis points to 8% is −18.40%. Thus, the estimate is not as good as when we used duration to approximate the percentage price change for a change in yield of only 10 basis points. How about if we use duration to approximate the percentage price change when the yield decreases by 200 basis points. The approximate percentage price change in this scenario is +21.32%, but the actual percentage price change as shown in Exhibit 3 in Chapter 3 is +25.04%.

Notice also in the two scenarios where we changed the yield by 200 basis points that the approximate percentage price change overestimated how much the bond's price would actually decline if the yield increased by 200 basis points and underestimates how much the bond's price would actually increase if the yield decreased by 200 basis points. We'll see why shortly.

Let's summarize what we found in our application of duration to approximate the percentage price change:

Yield	Percentage price change		
change (bp)	Approximate	Actual	Comment
+10	−1.066	−1.06	good job of estimating change
−10	+1.066	+1.07	good job of estimating change
+200	−21.32	−18.40	poor job; underestimates new price
−200	+21.32	+25.04	poor job; underestimates new price

Should any of this be a surprise to you? No, not if you read Chapter 3 and you evaluated equation (2) in terms of the properties for the price/yield relationship discussed in that chapter.

Look again at equation (2). Notice that whether the change in yield is an increase or a decrease, the approximate percentage price change will be the same except that the sign is reversed. This violates Property 3. Recall that Property 3 states that the percentage price change will not be the same for a large increase and decrease in yield by the same number of basis points. This is one reason why we see that the estimate is off for a 200 basis point yield change. We'll give another reason later on. Why did the duration estimate of the price change do a good job for a small change in yield of 10 basis points? Recall from Property 2 that the percentage price change will be approximately the same whether there is an increase or decrease in yield by a small number of basis points. Again, there is another reason which we will turn to now.

Exhibit 1: Price/Yield Relationship for an Option-Free Bond with a Tangent Line

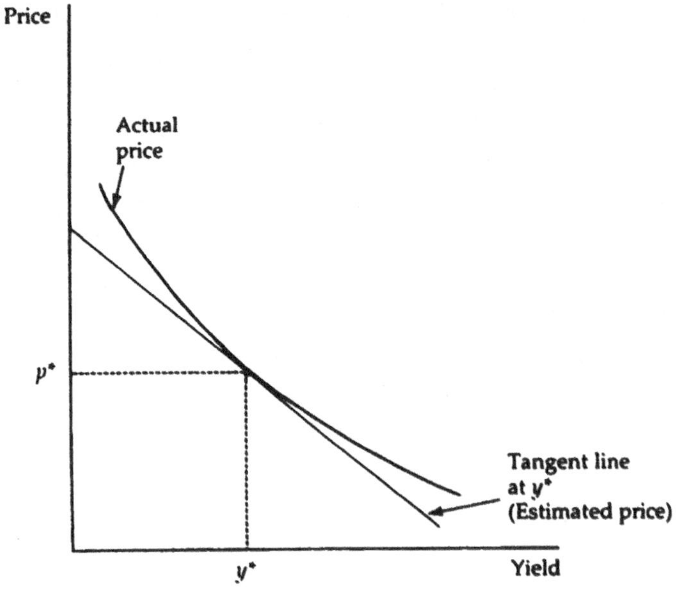

Graphical Depiction of Using Duration to Estimate Price Changes

In the previous chapter, we used the graph of the price/yield relationship to demonstrate the price volatility properties of bonds. We can use graphs here to illustrate what we observed in our examples about how duration estimates the percentage price change, as well as some other noteworthy points.

Recall the shape of the price/yield relationship for an option-free bond is convex. Exhibit 1 shows this relationship. In the exhibit a tangent line is drawn to the price/yield relationship at yield y^*. (For those unfamiliar with the concept of a tangent line, it is a straight line that just touches a curve at one point within a relevant (local) range.) The tangent line can be used to estimate the new price if the yield changes. If we draw a vertical line from any yield (on the horizontal axis), as in Exhibit 1, the distance between the horizontal axis and the tangent line represents the price approximated by using duration starting with the initial yield y^*.

Exhibit 2: Estimating the New Price Using a Tangent Line

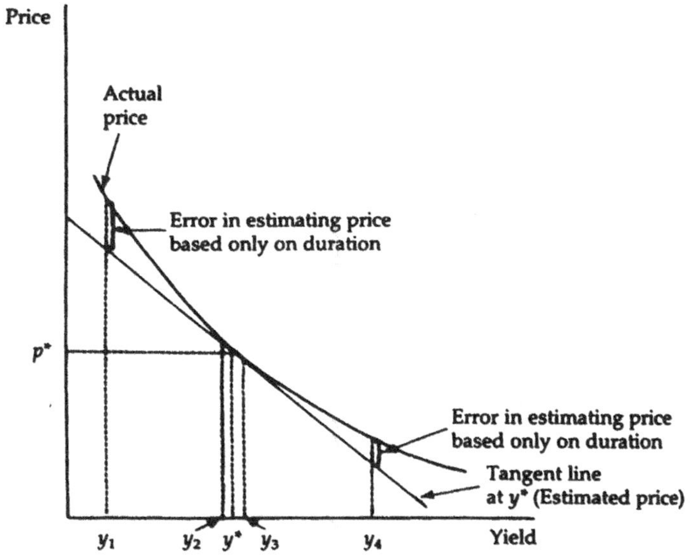

Now how is the tangent line that is used to approximate what the new price will be if yields change related to duration? Well, duration tells us the approximate percentage price change. Given the initial price and the approximate percentage price change provided by duration (i.e., as given by equation (2)), the approximate new price can be estimated. Mathematically, it can be demonstrated that the tangent line is the estimated price that is provided by duration.

This helps us understand why duration did an effective job of estimating the percentage price change, or equivalently, new price, when the yield changes by a small number of basis points. Look at Exhibit 2. Notice that for a small change in yield, the tangent line does not depart much from the price/yield relationship. Hence, when the yield changes up or down by 10 basis points, the tangent line does a good job of estimating the new price, as we found in our example.

Exhibit 2 also shows what happens to the estimate using the tangent line when the yield changes by a large number of basis points. Notice that the error in the estimate gets larger the further one moves from the initial yield. The estimate is poorer the more convex the bond. This is illustrated in Exhibit 3.

Exhibit 3: Estimating the New Price for a Large Yield Change for Bonds with Different Convexities

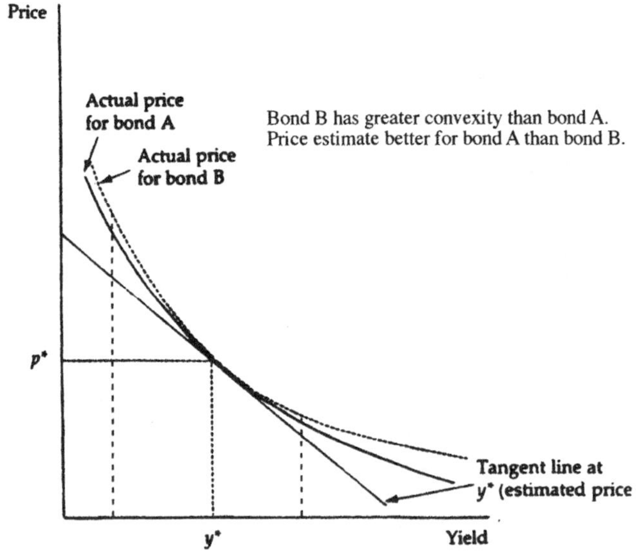

Also note that regardless of the magnitude in the yield change, the tangent line always underestimates what the new price will be for an option-free bond because the tangent line is below the price/yield relationship. This explains why we found in our illustration that when using duration we underestimated what the new price will be.

Rate Shocks and Duration Estimate

In calculating duration using equation (1), it is necessary to shock interest rates (yields) up and down by the same number of basis points to obtain the values for V_- and V_+. In our illustration, 20 basis points was arbitrarily selected. But how large should the shock be? That is, how many basis points should be used to shock the rate?

In Exhibit 4, the duration estimate for our four hypothetical bonds using equation (1) for rate shocks of 1 basis point to 200 basis points is reported. The duration estimates for the two 5-year bonds are not affected by the size of the shock. The two 5-year bonds are less convex than the two 20-year bonds. But even for the two 20-year bonds, for the size of the shocks reported in Exhibit 4 the duration estimates are not materially affected by the greater convexity.

Exhibit 4: Duration Estimates for Different Rate Shocks

Initial yield: 6%

Bond	1 bp	10 bps	20 bps	50 bps	100 bps	150 bps	200 bps
6% 5 year	4.27	4.27	4.27	4.27	4.27	4.27	4.27
6% 20 year	11.56	11.56	11.56	11.57	11.61	11.69	11.79
9% 5 year	4.07	4.07	4.07	4.07	4.07	4.08	4.08
9% 20 year	10.66	10.66	10.66	10.67	10.71	10.77	10.86

Thus, it would seem that the size of the shock is unimportant. However, the results reported in Exhibit 4 are for option-free bonds. When we deal with more complicated securities whose durations we want to estimate, the problem with small shocks is that divergences between actual and estimated price changes are magnified by dividing by a small change in rate in the denominator of equation (1). Moreover, small rate shocks that do not reflect the types of rate changes that may occur in the market do not permit the determination of how prices can change because expected cash flows may change when dealing with bonds with embedded options. In comparison, if large rate shocks are used, we encounter the asymmetry caused by convexity. Moreover, large rate shocks may cause dramatic changes in the expected cash flows for bonds with embedded options that may be far different from how the expected cash flows will change for smaller rate shocks.

What is done in practice by dealers and vendors of analytical systems? Each system developer uses rate shocks that they have found to be realistic based on historical rate changes.

Dollar Duration

Duration is related to percentage price change. However, for two bonds with the same duration, the dollar price change need not be the same. For example, consider two bonds, W and X. Suppose that both bonds have a duration of 5, but that W is trading at par while X is trading at 90. A 100 basis point change for both bonds will change the price by approximately 5%. This means a price change of $5 (5% times $100) for W and a price change of $4.5 (5% times $90) for X.

The dollar price volatility of a bond can be measured by multiplying duration by the bond's dollar price and the number of basis points (in decimal form). That is:

$$\text{Dollar price change} = -\text{Duration} \times \text{Dollar price} \times \Delta y \qquad (3)$$

For example, for our 9% 20-year bond selling to yield 6%, the dollar price is 134.6722 and the duration is 10.66. For a 10 basis point increase in yield (i.e., $\Delta y = +0.001$), the dollar price change is:

$$\begin{aligned}\text{Dollar price change} &= -10.66 \times 134.6722 \times (+0.001)\\ &= -1.4356\end{aligned}$$

This is close to the actual price change of 1.4250 (from 134.6722 to 133.2472).

The dollar price change for a 100 basis point change in yield involves substituting 0.01 for Δy into equation (3) obtaining:

$$\text{Dollar price change} = -\text{Duration} \times \text{Dollar price} \times (0.01)$$

or equivalently,

$$\text{Dollar price change} = -\text{Duration} \times \text{Dollar price}/100 \qquad (4)$$

The dollar price change for a 100 basis point change in yield as given by equation (4) is referred to by some market participants as *dollar duration*. Some market participants use the term dollar duration in a generic way meaning simply the dollar price change when rates change as given by equation (3). For a one basis point change in yield, the dollar price change will give the same value as the *price value of a basis point* or *dollar value of an 01* used by some market participants to quantify dollar price changes.

The dollar duration for a 100 basis point change in yield (up or down) for bonds W and X is:

$$\begin{aligned}&\text{For bond W: Dollar duration} = 5 \times 100 \times 0.01 = 5.0\\ &\text{For bond X: Dollar duration} = 5 \times 90 \times 0.01 = 4.5\end{aligned}$$

Modified Duration versus Effective Duration

One form of duration that is cited by practitioners is *modified duration*. Modified duration is the approximate percentage change in a bond's price for a 100 basis point change in yield *assuming that the bond's expected cash flows do not change when the yield changes*. What this means is that in calculating the values of V_- and V_+ in equation (1), the same cash flows used to calculate V_0 are used. Therefore, the change in the bond's price when the yield is changed is due solely to discounting at the new yield level.

The assumption that the cash flows will not change when the yield is changed makes sense for option-free bonds such as noncallable Treasury securities. This is because the payments made by the U.S. Department of the Treasury to holders of its obligations do not change when interest rates change. However, the same cannot be said for bonds with embedded options (i.e., callable and putable bonds and mortgage-backed securities). For these securities, a change in yield may alter the expected cash flows.

In Chapter 3 we showed the price/yield relationship for callable and prepayable bonds. We also gave an illustration in Chapter 3 that showed how when yields change the expected cash flows may change on a prepayable security and how, in turn, the new price changes. Failure to recognize how changes in yield can alter the expected cash flows will produce two values used in the numerator of equation (1) that are not good estimates of how the price can change. The duration is then not a good number to use to estimate how the price will change.

When we discuss in later chapters valuation models for bonds with embedded options, we will see how these models take into account how changes in yield will affect the expected cash flows. Thus, when V_- and V_+ are the values produced from these valuation models, the resulting duration takes into account both the discounting at different interest rates and how the expected cash flows may change. When duration is calculated in this manner, it is referred to as *effective duration* or *option-adjusted duration*. Exhibit 5 summarizes the distinction between modified duration and effective duration.

The difference between modified duration and effective duration for bonds with an embedded option can be quite dramatic. For example, a callable bond could have a modified duration of 5 but an effective duration of only 3. For certain collateralized mortgage obligations, the modified duration could be 7 and the effective duration 20! Thus, using modified duration as a measure of the price sensitivity of a security to changes in yield would be misleading. The more appropriate measure for any bond with an embedded option is effective duration.

Exhibit 5: Modified Duration versus Effective Duration

Duration

Interpretation: Generic description of the sensitivity of a bond's price (as a percentage of initial price) to a change in yield

Modified Duration	*Effective Duration*
Duration measure in which it is assumed that yield changes do not change the expected cash flows	Duration measure in which recognition is given to the fact that yield changes may change the expected cash flows

Macaulay Duration

It is worth comparing the relationship between modified duration to the another duration measure that is commonly cited by market participants. Modified duration can also be written as:[1]

$$\frac{1}{(1+\text{yield}/k)}\left[\frac{1\times \text{PVCF}_1 + 2\times \text{PVCF}_2 + \ldots + n\times \text{PVCF}_n}{k\times \text{Price}}\right] \quad (5)$$

where

k = number of periods, or payments, per year (e.g., k = 2 for semiannual-pay bonds and k = 12 for monthly-pay bonds)

n = number of periods until maturity (i.e., number of years to maturity times k)

yield = yield to maturity of the bond

PVCF_t = present value of the cash flow in period t discounted at the yield to maturity

The expression in the brackets of the modified duration formula given by equation (5) is a measure formulated in 1938 by Frederick Macaulay.[2] This measure is popularly referred to as *Macaulay duration*. Thus, modified duration is commonly expressed as:

$$\text{Modified duration} = \frac{\text{Macaulay duration}}{(1+\text{yield}/k)}$$

[1] More specifically, this is the formula for modified duration for a bond on a coupon anniversary date.

[2] Frederick Macaulay, *Some Theoretical Problems Suggested by the Movement of Interest Rates, Bond Yields, and Stock Prices in the U.S. Since 1856* (New York: National Bureau of Economic Research, 1938).

The general formulation for duration as given by equation (1) provides a short-cut procedure for determining a bond's modified duration. Because it is easier to calculate the modified duration using the short-cut procedure, most vendors of analytical software will use equation (1) rather than equation (5) to reduce computation time.

However, it must be clearly understood that modified duration is a flawed measure of a bond's price sensitivity to interest rate changes for a bond with an embedded option and therefore so is Macaulay duration. In fact, it is strongly recommended that if you have the formula for modified duration as given by equation (5) on a spreadsheet you do the following. Highlight the file and hit the *delete* key. The file with the spreadsheet will be destroyed. Why destroy it? The use of the formula for duration given by equation (5) misleads the user because it masks the fact that changes in the expected cash flows must be recognized for bonds with embedded options. For those who argue that the formula can still be used for option-free bonds, they're right. But, so what? You get the same estimate for duration using equation (1).

Other Interpretations of Duration

Earlier in this chapter, the following definition was provided for duration: the approximate percentage change in price for a 100 basis point change in rates. That definition is the most relevant for what a manager or investor is attempting to use duration for. In fact, if you understand this definition, you never need to use the equation for the approximate percentage price change given by equation (2) nor the equation for the approximate dollar price change given by equation (3).

Let's see why. Suppose you own a bond with a market value of $10 million and a duration (properly calculated) of 6. Suppose you want to approximate how much the dollar price change will be for this bond if rates rise by 50 basis points. It's simple. For a 100 basis point rise in yield the bond's value will change by approximately 1% or $100,000 (1% times the market value of $10 million). For a 50 basis point yield change, the change in the dollar value of the bond will be half the amount or $50,000.

Now let's look at some other definitions or interpretations of duration that appear in publications and are cited in discussions by managers with their clients.

Duration is the "First Derivative"

Sometimes a market participant will refer to duration as the "first derivative of the price/yield function" or simply the "first derivative." Wow! Sounds impressive. First, "derivative" here has nothing to do with "derivative instruments" (i.e., futures, swaps, options, etc.) A derivative as used in this context is obtained by differentiating a mathematical function. There are first derivatives, second derivatives, etc. When market participants say that duration is the first derivative, here is what they mean. If it were possible to write a mathematical equation for a bond in closed form, the first derivative would be the result of differentiating that equation the first time. Even if you don't know how to do the process of differentiation to get the first derivative, it sounds like you are really smart since it suggests you understand calculus! However, it is a useless interpretation and operationally meaningless for most bonds.

Let's look at this one at a time. Why is it a useless interpretation? Go back to the $10 million bond position with a duration of 6. Suppose a client is concerned with the exposure of the bond to changes in interest rates. Now, tell that client the duration is 6 and that it is the first derivative of the price function for that bond. What have you told the client? Not much. In contrast, tell that client that the duration is 6 and that duration is the approximate price sensitivity of a bond to a 100 basis point change in rates and you've told them a lot more with respect the bond's risk exposure to rate changes.

Why is it operationally meaningless for most bonds? Because for many bonds you cannot determine the bond's value by solving a closed-form mathematical expression. This will become clear when we discuss models such as the binomial model and Monte Carlo simulation model to value bonds with embedded options. You'll see how to get the two values to substitute into the numerator of equation (1). But you can't get a duration by taking a first derivative when these valuation models are used.

Thus, telling a client that duration is a first derivative is what can be viewed as the pretentious definition of duration. In the highly quantitative field of bond portfolio management, it sounds impressive that duration is obtained from calculus. Clients, however, are not concerned with a manager's ability to differentiate mathematical functions. They are impressed with performance and risk management. If a manager wants to show a client that he or she is well acquainted with calculus, the manager can send the client a college transcript with the impressive grades earned in calculus courses.

Before going on to another interpretation, it is important to put equation (1) for obtaining a duration estimate in the context of calculus. When studying calculus one is interested in knowing how given a mathematical function, the change in the value of the independent variable will change the value of the dependent variable. In terms of bond valuation, one wants to know how the change in yield (the independent variable) will change the value (the dependent variable). Calculus tells us that this can be done by using derivatives. In particular, the first derivative gives us a first approximation of how price will change. A 14-year old who knows algebra and can use a spreadsheet will ask, why bother with a first derivative? The 14-year old says give me the equation for the price of the bond and I will put it in my spreadsheet. If someone wants to know how the price will change if yield changes, the spreadsheet gives the solution much faster than a mathematician can by using derivatives.

Duration is Some Measure of Time

When the concept of duration was originally introduced by Macaulay in 1938, he used it as a gauge of the time that the bond was outstanding. Subsequently, duration has too often been thought of in temporal terms, i.e., years. That is most unfortunate for two reasons.

First, in terms of dimensions, there is nothing wrong with expressing duration in terms of years because that is the proper dimension of this value. But the proper interpretation is that duration is the price volatility of a zero-coupon bond with that number of years to maturity. So, when a manager says a bond has a duration of 4 years, it is not useful to think of this measure in terms of the time it takes to recoup principal on some weighted average time basis, but that the bond has the price sensitivity to rate changes of a 4-year zero-coupon bond.

Second, thinking of duration in terms of years makes it difficult for managers and their clients to understand the duration of some complex securities. Here are a few examples. For a mortgage-backed security that is an interest-only (IO) security, the duration is negative. What does a negative number of, say, –4 mean? In terms of our interpretation as a percentage price change, it means that when rates change by 100 basis points, the price of the bond changes by about 4% but the change is in the same direction as the change in rates.

As a second example, and one we will look at more closely in the next chapter, consider a security called an inverse floater. The underlying collateral for such a security might be loans with 25 years to final maturity. However, an inverse floater can have a duration that easily exceeds 25. This doesn't make sense to a manager or client who uses a temporal definition for duration.

As a final example, consider derivative instruments. We'll discuss the duration of these instruments in Chapter 8. Consider the duration of an option that expires in one year. Suppose that it is reported that its duration is 60. What does that mean? To someone who interprets duration in terms of time, does that mean 60 years, 60 days, 60 seconds? It doesn't mean any of these. It simply means that the option tends to have the price sensitivity to rate changes of a 60-year zero-coupon bond.

Forget First Derivatives and Temporal Definitions

The bottom line is that one should not care if it is technically correct to think of duration in terms of years (volatility of a zero-coupon bond) or in terms of first derivatives. There are even some who interpret duration in terms of the "half life" of a security. Subject to the limitations that we will describe as we proceed in this book, duration is used as a measure of the sensitivity of a security's price to changes in yield. We will fine tune this definition as we move along.

Users of this risk parameter are interested in what it tells them about the price sensitivity of a bond (or a portfolio) to changes in rates. Duration provides the investor with a feel for the dollar price exposure or the percentage price exposure when rates change. Try the following definitions on a client who has a portfolio with a duration of 4 and see which one the client finds most useful for understanding the risk exposure of the portfolio when rates change:

Definition 1: The duration of 4 for your portfolio indicates that the portfolio's value will change by approximately 4% if rates change by 100 basis points.

Definition 2: The duration of 4 for your portfolio is the first derivative of the price function for the bonds in the portfolio.

Definition 3: The duration of 4 for your portfolio is the weighted average number of years to receipt of the present value of the cash flows of the portfolio.

If you find that clients really understand the last two definitions better than the first, then send me a letter with the names of the clients and why they find it more useful and I will refund the cost of the book![3]

Portfolio Duration

A portfolio's duration can be obtained by calculating the weighted average of the duration of the bonds in the portfolio. The weight is the proportion of the portfolio that a security comprises. Mathematically, a portfolio's duration can be calculated as follows:

$$w_1 D_1 + w_2 D_2 + w_3 D_3 + \ldots + w_K D_K$$

where

w_i = market value of bond i/market value of the portfolio
D_i = duration of bond i
K = number of bonds in the portfolio

To illustrate this calculation, consider the following 3-bond portfolio in which all three bonds are option free:

Bond	Par amount owned	Market Value
10% 5-year	$4 million	$4,000,000
8% 15-year	5 million	4,231,375
14% 30-year	1 million	1,378,586

In this illustration, it is assumed that the next coupon payment for each bond is six months from now. The market value for the portfolio is $9,609,961. Since each bond is option free, the mod-

[3] This offer is conditional upon permission to reprint the name of the client and receipt of a letter granting permission to reprint.

ified duration can be used. The market price per $100 par value of each bond, its yield, and its duration are given below:

Bond	Price ($)	Yield (%)	Duration
10% 5-year	100.0000	10	3.861
8% 15-year	84.6275	10	8.047
14% 30-year	137.8590	10	9.168

In this illustration, K is equal to 3 and:

$$\begin{aligned} w_1 &= \$4{,}000{,}000/\$9{,}609{,}961 = 0.416 & D_1 &= 3.861 \\ w_2 &= \$4{,}231{,}375/\$9{,}609{,}961 = 0.440 & D_2 &= 8.047 \\ w_3 &= \$1{,}378{,}586/\$9{,}609{,}961 = 0.144 & D_3 &= 9.168 \end{aligned}$$

The portfolio's duration is:

$$0.416\,(3.861) + 0.440\,(8.047) + 0.144\,(9.168) = 6.47$$

A portfolio duration of 6.47 means that for a 100 basis point change in the yield for *all* three bonds, the market value of the portfolio will change by approximately 6.47%. But keep in mind, the yield on all three bonds must change by 100 basis points for the duration measure to be useful. This is a critical assumption and its importance cannot be overemphasized. We introduced this assumption in Chapter 2 and shall return to it in later chapters.

An alternative procedure for calculating the duration of a portfolio is to calculate the dollar price change for a given number of basis points for each security in the portfolio and then adding up all the price changes. Dividing the total of the price changes by the initial market value of the portfolio produces a percentage price change that can be adjusted to obtain the portfolio's duration.

For example, consider the 3-bond portfolio shown above. Suppose that we calculate the dollar price change for each bond in the portfolio based on its respective duration for a 50 basis point change in yield. We would then have:

Bond	Market value	Duration	Change in value for 50 bp yield change
10% 5-year	$4,000,000	3.861	$77,220
8% 15-year	4,231,375	8.047	170,249
14% 30-year	1,378,586	9.168	63,194
		Total	$310,663

Thus, a 50 basis point change in all rates changes the market value of the 3-bond portfolio by $310,663. Since the market value of the portfolio is $9,609,961, a 50 basis point change produced a change in value of 3.23% ($310,663 divided by $9,609,961). Since duration is the approximate percentage change for a 100 basis point change in rates, this means that the portfolio duration is 6.46 (found by doubling 3.23). This is the same value for the portfolio's duration as found earlier.

Contribution to Portfolio Duration

Some portfolio managers look at their exposure to an issue or to a sector in terms of the percentage of that issue or sector in the portfolio. A better measure of exposure of an individual issue or sector to changes in interest rates is in terms of its contribution to the portfolio duration. This is found by multiplying the percentage that the individual issue or sector is of the portfolio by the duration of the individual issue or sector. That is,

$$\text{Contribution to portfolio duration}$$
$$= \frac{\text{Market value of issue or sector}}{\text{Market value of portfolio}} \times \text{Duration of issue or sector}$$

The exposure can also be cast in terms of dollar exposure. To do this, the dollar duration of the issue or sector is used instead of the duration of the issue or sector.

A portfolio manager who wants to determine the contribution to portfolio duration of a sector relative to the contribution of the same sector in a broad-based market index can compute the difference between the two contributions.

Allowing for Leverage and Derivatives in Computing Duration

The question is why bother looking at dollar price changes for each position in the portfolio if the same duration is computed by just calculating a weighted average of the durations? The reason is that when a manager borrows to leverage a portfolio and/or uses derivatives, it is easier to compute the portfolio's duration using this approach. The portfolio is then composed of the assets, liabilities, and derivatives. The percentage price change of a portfolio that includes borrowed funds and derivatives is equal to:

	Dollar price change of all the bonds when rates change
–	Dollar price change of the liabilities when rates change
+	Dollar price change of the derivatives when rates change
	Total change in the portfolio value when rates change

Dividing the total change in the portfolio value by the initial value of the portfolio and adjusting based on the number of basis points used to change rates gives the duration of the portfolio.

If the liabilities are short-term, then the value of a short-term liability like that of a short-term asset will be small. In Chapter 8, we look at how to calculate the dollar price change for derivative instruments.

To illustrate the above calculation of portfolio duration, suppose that in our previous portfolio $2 million was borrowed to buy the securities in our 3-bond portfolio and that there are no derivatives in the portfolio. Since $2 million was borrowed, the amount of the client's funds invested (i.e., the equity) is $7,609,961. The client is interested in how the rate changes will affect the equity investment of $7,609,961. Suppose further that the funds are borrowed via a 3-month reverse repurchase agreement so that the duration of the liabilities is close to zero and the dollar price change in the liabilities for a 50 basis point change in rates is close to zero. Then the change in the value of the portfolio for a 50 basis point change in rates is as follows:

	Dollar price change of the bonds	$310,663
–	Dollar price change of the liability	0
	Total change in portfolio value	$310,663

Thus, the percentage change in the portfolio's value for a 50 basis point change in rates is 4.08% ($310,663 divided by $7,609,961). The portfolio's duration is then 8.16. The higher duration with the $2 million short-term reverse repo borrowing (8.16 versus 6.47) is due to the leveraging of the portfolio.

Some Applications

Let's look at two applications of duration to portfolio management. The first is in constructing swap trades. In this context, a swap trade is an exchange of one or more bonds for one or more other bonds. The second is altering the duration of a portfolio.

Duration-Weighted Swap Trades

Yield spread strategies involve positioning a portfolio to capitalize on expected changes in yield spreads between sectors of the bond market. Swapping (or exchanging) one bond for another when the manager believes that the prevailing yield spread between two bonds in the market is out of line with their historical yield spread, and that the yield spread will realign by the end of the investment horizon, is called an *intermarket spread swap*. Individual security selection strategies involve identifying mispriced securities and taking a position in those securities so as to benefit when the market realigns. The most common strategy identifies an issue as undervalued because either (1) its yield is higher than that of comparably rated issues, or (2) its yield is expected to decline (and price therefore rise) because credit analysis indicates that its rating will improve.

What is critical in assessing yield spread and individual security selection strategies when one of these swaps is being contemplated is to compare positions that have the same dollar duration. To understand why, consider two bonds, A and B. Suppose that the price of bond A is 80 and has a duration of 5, while bond B has a price of 90 and has a duration of 4. Since duration is the approximate percentage price change per 100 basis point change in yield, a 100 basis point change in yield for bond A would change its price by about 5%. Based on a price of 80, its price will change by about \$4. Thus, its dollar duration for a 100 basis point change in yield is \$4 per \$80 of market value. Similarly, for bond B, its dollar duration for a 100 basis point change in yield per \$90 of market value can be determined. In this case it is \$3.6. So, if bonds A and B are being considered as alternative investments in some strategy other than one based on anticipating interest rate movements, the amount of each bond in the strategy should be such that they will both have the same dollar duration.

To illustrate this, suppose that a manager owns \$10 million of par value of bond A which has a market value of \$8 million. The dollar duration of bond A per 100 basis point change in yield for the \$8 million market value is \$400,000. Suppose further that this manager is considering swapping bond A that she owns in her portfolio for bond B. If the manager wants to have the same interest rate exposure (i.e., dollar duration) for bond B that she currently has for bond A, she will buy a market value amount of bond B with the same dollar duration. If the manager purchased \$10 million of *par value* of bond B and therefore \$9 million of *market value* of bond B, the dollar value change per 100 basis change in yield would be only \$360,000. If, instead, the manager purchased \$10 million of *market value* of bond B, the dollar duration per 100 basis point change in yield would be \$400,000. Since bond B is trading at 90, \$11.11 million of par value of bond B must be purchased to keep the dollar duration of the position for bond B the same as for bond A.

Mathematically, this problem can be expressed as follows. Let:

$\$D_A$ = dollar duration per 100 basis point change in yield for bond A for the market value of bond A held
D_B = duration for bond B
MV_B = market value of bond B needed to obtain the same dollar duration as bond A

Then, the following equation sets the dollar duration for bond A equal to the dollar duration for bond B:

$$\$D_A = (D_B/100)\ MV_B$$

Solving for MV_B,

$$MV_B = \$D_A/(D_B/100)$$

Dividing by the price per \$1 of par value of bond B gives the par value of B that has an approximately equivalent dollar duration as bond A.

In our illustration, $\$D_A$ is \$400,000 and D_B is 4, then

$$MV_B = \$400{,}000/(4/100) = \$10{,}000{,}000$$

Since the market value of bond B is 90 per \$100 of par value, the price per \$1 of par value is 0.9. Dividing \$10 million by 0.9 indicates that the par value of bond B that should be purchased is \$11.11 million.

Failure to adjust a trade that is based on some expected change in yield spread so as to keep the dollar duration the same means that the outcome of the portfolio will be affected by not only the expected change in the yield spread but also a change in the yield level. Thus, a manager would be making a conscious yield spread bet and possibly an undesired bet on the level of interest rates.

Controlling Interest Rate Risk

The general principle in controlling interest rate risk is to combine the dollar value exposure of the current portfolio and that of another position so that it is equal to the target dollar exposure. This means that the manager must be able to accurately measure the dollar exposure of both the current portfolio and the other position employed to alter the exposure. We will refer to the other position that is used to adjust the current portfolio to achieve the target dollar exposure as the "controlling position." The controlling position could be simply the sale of cash market instruments in the portfolio, the short sale of Treasuries, the purchase of bonds, and/or positions in derivative instruments.

Dollar duration can be used to approximate the change in the dollar value of a bond or bond portfolio to changes in interest rates. Suppose that a manager has a $250 million portfolio with a duration of 5 and wants to reduce the duration to 4. Thus, the target duration for the portfolio is 4. Given the target duration, a target dollar duration for say a 50 basis point rate change can be obtained. A target duration of 4 means that for a 100 basis point change in rates (assuming a parallel shift in rates of all maturities), the target percentage change in the portfolio's value is 4%. For a 50 basis point change, the target percentage change in the portfolio's value is 2%. Multiplying the 2% by $250 million gives a target dollar duration of $5 million for a 50 basis point change in rates.

The manager must then determine the dollar duration of the current portfolio for a 50 basis point change in rates. Since the current duration for the portfolio is 5, the current dollar duration for a 50 basis point change in interest rates is $6.25 million. The target dollar duration is then compared to the current dollar duration. The difference between the two dollar durations is the dollar exposure that must be provided by the controlling position. If the target dollar duration exceeds the current dollar duration, a controlling position must be such that it increases the dollar exposure by the difference. If the target dollar duration is less than the current dollar duration, a controlling position must be created such that it decreases the dollar exposure by the difference.

Once a controlling position is taken, the portfolio's dollar duration is equal to the current dollar duration without the controlling position plus the dollar duration of the controlling position. That is,

Portfolio's dollar duration
= Current dollar duration without controlling position
+ Dollar duration with controlling position

The objective is to control the portfolio's interest rate risk by establishing a controlling position such that the portfolio's dollar duration is equal to the target dollar duration. That is,

Portfolio's dollar duration = Target dollar duration

or, equivalently,

Target dollar duration
= Current dollar duration without controlling position
+ Dollar duration of controlling position (6)

Over time, the portfolio's dollar duration will move away from the target dollar duration. The manager can alter the controlling position to adjust the portfolio's dollar duration to the target dollar duration.

In Chapter 8 where we discuss the price volatility characteristics and duration of derivative instruments, we will see how these instruments can be used to alter the dollar duration of a portfolio.

CONVEXITY

The duration measure indicates that regardless of whether interest rates increase or decrease, the approximate percentage price change is the same. However, as we noted earlier, this does not agree with Property 3 of a bond's price volatility. Specifically, while for small changes in yield the percentage price change will be the same for an increase or decrease in yield, for large changes in yield this is not true. This suggests that duration is only a good approximation of the percentage price change for a small change in yield.

We demonstrated this earlier using a 9% 20-year bond selling to yield 6% with a duration of 10.66. For a 10 basis point change in yield, the estimate was right on the money for both an increase or decrease in yield. However, for a 200 basis point change in yield the approximate percentage price change was off considerably.

The reason for this result is that duration is in fact a first approximation for a small change in yield. The approximation can be improved by using a second approximation. This approximation is referred to as "convexity." *The use of this term in the industry is unfortunate since the term convexity is also used to describe the shape or curvature of the price/yield relationship.* The *convexity measure* of a security can be used to approximate the change in price that is not explained by duration.

Convexity Measure

The convexity measure of a bond can be approximated using the following formula:

$$\text{Convexity measure} = \frac{V_+ + V_- - 2V_0}{2V_0(\Delta y)^2} \qquad (7)$$

where the notation is the same as used earlier for duration as given by equation (1).

For our hypothetical 9% 20-year bond selling to yield 6%, we know that for a 20 basis point change in yield ($\Delta y = 0.002$):

$$V_0 = 134.6722,\ V_- = 137.5888,\ \text{and}\ V_+ = 131.8439$$

Substituting these values into the convexity measure given by equation (7):

$$\text{Convexity measure} = \frac{131.8439 + 137.5888 - 2(134.6722)}{2(134.6722)(0.002)^2}$$

$$= 81.96$$

We'll see how to use this convexity measure shortly. Before doing so, there are three points that should be noted. First, there is no simple interpretation of the convexity measure as there is for duration. Second, it is more common for market participants to refer to the value computed in equation (7) as the "convexity of a bond" rather than the "convexity measure of a bond." Finally, the convexity measure reported by dealers and vendors will differ for an option-free bond. The reason is that the value obtained from equation (7) will be scaled for the reason explained after we demonstrate how to use the convexity measure.

Convexity Adjustment to Percentage Price Change

Given the convexity measure, the approximate percentage price change adjustment due to the bond's convexity (i.e., the percentage price change not explained by duration) is:

$$\text{Convexity adjustment to percentage price change} \\ = \text{Convexity measure} \times (\Delta y)^2 \times 100 \quad (8)$$

For example, for the 9% coupon bond maturing in 20 years, the convexity adjustment to the percentage price change based on duration if the yield increases from 6% to 8% is

$$81.96 \times (0.02)^2 \times 100 = 3.28$$

If the yield decreases from 6% to 4%, the convexity adjustment to the approximate percentage price change based on duration would also be 3.28%.

The approximate percentage price change based on duration and the convexity adjustment is found by adding the two estimates. So, for example, if yields change from 6% to 8%, the estimated percentage price change would be:

Estimated change approximated by duration	=	−21.32%
Convexity adjustment	=	+3.28%
Total estimated percentage price change	=	−18.04%

The actual percentage price change is −18.40%.

For a decrease of 200 basis points, from 6% to 4%, the approximate percentage price change would be as follows:

Estimated change approximated by duration	=	+21.32%
Convexity adjustment	=	+3.28%
Total estimated percentage price change	=	+24.60%

The actual percentage price change is +25.04%. Thus, duration combined with the convexity adjustment does a good job of estimating the sensitivity of a bond's price change to large changes in yield.

Notice that when the convexity measure is positive, we have the situation described earlier that the gain is greater than the loss for a given large change in rates. That is, the bond exhibits positive convexity. We can see this in the example above. However, if the convexity measure is negative, we have the situation where the loss will be greater than the gain. For example, suppose that a callable bond has an effective duration of 4 and a convexity measure of –30. This means that the approximate percentage price change for a 200 basis point change is 8%. The convexity adjustment for a 200 basis point change in rates is then

$$-30 \times (0.02)^2 \times 100 = -1.2$$

Thus, the convexity adjustment is –1.2%. Therefore, the approximate percentage price change after adjusting for convexity is:

Estimated change approximated by duration	=	–8.0%
Convexity adjustment	=	–1.2%
Total estimated percentage price change	=	–9.2%

For a decrease of 200 basis points, the approximate percentage price change would be as follows:

Estimated change approximated by duration	=	+8.0%
Convexity adjustment	=	–1.2%
Total estimated percentage price change	=	+6.8%

Notice that the loss is greater than the gain — a property called negative convexity that we discussed in Chapter 3.

Scaling the Convexity Measure

The convexity measure as given by equation (7) means nothing in isolation. It is the substitution of the computed convexity measure into equation (8) that provides the estimated adjustment for convexity. Therefore, it is possible to scale the convexity measure in any way and obtain the same convexity adjustment.

For example, in some books the convexity measure is defined as follows:

$$\text{Convexity measure} = \frac{V_+ + V_- - 2V_0}{V_0(\Delta y)^2} \tag{9}$$

Equation (9) differs from equation (7) since it does not include 2 in the denominator. Thus, the convexity measure computed using equation (9) will be double the convexity measure using equation (7). So, for our earlier illustration, since the convexity measure using equation (7) is 81.96, the convexity measure using equation (9) would be 163.92.

Which is correct, 81.96 or 163.92? Both. The reason is that the corresponding equation for computing the convexity adjustment would not be given by equation (8) if the convexity measure is obtained from equation (9). Instead, the corresponding convexity adjustment formula would be:

$$\begin{aligned}&\text{Convexity adjustment to percentage price change}\\&\quad = (\text{Convexity measure}/2) \times (\Delta y)^2 \times 100\end{aligned} \tag{10}$$

Equation (10) differs from equation (8) in that the convexity measure is divided by 2. Thus, the convexity adjustment will be the same whether one uses equation (7) to get the convexity measure and equation (8) to get the convexity adjustment or one uses equation (9) to compute the convexity measure and equation (9) to determine the convexity adjustment.

Some dealers and vendors scale in a different way. One can also compute the convexity measure as follows:

$$\text{Convexity measure} = \frac{V_+ + V_- - 2V_0}{2V_0(\Delta y)^2(100)} \tag{11}$$

Equation (11) differs from equation (7) by the inclusion of 100 in the denominator. In our illustration, the convexity measure would be 0.8196 rather than 81.96 using equation (7). The convexity adjustment formula corresponding to the convexity measure given by equation (11) is then

Convexity adjustment to percentage price change
$$= \text{Convexity measure} \times (\Delta y)^2 \times 10{,}000 \qquad (12)$$

Similarly, one can express the convexity measure as shown in equation (13):

$$\text{Convexity measure} = \frac{V_+ + V_- - 2V_0}{V_0(\Delta y)^2(100)} \qquad (13)$$

For the bond we have been using in our illustrations, the convexity measure is 1.6392. The corresponding convexity adjustment is:

Convexity adjustment to percentage price change
$$= (\text{Convexity measure}/2) \times (\Delta y)^2 \times 10{,}000 \qquad (14)$$

Consequently, the convexity measures (or just simply convexity as it is referred to by some market participants) that could be reported for this option-free bond are 81.96, 163.92, 0.8196, or 1.6392. All of these values are correct, but they mean nothing in isolation. To use them to obtain the convexity adjustment requires knowing how they are computed so that the correct convexity adjustment formula is used.

It is also important to understand this when comparing the convexity measures reported by dealers and vendors. For example, if one dealer shows a manager Bond A with a duration of 4 and a convexity measure of 50, and a second dealer shows the manager Bond B with a duration of 4 and a convexity measure of 80, which bond has the greater percentage price change response to changes in interest rates? Since the duration of the two bonds is identical, the bond with the larger convexity measure will change more when rates decline. However, not knowing how the two dealers computed the convexity measure means that the manager does not know which bond will have the greater convexity adjustment. If the first dealer used equation (7) while the second dealer used equation (9), then the convexity measures must be adjusted in terms of either equation. For example, using equation (7), the convexity measure of 80 computed using equation (9) is equal to a convexity measure of 40 based on equation (7).

Derivation of the Convexity Measure and Convexity Adjustment

The formulas for the convexity measure and the convexity adjustment were given without any explanation of how they were determined. They are derived from a mathematical property in calculus. This property says that a mathematical function can be approximated by a series of derivatives. The first derivative provides the first approximation, the second derivative is the improvement to the first approximation, the third derivative is the improvement to the first two approximations, etc.

It turns out that the first derivative is related to the duration estimate of the percentage price change and the second derivative is related to the convexity measure/convexity adjustment. Thus, some market participants refer to the convexity measure/convexity adjustment as the "second derivative." As in the case of interpreting duration, it is not a very insightful interpretation.

One might ask, is there a corresponding approximation above the second derivative? While one can derive an adjustment to improve upon the approximation based on duration and the convexity adjustment, it turns out that with just these two parameters most of the percentage price change of a bond can be explained. Thus, market participants at this time have not developed higher order measures.

Modified Convexity and Effective Convexity

The prices used in equation (7) to calculate convexity can be obtained by either assuming that when the yield changes the expected cash flows do not change or they do change. In the former case, the resulting convexity is referred to as *modified convexity*. (Actually, in the industry, convexity is not qualified by the adjective "modified.") *Effective convexity*, in contrast, assumes that the cash flows do change when yields change. This is the same distinction made for duration.

As with duration, for bonds with embedded options there can be quite a difference between the calculated modified convexity and effective convexity. In fact, for all option-free bonds, either convexity measure will have a positive value. For bonds with embedded options, the calculated effective convexity can be negative when the calculated modified convexity gives a positive value.

Portfolio Convexity Measure

The procedure for calculating the convexity measure for a portfolio is the same as for calculating a portfolio's duration. That is, the convexity measure for each bond in the portfolio is computed. Either equation (7), (9), (11), or (13) can be used. Then, the weighted average of the convexity measure for the bonds in the portfolio is computed to get the portfolio's convexity measure.

When combining the estimated percentage price change for the portfolio due to duration and the convexity adjustment, the equation used to obtain the latter depends on the equation used to compute the convexity measure.

SUMMARY

Duration is a measure of the sensitivity of the price of a bond or the value of a portfolio to changes in interest rates. A useful working definition is that duration is the approximate percentage change in the price of a bond (or value of a portfolio) for a 100 basis point change in rates. Duration is estimated by shocking rates up and down by a small number of basis points and looking at how the price changes. The duration estimate is dependent on a good valuation model. While duration measures the percentage price change, dollar duration measures the dollar price change of a bond or portfolio.

In computing the new prices when rates are shocked, the new prices can reflect either no change in the expected cash flows when yields change or changes in the expected cash flows resulting from the change in yield. When the prices used to compute duration when rates are shocked assume that the expected cash flows are unchanged, the resulting duration calculation is called modified duration; when rates are shocked and the expected cash flows are allowed to change in deriving the new prices, then the resulting duration is called effective duration. It is effective duration that is the appropriate measure to use for bonds with embedded options.

The duration of a portfolio is just the weighted average of the duration of the bonds in the portfolio. A leveraged portfolio can be computed by looking at the sensitivity of the bonds in the portfolio to rate changes and relating that change to the amount of the equity investment (i.e., the amount without borrowing). The duration of a portfolio with derivative instruments can be computed once the sensitivity of each derivative instrument to rate changes is estimated.

Duration is the first approximation as to how the price of a bond or value of a portfolio will change when rates change. A second approximation can be used to improve the estimate of the price change obtained from duration. The second approximation is sometimes called "convexity." More specifically, a convexity measure can be computed and then the convexity adjustment to the percentage price change can be made. By adjustment it is meant that the approximate percentage price change as estimated by duration is adjusted. The convexity adjustment formula depends on how the convexity measure is defined. Thus, dealers and vendors may report different convexity measures for an option-free bond but come up with the same convexity adjustment for a given change in yield. As with duration, a modified convexity and effective convexity measure can be computed.

Chapter 5

Duration Measures for Bonds with Embedded Options and Foreign Bonds

In the previous chapter we saw how to compute the duration of an option-free bond and the distinction between modified duration and effective duration. Effective duration is the appropriate measure for bonds with embedded options. In this chapter we focus on how to compute the effective duration for bonds with embedded options. This includes callable bonds, putable bonds, and floating-rate securities. We will see that floating-rate securities even if they are not callable or putable have an embedded option. This is because most have a cap (i.e., maximum interest rate) which is effectively an option that the investor has given to the issuer. Along the way we will discuss other duration measures — spread duration, index duration, and volatility duration. The durations presented here are appropriate for agency debentures, corporates, and municipals. (In Chapter 6, we cover mortgage-backed securities.) At the end of the chapter, we discuss the contribution to a portfolio's duration of including foreign bonds.

In the previous chapter we emphasized that to estimate the effective duration of a bond, it is necessary to have a good valuation model. The model used for valuing agency debentures, corporates, and municipals with embedded options is the *binomial model*. Therefore, we begin this chapter with a brief review of this valuation model.

THE BINOMIAL MODEL

The model used to value agency debentures, corporates, and municipals with embedded options is the binomial model.[1] In this section,

[1] The model described in this section was presented in Andrew J. Kalotay, George O. Williams, and Frank J. Fabozzi, "A Model for the Valuation of Bonds with Embedded Options," *Financial Analysts Journal* (May-June 1993), pp. 35-46.

we will describe this model. The focus here is on the general principles of the methodology and the assumptions made in constructing the model. This will also be our focus when we discuss how to value mortgage-backed securities using the Monte Carlo simulation model described in Chapter 6. In all valuation models, assumptions are made. The risk that these assumptions may be wrong, leading to values predicted by the model being wrong and therefore the effective duration estimated being wrong, is called *modeling risk.* As we proceed, we will introduce measures that have been developed to see how sensitive the estimates are to modeling risk.

To illustrate the binomial model, we start with the on-the-run yield curve for the particular issuer whose bonds we want to value. The starting point is the Treasury's on-the-run yield curve. To obtain a particular issuer's on-the-run yield curve, an appropriate credit spread is added to each on-the-run Treasury issue. The credit spread need not be constant for all maturities. For example, the credit spread may increase with maturity. In our illustration, we use the hypothetical on-the-run issues for an issuer shown in Exhibit 1. Each bond is trading at par value (100) so the coupon rate is equal to the yield. We will simplify the illustration by assuming annual-pay bonds.

Binomial Interest Rate Tree

Once we allow for embedded options, consideration must be given to interest rate volatility. This is done by introducing a *binomial interest rate tree*. This tree is nothing more than a graphical depiction of the 1-period or short rates over time based on some assumption about interest rate volatility. How this tree is constructed is illustrated below.

Exhibit 1: On-the-Run Yield Curve and Spot Rates for an Issuer

Maturity (Years)	Yield (%)	Market Price ($)	Spot Rate (%)
1	3.5	100	3.5000
2	4.2	100	4.2147
3	4.7	100	4.7345
4	5.2	100	5.2707

Exhibit 2: Four-Year Binomial Interest Rate Tree

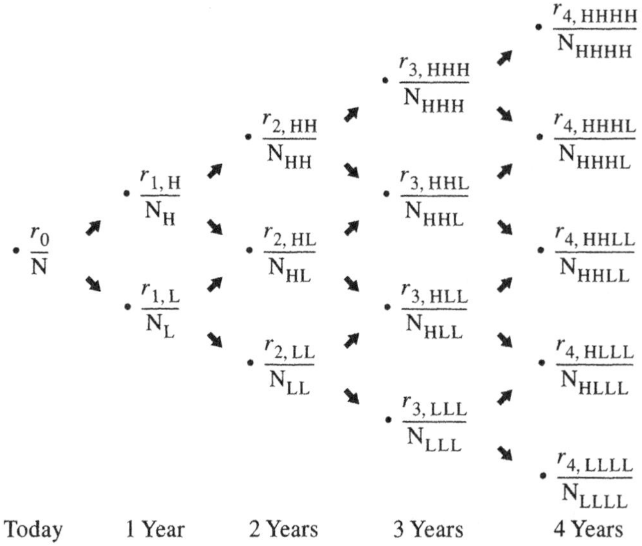

Exhibit 2 shows an example of a binomial interest rate tree. In this tree, each node (bold circle) represents a time period that is equal to one year from the node to its left. Each node is labeled with an N, representing node, and a subscript that indicates the path that the 1-year rate took to get to that node. L represents the lower of the two 1-year rates and H represents the higher of the two 1-year rates. For example, node N_{HH} means to get to that node the following path for 1-year rates occurred: the 1-year rate realized is the higher of the two rates in the first year and then the higher of the 1-year rates in the second year.[2]

Look first at the point denoted by just N in Exhibit 2. This is the root of the tree and is nothing more than the current 1-year spot rate, or equivalently the current 1-year rate, which we denote by r_0. What we have assumed in creating this tree is that the 1-year rate can take on two possible values the next period and that the two rates have the same probability of occurring. One rate will be higher than the other. It is assumed that the 1-year rate can evolve over time based on a random process called a lognormal random walk with a certain volatility.

---

[2] Note that N_{HL} is equivalent to N_{LH} in the second year and that in the third year N_{HHL} is equivalent to N_{HLH} and N_{LHH}, and that N_{HLL} is equivalent to N_{LLH}. We have simply selected one label for a node rather than clutter up the figure with redundant information.

We use the following notation to describe the tree in the first year. Let

σ = assumed volatility of the 1-year rate
$r_{1,L}$ = the lower 1-year rate one year from now
$r_{1,H}$ = the higher 1-year rate one year from now

The relationship between $r_{1,L}$ and $r_{1,H}$ is as follows:

$$r_{1,H} = r_{1,L}(e^{2\sigma})$$

where e is the base of the natural logarithm 2.71828.

For example, suppose that $r_{1,L}$ is 4.4448% and σ is 10% per year, then:

$$r_{1,H} = 4.4448\%(e^{2\times 0.10}) = 5.4289\%$$

In the second year, there are three possible values for the 1-year rate, which we will denote as follows:

$r_{2,LL}$ = 1-year rate in second year assuming the lower rate in the first year and the lower rate in the second year
$r_{2,HH}$ = 1-year rate in second year assuming the higher rate in the first year and the higher rate in the second year
$r_{2,HL}$ = 1-year rate in second year assuming the higher rate in the first year and the lower rate in the second year or equivalently the lower rate in the first year and the higher rate in the second year

The relationship between $r_{2,LL}$ and the other two 1-year rates is as follows:

$$r_{2,HH} = r_{2,LL}(e^{4\sigma}) \text{ and } r_{2,HL} = r_{2,LL}(e^{2\sigma})$$

So, for example, if $r_{2,LL}$ is 4.6958%, then assuming once again that σ is 10%, then

$$r_{2,HH} = 4.6958\%(e^{4\times 0.10}) = 7.0053\%$$

and

$$r_{2,HL} = 4.6958\%(e^{2\times 0.10}) = 5.7354\%$$

Exhibit 3: Four-Year Binomial Interest Rate Tree with 1-Year Rates*

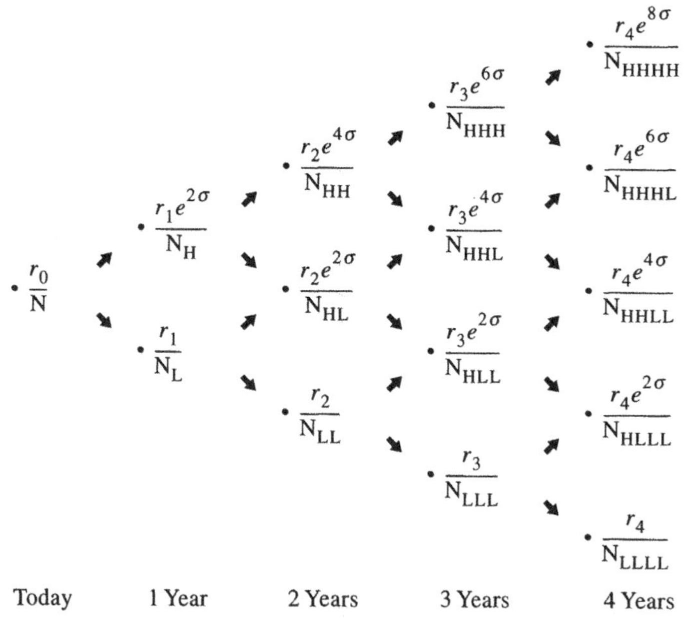

* r_t equals forward 1-year lower rate

In the third year there are four possible values for the 1-year rate, which are denoted as follows: $r_{3,HHH}$, $r_{3,HHL}$, $r_{3,HLL}$, and $r_{3,LLL}$, and whose first three values are related to the last as follows:

$$r_{3,HHH} = (e^{6\sigma})\, r_{3,LLL};\ r_{3,HHL} = (e^{4\sigma})\, r_{3,LLL};\ r_{3,HLL} = (e^{2\sigma})\, r_{3,LLL}$$

Exhibit 2 shows the notation for a 4-year binomial interest rate tree. We can simplify the notation by letting r_t be the 1-year rate t years from now for the lower rate since all the other short rates t years from now depend on that rate. Exhibit 3 shows the interest rate tree using this simplified notation.

Before we go on to show how to use this binomial interest rate tree to value bonds, let's focus on two issues here. First, what does the volatility parameter σ represent? Second, how do we find the value of the bond at each node?

Volatility and the Standard Deviation

It can be shown that the standard deviation of the 1-year rate is equal to $r_0\sigma$.[3] The standard deviation is a statistical measure of volatility. In Chapter 9, we will explain the concept of standard deviation and in Chapter 10 show how it is measured. What is important to understand here is that the interest rate volatility assumption is an input into the binomial model and therefore is one of those modeling risks we mentioned earlier.

It is important to see that the process that we assumed generates the binomial interest rate tree (or equivalently the short rates), implies that volatility is measured relative to the current level of rates. For example, if σ is 10% and the 1-year rate (r_0) is 4%, then the standard deviation of the 1-year rate is 4% × 10% = 0.4% or 40 basis points. However, if the current 1-year rate is 12%, the standard deviation of the 1-year rate would be 12% × 10% or 120 basis points.

Determining the Value at a Node

To find the value of the bond at a node, we first calculate the bond's value at the two nodes to the right of the node we are interested in. For example, in Exhibit 3, suppose we want to determine the bond's value at node N_H. The bond's value at node N_{HH} and N_{HL} must be determined. Hold aside for now how we get these two values because as we will see, the process involves starting from the last year in the tree and working backwards to get the final solution we want, so these two values will be known.

Effectively what we are saying is that if we are at some node, then the value at that node will depend on the future cash flows. In turn, the future cash flows depend on (1) the bond's value one year from now and (2) the coupon payment one year from now. The latter is known. The former depends on whether the 1-year rate is the higher or lower rate. The bond's value depending on whether the rate is the higher or lower rate is reported at the two nodes to the right of the node that is the focus of our attention. So, the cash flow at a node will be either (1) the bond's value if the short rate is the

---

[3] This can be seen by noting that $e^{2\sigma} \cong 1 + 2\sigma$. Then the standard deviation of the 1-period rate is

$$\frac{re^{2\sigma} - r}{2} \approx \frac{r + 2\sigma r - r}{2} = \sigma r$$

higher rate plus the coupon payment, or (2) the bond's value if the short rate is the lower rate plus the coupon payment. For example, suppose that we are interested in the bond's value at N_H. The cash flow will be either the bond's value at N_{HH} plus the coupon payment, or the bond's value at N_{HL} plus the coupon payment.

To get the bond's value at a node we follow the fundamental rule for valuation: the value is the present value of the expected cash flows. The appropriate discount rate to use is the 1-year rate at the node. Now there are two present values in this case: the present value if the 1-year rate is the higher rate and one if it is the lower rate. Since it is assumed that the probability of both outcomes is equal, an average of the two present values is computed. This is illustrated in Exhibit 4 for any node assuming that the 1-year rate is *r** at the node where the valuation is sought and letting:

V_H = the bond's value for the higher 1-year rate
V_L = the bond's value for the lower 1-year rate
C = coupon payment

Using our notation, the cash flow at a node is either:

$V_H + C$ for the higher 1-year rate
or $V_L + C$ for the lower 1-year rate

The present value of these two cash flows using the 1-year rate at the node, *r**, is:

Exhibit 4: Calculating a Value at a Node

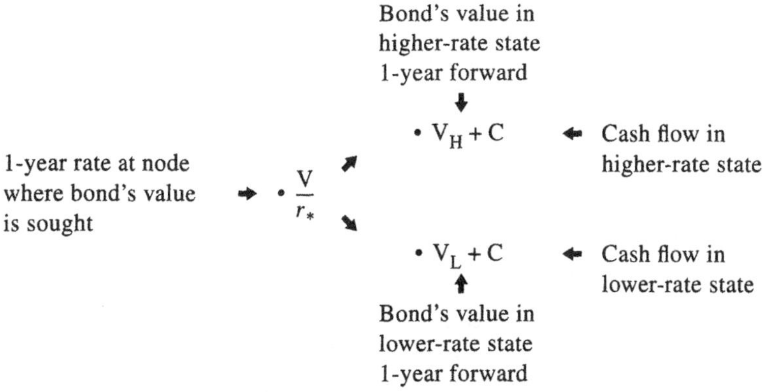

$$\frac{V_H + C}{(1 + r_*)} = \text{present value for the higher 1-year rate}$$

$$\frac{V_L + C}{(1 + r_*)} = \text{present value for the lower 1-year rate}$$

Then, the value of the bond at the node is found as follows:

$$\text{Value at a node} = \frac{1}{2}\left[\frac{V_H + C}{(1 + r_*)} + \frac{V_L + C}{(1 + r_*)}\right]$$

Constructing the Binomial Interest Rate Tree

What we have not explained thus far is how one goes about constructing the binomial interest rate tree. Actually, it is not essential to understand how the tree is constructed in order to use the tree to obtain the value of a bond and therefore how to use the tree to obtain a bond's effective duration. However, for closure the general principles are discussed.

The tree must be constructed such that it is calibrated to the on-the-run Treasuries or the on-the-run for the issuer. This means that if an on-the-run issue is valued using the tree, the value produced by the model will be the observed market value for the on-the-run. This is equivalent to saying that the model is "arbitrage free." That is, the model doesn't give a value that suggests that the user can arbitrage based on the market value.

The construction of the tree is an iterative process. Using the yield curve in Exhibit 1, it begins with the 1-year rate at the base of the tree. Then based on some volatility assumption and the yield on the 2-year on-the-run, the rates at the 1-year nodes are found as follows. An arbitrary rate is selected for the lower rate. Given the relationship between the lower and higher rates given above, the higher rate is determined. Now we have a proposed tree with the 1-year rates at the nodes. Using the procedure for valuing a bond explained later, the 2-year on-the-run is valued. If the model does not produce a value for the 2-year on-the-run that is equal to its market value (100 in our illustration), then the lower rate we used is not the correct rate. The procedure then involves trying another lower rate until a rate is found that will provide a tree with 1-year rates that will generate the value for the on-the-run equal to that issue's market value.

Given the 1-year rates, the 2-year rates are found by using the 3-year on-the-run issue. The procedure again involves arbitrarily selecting a rate for the 2-year lower node and then given the volatility assumption, computing the corresponding rates for the other two 2-year rates. The 3-year on-the-run is then valued using these three 2-year rates and the previously determined 1-year rates. If the value produced by the tree is not equal to the market value of the 3-year on-the-run issue, a different 2-year rate is tried for the lower rate. The process continues until the 2-year lower rate generates a tree that produces a value for the 3-year on-the-run issue equal to its market value.

Following the same procedure, the rates at all the nodes are determined using the corresponding on-the-run issue. Exhibit 5 shows the binomial tree based on the on-the-run issues in Exhibit 1 and assuming a 10% volatility. How do we know the binomial interest rate tree shown in Exhibit 5 is the correct one? After we see how to use the tree to value a bond, try valuing each bond in Exhibit 1 to determine if the binomial model produces a value equal to the corresponding market value in Exhibit 1.

Exhibit 5: Binomial Interest Rate Tree for Valuing Up to a 4-Year Bond for Issuer (10% Volatility Assumed)

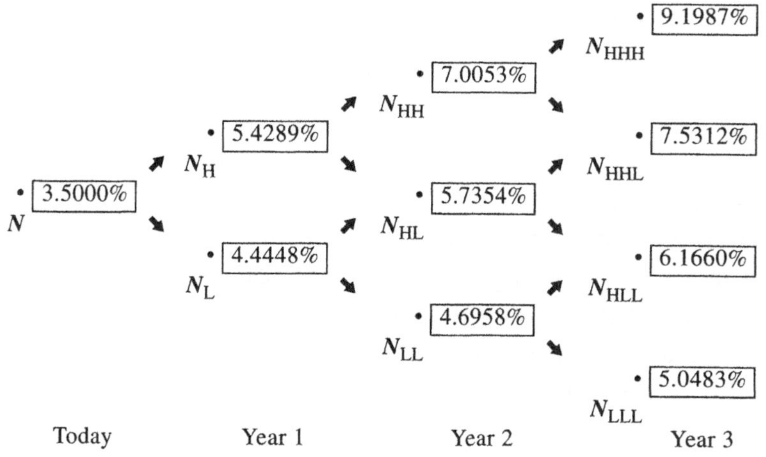

Valuing Bonds with the Tree

Now let's see how to value an option-free bond, a callable bond, a putable bond, a capped floater, and structured notes using the tree. Once we understand this, in a later section we will see how the binomial model can be used to generate the values needed in the effective duration formula when rates are shocked.

Valuing an Option-Free Bond with the Tree

Consider an option-free bond with four years remaining to maturity and a coupon rate of 6.5%. The value of this bond can be calculated by discounting each cash flow at the spot rates provided in Exhibit 1 as shown below:

$$\frac{\$6.5}{(1.035)^1} + \frac{\$6.5}{(1.042147)^2} + \frac{\$6.5}{(1.047345)^3} + \frac{\$100 + \$6.5}{(1.052707)^4}$$
$$= \$104.643$$

An option-free bond that is valued using the binomial interest rate tree should have the same value as discounting by the spot rates.

Exhibit 5 shows the 1-year rates or binomial interest rate tree that can then be used to value any bond for this issuer with a maturity up to four years. To illustrate how to use the binomial interest rate tree, consider once again the 6.5% option-free bond with four years remaining to maturity. Also assume that the issuer's on-the-run yield curve is the one in Exhibit 1, hence the appropriate binomial interest rate tree is the one in Exhibit 5. Exhibit 6 shows the various values in the discounting process and produces a bond value of $104.643.

This value is identical to the bond value found when we discounted at the spot rates. This clearly demonstrates that the valuation model is consistent with the standard valuation model for an option-free bond. Furthermore, try valuing each of the on-the-run issues in Exhibit 1 using the procedure for valuing an option-free bond using the tree. You will find that the binomial model will give a value equal to the market value of each on-the-run issue — 100 for all of the issues in Exhibit 1.

Exhibit 6: Valuing an Option-Free Bond with Four Years to Maturity and a Coupon Rate of 6.5% (10% Volatility Assumed)

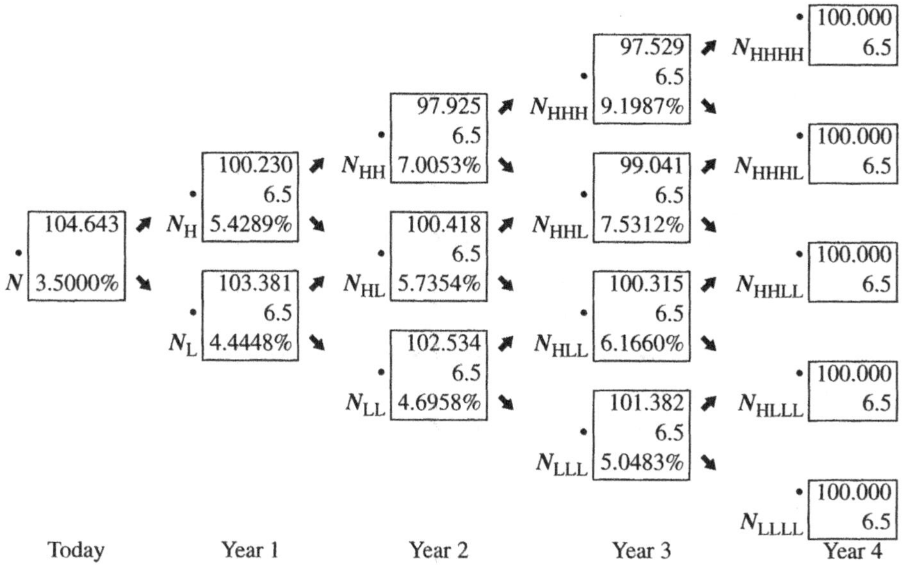

Valuing a Callable Bond

Now we will demonstrate how the binomial interest rate tree can be applied to value a callable bond. The valuation process proceeds in the same fashion as in the case of an option-free bond, but with one exception: when the call option may be exercised by the issuer, the bond value at a node must be changed to reflect the lesser of its values if it is not called (i.e., the value obtained by applying the recursive valuation formula described above) and the call price.

For example, consider a 6.5% bond with four years remaining to maturity that is callable in one year at $100. Exhibit 7 shows two values at each node of the binomial interest rate tree. The discounting process explained above is used to calculate the first of the two values at each node. The second value is the value based on whether the issue will be called. For simplicity, let's assume that this issuer calls the issue if the bond's value exceeds the call price. Then, in Exhibit 7 at nodes N_L, N_H, N_{LL}, N_{HL}, N_{LLL}, and N_{HLL} the values from the recursive valuation formula are $101.968, $100.032, $101.723, $100.270, $101.382, and $100.315. These values exceed the assumed call price ($100) and therefore the second value is $100 rather than the calculated value. It is the second value that is used in subsequent calculations. The root of the tree indicates that the value for this callable bond is $102.899.

The question that we have not addressed in our illustration, which is nonetheless important, is the circumstances under which the issuer will call the bond. A detailed explanation of the call rule is beyond the scope of this chapter. Basically, it involves determining when it would be economic for the issuer on an after-tax basis to call the issue. However, it should be noted that the rules for calling vary by broker/dealers and vendors of analytical systems. Unfortunately, there is no way to determine how significant the call rules are on the resulting value produced by the model.

Exhibit 7: Valuing a Callable Bond with Four Years to Maturity, a Coupon Rate of 6.5%, and Callable in One Year at 100 (10% Volatility Assumed)

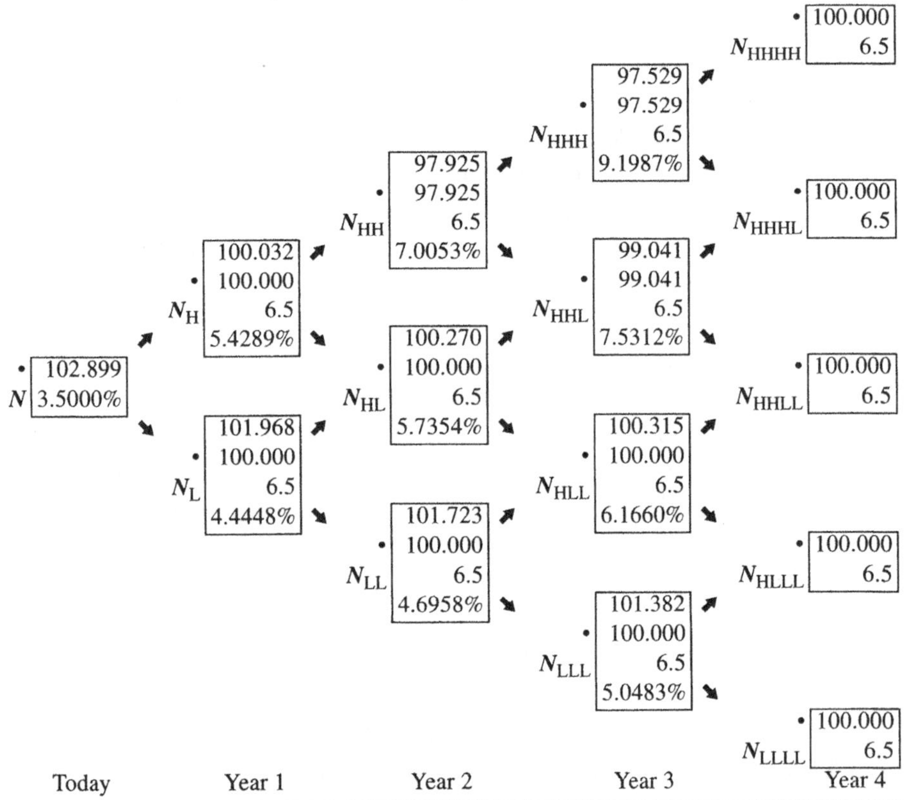

Exhibit 8: Valuing a Putable Bond with Four Years to Maturity, a Coupon Rate of 6.5%, and Putable in One Year at 100 (10% Volatility Assumed)

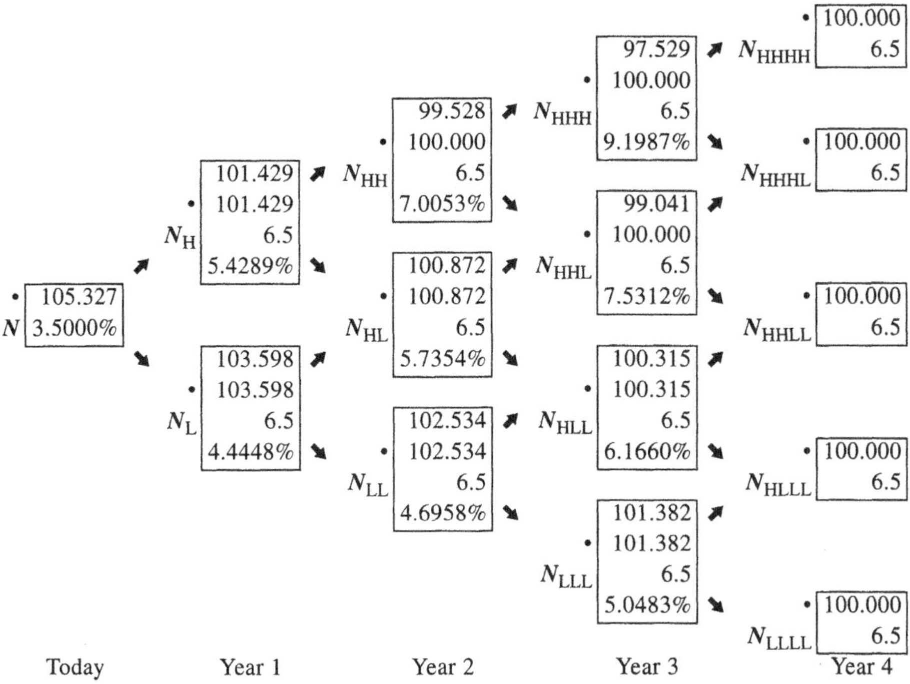

Valuing a Putable Bond

A putable bond is one in which the bondholder has the right to force the issuer to pay off the bond prior to the maturity date. To illustrate how the binomial model can be used to value a putable bond, suppose that a 6.5% bond with four years remaining to maturity is putable in one year at par ($100). Also assume that the appropriate binomial interest rate tree for this issuer is the one in Exhibit 5 and the bondholder exercises the put if the bond's price is less than par.

Exhibit 8 shows the binomial interest rate tree with the bond value altered at three nodes (N_{HH}, N_{HHH}, and N_{HHL}) because the bond value at these nodes is less than $100, the assumed value at which the bond can be put. The value of this putable bond is $105.327.

The binomial model can also be used to value a bond that is both callable and putable.

Exhibit 9: Valuing a Floating-Rate Note with a 7.25% Cap

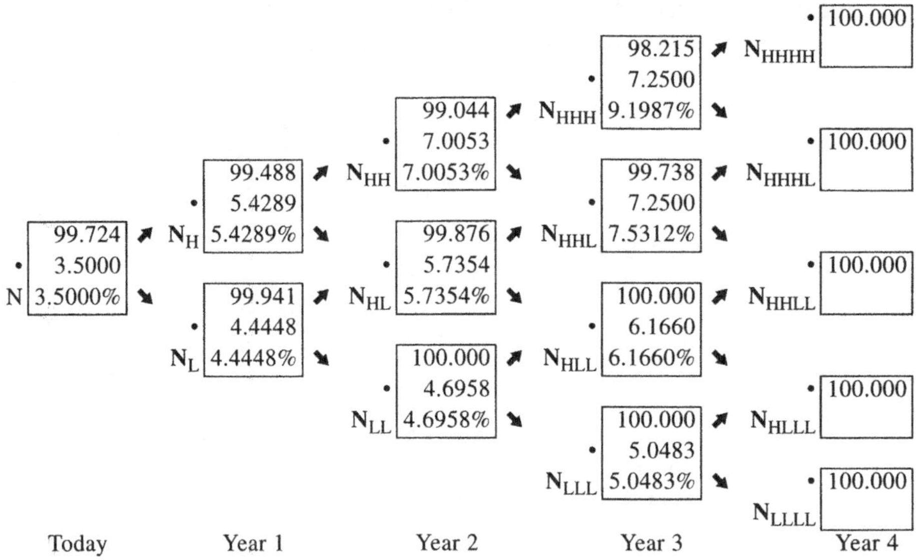

Note: The coupon rate shown at a node is the coupon rate to be received in the next year.

Valuing a Capped Floating-Rate Note

The valuation of a capped floating-rate note using the binomial model requires that the coupon be computed at every node where the node represents a coupon reset date. The coupon is determined by the coupon formula. At each node, the interest rate in the binomial tree is the short-term rate. However, the coupon at each node is determined by the reference rate in the coupon formula. Thus, to determine the coupon at a node, a relationship between the reference rate used in the coupon formula and the short-term rate used to generate the interest rate tree must be assumed.

In our illustration, we will assume that the reference rate for the coupon formula is the same as the short-term rate generated by the tree (i.e., the 1-year rate). Moreover, we will assume that the coupon reset is every year and the coupon formula is the 1-year rate flat (i.e., no spread). Exhibit 9 shows the binomial tree and the relevant values at each node for a floater whose coupon rate is the 1-year rate flat and in which there is a 7.25% cap. The valuation procedure is identical to that for the other callable and putable bonds described above with one exception. While the coupon rate is set at the beginning of the period, it is paid in arrears. In the valuation procedure, the coupon rate set for the next period is shown in the box at which the rate is determined.

Exhibit 9 shows how this floater would be valued. At each node where the short rate exceeds 7.25%, a coupon of $7.25 is substituted. The value of this capped floater is $99.724.

Valuing Structured Notes

Structured notes have an unusual coupon rate formula. The coupon rate can be based on either an interest rate, a non-interest rate financial index, or a nonfinancial index. Structured notes for which the coupon rate is based on an interest rate can generally be valued using the binomial model. We will illustrate how using a step-up callable note.

Step-up callable notes are callable instruments whose coupon rate is increased (i.e., "stepped up") at designated times. When the coupon rate is increased only once over the security's life, it is said to be a single step-up callable note. A multiple step-up callable note is a step-up callable note whose coupon rate is increased more than one time over the life of the security.

To illustrate how the binomial model can be used to value a single step-up callable note, suppose that a 4-year step-up callable note pays 4.25% for two years and then 7.5% for two more years. Assume that this note is callable at par at the end of Year 2 and Year 3. We will use the binomial interest rate tree given in Exhibit 5 to value this note.

The valuation procedure is identical to that performed in Exhibit 7 except that the coupon in the box at each node reflects the step-up terms. Exhibit 10 shows that the value of the single step-up callable note is $100.031.

Option-Adjusted Spread

Suppose the market price of the 4-year 6.5% callable bond is $102.218 and the theoretical value assuming 10% volatility is $102.899. This means that this bond is cheap by $0.681 according to the valuation model. Bond market participants prefer to think not in terms of a bond's price being cheap or expensive in dollar terms but rather in terms of a yield spread — a cheap bond trades at a higher yield spread and an expensive bond at a lower yield spread.

Exhibit 10: Valuing a Single Step-Up Callable Note with Four Years to Maturity, Callable in Two Years at 100 (10% Volatility Assumed)

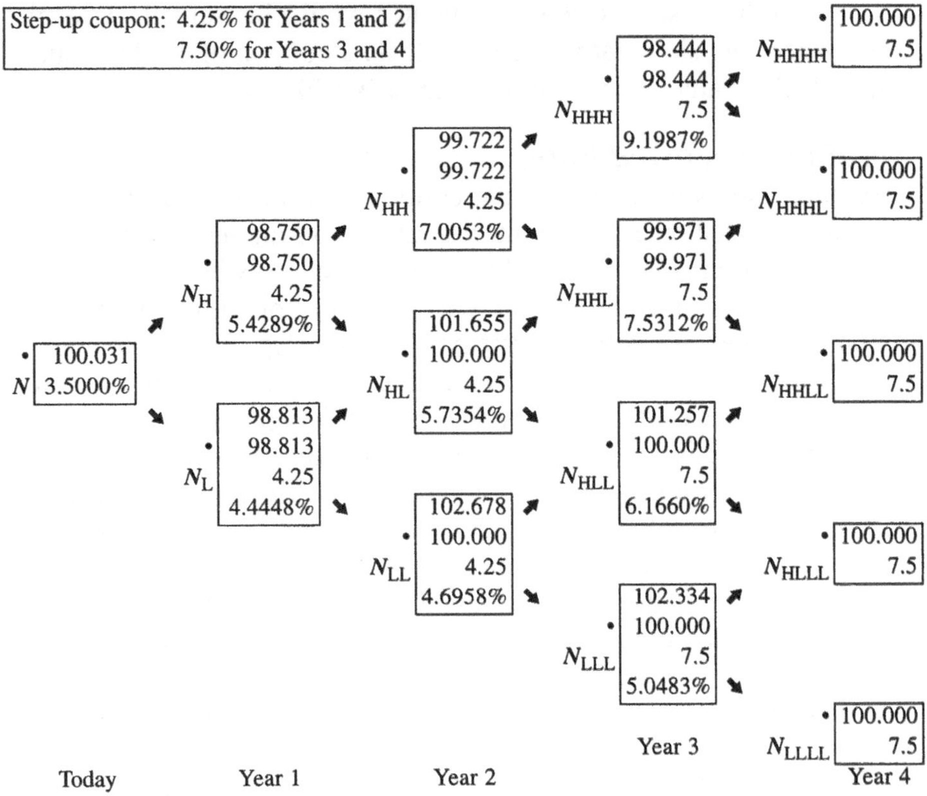

The option-adjusted spread (OAS) is the constant spread that when added to all the rates on the binomial interest rate tree will make the theoretical value equal to the market price. In our illustration, if the market price is \$102.218, the OAS would be the constant spread added to every rate in Exhibit 5 that will make the theoretical value equal to \$102.218. The solution in this case would be 35 basis points.

As with the value of a bond with an embedded option, the OAS will depend on the volatility assumption. For a given bond price, the higher the interest rate volatility assumed, the lower the OAS for a callable bond and the higher the OAS for a putable bond. For example, if volatility is 20% rather than 10%, it can be demonstrated that the OAS would be –6 basis points.

This illustration clearly demonstrates the importance of the volatility assumption. Assuming volatility of 10%, the OAS is 35 basis points. At 20% volatility, the OAS declines and, in this case, is negative and therefore overvalued.

Consequently, in comparing the OAS of dealer firms, it is critical to compare the volatility assumed. Moreover, it is important to inquire as to the benchmark on-the-run yield curve used in generating the binomial tree. Some dealers use the Treasury on-the-run issues. As a result, the OAS is capturing the credit spread. In contrast, some vendors and dealers use the issuer's on-the-run issue which embodies the issuer's credit risk. This is the approach used in our illustrations.

COMPUTING EFFECTIVE DURATION AND CONVEXITY WITH THE BINOMIAL MODEL

In Chapter 4, we explained how the duration for a bond can be calculated using the following formula:

$$\text{Duration} = \frac{V_- - V_+}{2V_0(\Delta y)100} \tag{1}$$

Whether the resulting duration is modified duration or effective duration depends on whether the two values in the numerator are obtained by assuming that the cash flows do not change when rates change — modified duration — or when rates change the expected cash flows change — effective duration. When the binomial model is used to generate the values in the numerator, the resulting duration is effective duration because as we will see, the model allows for changes in cash flows when rates change.

Let's look at how to calculate the effective duration using the binomial model. The procedure for calculating the value of V_+ to use in equation (1) is as follows:

Step 1: Calculate the option-adjusted spread (OAS) for the issue.

Step 2: Shift the on-the-run yield curve up by a small number of basis points (Δy).

Step 3: Construct a binomial interest rate tree based on the new yield curve in Step 2.

Step 4: To each of the 1-period rates in the binomial interest rate tree, add the OAS to obtain an "adjusted tree."

Step 5: Use the adjusted tree found in Step 4 to determine the value of the bond, which is V_+

To determine the value of V_-, the same five steps are followed except that in Step 2, the on-the-run yield curve is shifted down by a small number of basis points (Δy).

To illustrate how V_+ and V_- are determined in order to calculate effective duration, we will use the same on-the-run yield curve used in Exhibit 1 and assume an interest rate volatility of 10%. The hypothetical 4-year callable bond with a coupon rate of 6.5%, callable at par, and selling at \$102.218 used to illustrate the binomial model will be used in this illustration to demonstrate how to calculate the effective duration. As indicated earlier, the OAS for this issue is 35 basis points.

Exhibit 11 shows the adjusted tree by shifting the yield curve up by an arbitrarily small number of basis points, 25 basis points, and then adding 35 basis points (the OAS) to each 1-year rate. The adjusted tree is then used to value the bond. The resulting value, V_+, is \$101.621. Exhibit 12 shows the adjusted tree by shifting the yield curve down by 25 basis points and then adding 35 basis points to each 1-year rate. The resulting value, V_-, is \$102.765.

Therefore, Δy is 0.0025, V_+ is 101.621, V_- is 102.765, and V_0 is 102.218. The effective duration is then

$$\text{Effective duration} = \frac{102.765 - 101.621}{2(102.218)(0.0025)} = 2.24$$

While our illustration is for a callable bond, the same procedure is used to compute based on the binomial model the effective duration of a putable bond, a bond both callable and putable, a capped floater, and an interest-sensitive structured note.

When the binomial model is used to value a security, the values used in equation (1) to calculate effective duration can be used to calculate the effective convexity measure or simply effective convexity. The formula for effective convexity is:

*Exhibit 11: Determination of V_+ for Calculating Effective Duration and Convexity**

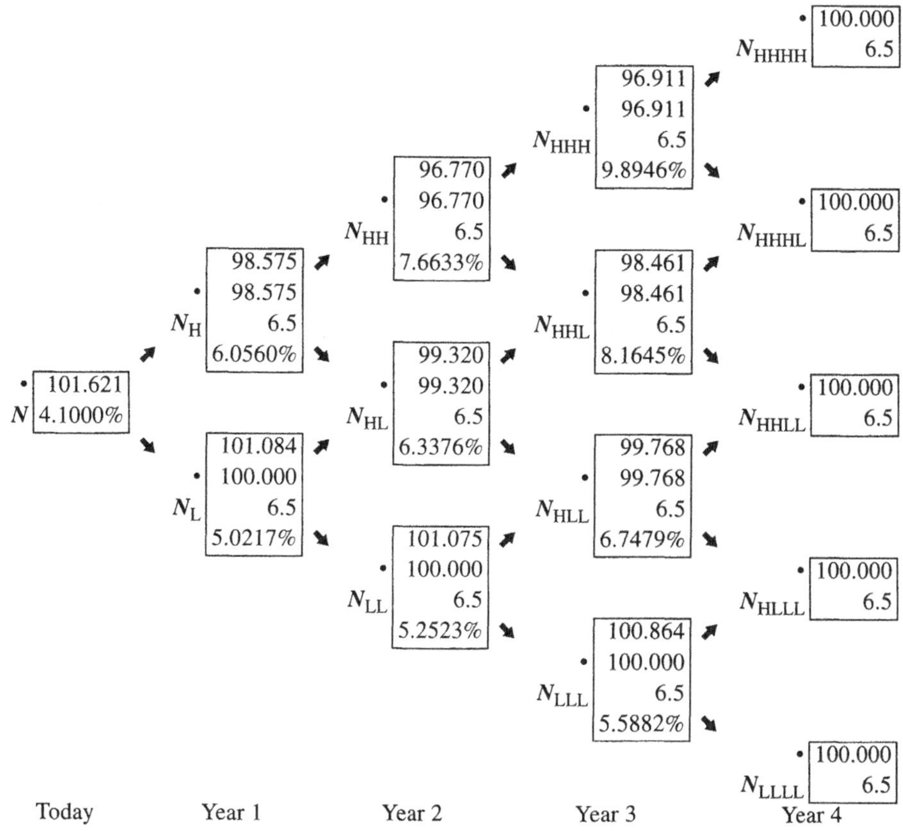

* +25 basis point shift in on-the-run yield curve.

$$\text{Convexity measure} = \frac{V_+ + V_- - 2V_0}{2V_0(\Delta y)^2} \tag{2}$$

For our hypothetical 4-year callable bond, the effective convexity measure is:

$$\text{Effective convexity measure} = \frac{101.621 + 102.765 - 2(102.218)}{2(102.218)(0.0025)^2}$$

$$= -39.1321$$

Notice that this callable bond exhibits negative convexity.

*Exhibit 12: Determination of V_ for Calculating Effective Duration and Convexity**

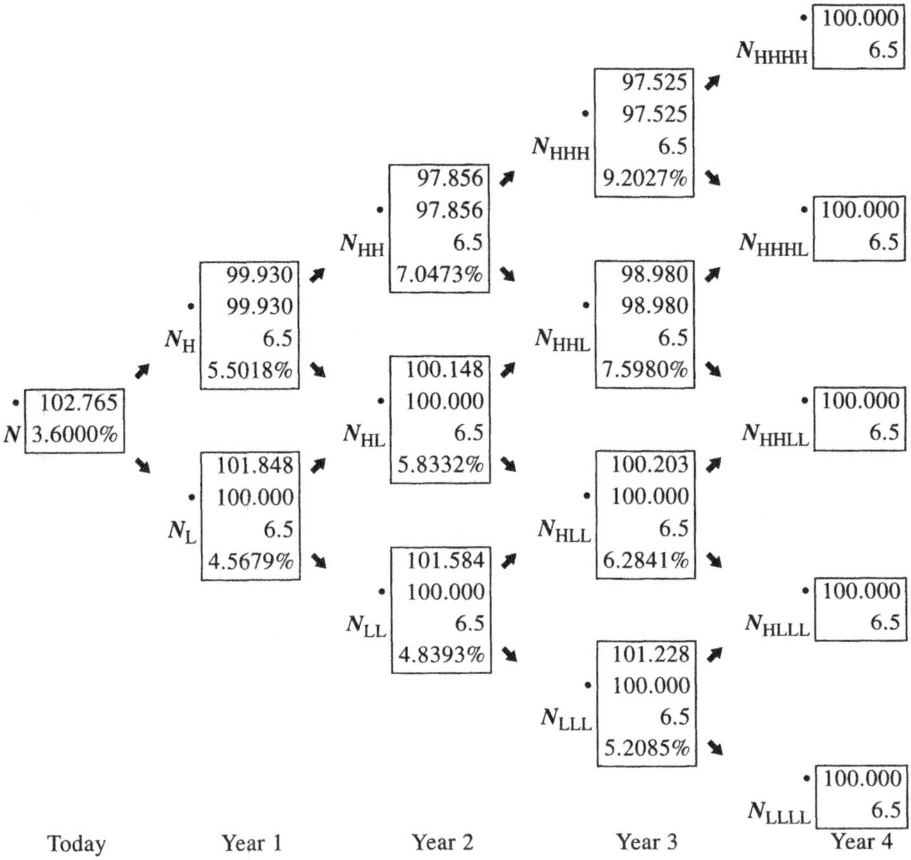

* –25 basis point shift in on-the-run yield curve.

OTHER DURATION MEASURES

There are a variety of other measures of duration that relate to both fixed-rate bonds and floating-rate securities. We discuss these below.

Spread Duration for Fixed-Rate Bonds

Duration is a measure of the change in the value of a bond when rates change. The interest rate that is assumed to shift is the Treasury rate. However, for non-Treasury securities, the yield is equal to the Treasury yield plus a spread to the Treasury yield curve. As explained in Chapter 2, the price of a bond exposed to credit risk can change even though Treasury yields are unchanged because the spread required by the market changes. A measure of how a non-Treasury issue's price will change if the spread sought by the market changes is called *spread duration*.

The problem is, what spread is assumed to change? There are three spread measures that are used for fixed-rate bonds: nominal spread, zero-volatility spread, and option-adjusted spread.

The *nominal spread* is the traditional spread measure. That is, it is the difference between the yield on a non-Treasury issue and the yield on a comparable maturity Treasury issue. Thus, spread duration when spread is defined as the nominal spread indicates the approximate percentage change in price for a 100 basis point change in the nominal spread holding the Treasury yield constant.

The *zero-volatility spread*, also called the *static spread*, is the spread that when added to the Treasury spot rate curve will make the present value of the cash flows (when discounted at the spot rates plus the spread) equal to the price of the bond plus accrued interest. It is a spread over the Treasury spot rate curve. When spread is defined in this way, spread duration is the approximate percentage change in price for a 100 basis point change in the zero-volatility spread holding the Treasury spot rate curve constant.

As we explained in this chapter, the option-adjusted spread is another spread measure. Spread duration based on OAS can be interpreted as the approximate percentage change in price of a non-Treasury issue for a 100 basis point change in the OAS, holding the Treasury rate constant. So, for example, if a bond has a spread duration of 4, this means that if the OAS changes by 20 basis points, the price of the issue will change by approximately 0.8% (0.04 times 0.002×100).

The procedure for calculating a spread duration where the spread is defined as the OAS is as follows. In the binomial model, the binomial tree is kept constant but the OAS is shocked up and down by the same number of basis points. In equation (1) the two values in the numerator are then the values when the OAS is reduced and when it is increased.

How do you know whether a spread duration for a fixed-rate bond is a spread based on the nominal spread, zero-volatility spread, or the OAS? You don't. You must ask the broker/dealer or vendor of the analytical system. For example, in the Capital Management Sciences analytical system two duration measures are reported: spread duration and zero-volatility spread duration. It is clear what the latter is. The former is spread duration using OAS as the spread measure.

To add further to the confusion of spread duration, consider the term "OAS duration" that is referred to by some market participants. What does that mean? On the one hand, it could mean simply the spread duration that we just described. On the other hand, many market participants have used it interchangeably with the term effective duration. Once again, the only way to know what an OAS duration is measuring is to ask the broker/dealer or vendor.

Later in this chapter we will see how to compute a spread duration measure for a portfolio.

Volatility Duration

In discussing the binomial model, one important assumption that is made is the interest rate volatility. In our illustration we used 10%. The volatility assumption has an important impact on the theoretical value. More specifically, the higher the expected volatility, the higher the value of an option. The same is true for an option embedded in a bond. Correspondingly, this affects the value of the bond with an embedded option.

For example, for a callable bond, a higher interest rate volatility assumption means that the value of the embedded call option increases and, since the value of the option-free bond is not affected, the value of the callable bond must be lower. For a putable bond, higher interest rate volatility means that its value will be higher.

To illustrate this, suppose that a 20% volatility is assumed rather than 10%. Using the binomial model, the value of the hypothetical callable bond is $102.108 if volatility is assumed to be 20% compared to $102.899 if volatility is assumed to be 10%. The hypothetical putable bond at 20% volatility has a value of $106.010 compared to $105.327 at 10% volatility.

In the construction of the binomial interest rate, it was assumed that volatility is the same for each year. The methodology can be extended to incorporate a term structure of volatility.

The impact of interest rate volatility on the price of a bond can be quantified. This involves changing the interest rate volatility assumption by changing the volatility and recomputing the price. The prices computed by shocking volatility up and down are the values used in equation (1). If the volatility used is a term structure of volatility, then the interest rate volatility for each maturity is shocked by the same amount. In computing the sensitivity of the bond to a change in volatility, the OAS is held constant.

Vendors have different names for this measure that capture the sensitivity of a bond to changes in volatility. Some vendors call it *volatility risk* or *vega*, the latter term being used in the options market to assess the sensitivity of an option to changes in volatility. We'll discuss this in Chapter 8 where we cover options.

DURATION OF A FLOATING-RATE SECURITY

In Chapter 2, we explained the price sensitivity of a floater to changes in interest rates. We saw that the a floater's price will change depending on three factors: (1) time remaining to the next coupon reset date, (2) whether or not the cap is reached, and (3) whether the spread that the market wants changes. We described above how to compute the value of a capped floater. So, computing the effective duration of a capped floater using the binomial model is straightforward.

Two measures have been developed to estimate the sensitivity of a floater to each component of the coupon reset formula: the index and the spread. *Index duration* is a measure of the price sensitivity of a floater to changes in the reference rate (i.e., index) holding the spread constant. *Spread duration* measures a floater's price sensitivity to a change in the spread assuming that the reference rate is unchanged. As noted earlier, the term spread duration is also used to measure the sensitivity of the price of a fixed-rate bond when the spread changes where the spread is measured in terms of either nominal spread, zero-volatility spread, or OAS.

DURATION OF AN INVERSE FLOATER

An inverse floater is a security whose coupon rate changes inversely with the change in the reference rate. The typical coupon formula for an inverse floater is:

$$M - L \times (\text{Reference rate})$$

For example, an inverse floater's coupon formula may be:

$$30\% - 4 \times (\text{3-month LIBOR})$$

The reference rate for this inverse floater is 3-month LIBOR, M is 30%, and L is 4. So, if 3-month LIBOR at a coupon reset date is 5%, the coupon rate for the period is:

$$30\% - 4 \times (5\%) = 10\%$$

If 3-month LIBOR at the next reset date has declined to 4%, the coupon rate for the inverse floater is 14%. Thus, when the reference rate declines, the coupon rate increases.

If 3-month LIBOR is zero at a coupon reset date, the coupon formula specifies that the coupon rate is 30%. Thus, M is the maximum coupon rate or cap for an inverse floater.

Notice that if 3-month LIBOR is 7.5% at a coupon reset date, the coupon rate is zero. If 3-month LIBOR exceeds 7.5%, there will be a negative coupon rate indicated by the formula. Typically, a floor of zero will be placed on the inverse floater which in turn results in a cap for the floater.

The L in the coupon formula is referred to as the *coupon leverage* or *leverage*. It specifies the multiple by which the coupon rate will change when the reference rate changes (assuming the cap or the floor on the inverse floater is not reached).

Inverse floaters are created in several ways by dealers. One way is to take a fixed-rate bond (a fixed-rate tranche in the case of a collateralized mortgage obligation) and split it into a floater and an inverse floater. The floater/inverse floater package will redistribute the coupon interest from the fixed-rate bond between the two securities and do the same for the principal.

The duration of an inverse floater will be a multiple of the duration of the fixed-rate bond from which it is created. To see this, suppose that a 20-year fixed-rate bond with a *marke*t value of $100 million is split into a floater and an inverse floater with a *market* value of $80 million and $20, respectively. Assume also that the duration for the fixed-rate bond from which the floater/inverse floater combination is created is 8. For a 100 basis point change in interest rates, the fixed-rate bond's value will change by approximately 8% or $8 million (8% times $100 million). This means that by splitting the fixed-rate bond's value, the combined change in value for a 100 basis change in rates for the floater and inverse floater must be $8 million. If the duration of the floater is close to zero, this means that the entire $8 million change in value must come from the inverse floater. For this to occur, the duration of the inverse floater must be 40. That is, a duration of 40 will mean a 40% change in the value of the inverse floater for a 100 basis point change in interest rates and therefore a change in value of $8 million (40% times $20 million).

Notice from our illustration that the duration of the inverse floater is greater than the number of years to maturity of the fixed-rate bond used to create the inverse floater. That is, the maturity of the fixed-rate bond is 8 years and the duration of the inverse floater is 40. Portfolio managers who interpret duration in terms of years are confused that a security can have a duration greater than the fixed-rate bond from which it is created — a point we stressed in the previous chapter.

Another way to understand the duration of the inverse floater is to look at the economics underlying the security. An investor who owns a fixed-rate bond effectively owns a floater and an inverse floater. Owning these securities means being long these securities. Thus:

Long a fixed-rate bond
= Long a floater + Long an inverse floater

Equivalently, this can be expressed as:

Long an inverse floater
= Long a fixed-rate bond – Long a floater

Now look at the position of an investor who is long (owns) an inverse floater. That investor has two positions. First, the investor owns a fixed-rate bond from which the floater/inverse floater combination was created. But owning a fixed-rate bond means that the investor has purchased this bond. In our example, this means the investor owns $100 million market value of the fixed-rate bond. But remember that the investor paid $20 million for the inverse floater but effectively owns $100 million market value of a fixed-rate bond. Where did the funds come from to finance the difference between the $100 million fixed-rate bond and the $20 million invested to acquire the inverse floater? It must have come from the investor somehow borrowing funds. That is what the minus sign in front of the position "Long a floater" means in the above expression. The investor financed the $80 million to purchase the fixed-rate bond by borrowing on a floating-rate basis. Specifically, the investor borrowed $80 million and the funding rate is the coupon rate for the floater. Note also that the funding cost is capped by the cap on the floater.

Thus, one can describe the economic position of an investor in an inverse floater as a leveraged position in the fixed-rate bond. The investor has put up $20 million to buy $100 million of a fixed-rate bond and funded the balance ($80 million) on a floating-rate basis. This is why investors refer to an inverse floater as a security with *embedded leverage.* Consequently, the duration of the inverse floater will reflect the embedded leverage. In our example, the duration of the fixed-rate bond is 8. If an investor owns $20 million of this bond, the duration is 8. However, if the investor borrows $80 million to obtain the exposure to $100 million of the fixed-rate bond, the duration will be 5 times greater than the duration of $20 million of market value of the fixed-rate bond. That is, the duration is 40 (8×5). That is precisely what we found earlier for the duration of the inverse floater.

The duration will be less than the leveraged amount if the floater absorbs some of the change in value. Thus, recognition must be given to how the floater will change in value.

DURATION OF A MARKET INDEX

In the previous chapter we explained how the effective duration of a portfolio is computed. A portfolio's (effective) duration can be obtained by calculating the weighted average of the duration of the securities in the portfolio.

A market index is simply a portfolio. Let's look at how the duration of a broad-based bond market index is computed. Exhibit 13 shows for the four sectors of the Salomon Brothers' Broad-Investment Grade (BIG) Index the weights for each sector and the effective duration for each sector as of May 1, 1998. The effective duration for the index as reported by Salomon Brothers for that date was 4.53, calculated by multiplying the sector weights by the effective duration for the sector and summing. The effective duration for the index is found as follows:

$$W_{Tre}\,D_{Tre} + W_{GS}\,D_{GS} + W_{Mort}\,D_{Mort} + W_{Corp}\,D_{Corp}$$

where the subscripts *Tre*, *GS*, *Mort*, and *Corp* denote the Treasury, government sponsored, mortgage, and corporate sectors, respectively. Substituting the values reported in Exhibit 5 into the above equation we obtain the index's effective duration of 4.53:

$$0.4138\,(5.19) + 0.0738\,(4.81) + 0.2952\,(2.46) + 0.2172\,(5.99) = 4.53$$

The index's effective duration of 4.53 means that if the yield for all four sectors increased by 100 basis points and the OAS did not change, then the index's value will change by approximately 4.53%.

Exhibit 13: Data for the Salomon Brothers' BIG Index as of May 1, 1998

Sector	Sector weight (%)	Effective duration	Spread duration*
Treasury	41.38	5.19	0
Government sponsored	7.38	4.81	4.73
Mortgage	29.52	2.46	3.41
Corporate	21.72	5.99	5.89

* Spread is defined in terms of OAS.
Effective duration for index = 4.53
Spread duration for index = 2.63

PORTFOLIO SPREAD DURATION

Earlier we discussed the spread duration for an individual fixed-rate bond. The spread duration for a portfolio is found by computing a market weighted average of the spread duration for each sector. The same is true for a market index.

Let's use the data reported in Exhibit 13 for the Salomon Brothers' BIG Index on May 1, 1998 to illustrate this. The last column of the exhibit reports the spread duration for the credit sectors. Spread duration in this index is based on OAS. The spread duration for the index is found as follows:

$$0.4138\,(0) + 0.0738\,(4.73) + 0.2952\,(3.41) + 0.2172\,(5.89) = 2.63$$

The computed value of 2.63 agrees with the value reported at the bottom of Exhibit 13. This value is interpreted as follows: if the OAS of all credit sectors changes by 100 basis points while Treasury yields do not change, then the index's value will change by approximately 2.63%.

CONTRIBUTION TO DURATION OF FOREIGN BONDS

In describing how to compute the duration of a portfolio in the previous chapter, it was assumed that all the bonds are U.S.-dollar-pay bonds whose coupon rate is based on a U.S. rate. When a portfolio includes non-U.S. bonds or foreign bonds, the estimation of the contribution to a portfolio's duration by including a foreign bond is not straightforward.

For example, suppose a portfolio consists of government bonds of the United States, Germany, Canada, France, the U.K., and Japan. Suppose further that you are told that the duration of this portfolio comprised of both U.S. and foreign government bonds is 6. What does that mean? The quick interpretation is that if "rates" change by 100 basis points, the value of this portfolio will change by approximately 6%. But which country's rates changed by 100 basis points? Germany? Canada? France? the U.S.?

Japan? To interpret duration as we just did assumes that the rates of all countries change by 100 basis points. That is, it assumes that rates are perfectly correlated for all of these countries so that they move up and down in unison.

Obviously, this interpretation of duration is not meaningful Rather, a measure of duration for a U.S. portfolio that includes foreign bonds must recognize the correlation between the movement in rates in the U.S., and each non-U.S. country. Lee Thomas and Ram Willner suggest a methodology for computing the contribution of a foreign bond's duration to the duration of a domestic portfolio.[4]

The Thomas-Willner methodology begins by expressing the change in a bond's value in terms of a change in the foreign yield as follows:

Change in value of foreign bond
= Duration × Change in foreign yield × 100

From the perspective of a U.S. manager, the concern is the change in value of the foreign bond when domestic (U.S.) rates change. This can be determined by incorporating the relationship between changes in domestic (U.S.) rates and changes in foreign rates as follows:

Change in value of foreign bond = Duration
× (Change in foreign yield given a change in domestic yield)
× 100

The relationship between the change in domestic yield and the change in U.S. yield can be estimated empirically using monthly data for each country. The following relationship is estimated:

$$\Delta y_{f,t} = \alpha + \beta \, \Delta y_{\mathrm{US},t}$$

where

$\Delta y_{f,t}$ = change in a foreign bond's yield in month t
$\Delta y_{\mathrm{US},t}$ = change in U.S. yield in month time t

---

[4] Lee R. Thomas and Ram Willner, "Measuring the Duration of an Internationally Diversified Portfolio," *Journal of Portfolio Management* (Fall 1997), pp. 93-100.

Exhibit 14: Country Betas

Country	β	(t-stats)	R^2
Australia	1.04	(8.68)	0.49
Austria	0.23	(3.61)	0.13
Belgium	0.29	(3.00)	0.09
Canada	0.89	(8.67)	0.49
Denmark	0.48	(3.68)	0.14
France	0.51	(4.95)	0.23
Germany	0.42	(5.32)	0.26
Holland	0.45	(5.51)	0.27
Ireland	0.55	(4.65)	0.21
Italy	0.43	(2.53)	0.06
Japan	0.30	(2.75)	0.08
Spain	0.47	(2.82)	0.08
Sweden	0.49	(2.95)	0.09
Switzerland	0.25	(2.59)	0.07
UK	0.51	(4.30)	0.18

Source: Exhibit 1 in Ram Willner, "Improved Measurement of Duration Contributions of Foreign Bonds in Domestic Portfolios," Chapter 8 in Frank J. Fabozzi (ed.), *Perspectives on International Fixed Income Investing* (New Hope, PA: Frank J. Fabozzi Associates, 1998), p. 169.

and α and β are the parameters to be estimated for the countries whose bonds are candidates for inclusion in the portfolio. The parameter β_i is called the *country beta*. The duration that is attributed to a foreign bond in a U.S. portfolio is found by multiplying the country beta by the duration.

Exhibit 14 shows the estimated country betas for the period July 1992 to July 1997. For example, consider the U.K. This country's beta is 0.51. This means that if the duration for a U.K. bond is calculated to be 4, the duration contribution to a U.S. portfolio is not 4 but 4 times 0.51 or 2.04.

SUMMARY

When a bond has an embedded option, the appropriate duration measure is effective duration. The computation of this duration measure requires that a valuation model be used to determine the prices of a bond when rates change, allowing for the cash flows to change. The binomial model is used for valuing agency debentures, corporates, and municipals with embedded options. In the binomial model, an interest rate tree is created to value a bond. To obtain the effective duration of a bond, the tree is shifted (shocked) and a new tree is created to determine the prices used in the duration formula. The binomial model can be used to compute the duration and convexity of a callable bond, a putable bond, a capped floating-rate security, a structured note whose coupon rate is based on an interest rate, and a bond with multiple embedded options.

For a fixed-rate bond a spread duration can be computed. This is the approximate percentage change in the price of a bond if the Treasury yield is constant but the spread changes by 100 basis points. The problem is that the spread of a bond can be measured in several ways: nominal spread, zero-volatility spread, and option-adjusted spread. A spread duration for each can be computed. The manager must check with the dealer or vendor as to which spread measure is being computed or reported. Moreover, the term OAS duration is ambiguous because it can be a spread duration measure or it can mean the effective duration since many market participants use it in that way.

An input into the model for valuing bonds with embedded options is the expected yield volatility. The sensitivity of the bond's price to changes in the expected yield volatility can be estimated. This sensitivity is called volatility duration.

For a floating-rate bond an index duration and a spread duration can be computed. An index duration measures the price sensitivity of a floater to changes in the reference rate holding the spread constant. A spread duration can also be computed for a floater. It is the sensitivity of a floater to changes in the spread holding the reference rate constant.

For an inverse floating-rate security, the duration is a multiple of the duration of the fixed-rate bond from which the floater/inverse floater combination is created. Effectively, an inverse floater is a leveraged position in the fixed-rate bond, where the funds are borrowed on a floating-rate basis. Because of the embedded leverage, it should not be surprising if the duration of an inverse floater exceeds the number of years to maturity of the fixed-rate bond from which it is created.

For a foreign bond added to a U.S. portfolio, the duration of the foreign bond in terms of foreign rates must be adjusted to determine its contribution to the U.S. portfolio's duration. This is because a foreign bond's duration is the sensitivity of the bond to changes in the yield in that foreign country. Of concern to a U.S. manager that is considering the addition of a foreign bond to a U.S. portfolio is the sensitivity of the bond's price to changes in U.S. interest rates. The adjustment of the foreign bond's duration can be made based on an empirically estimated country beta. This measure is estimated from a regression showing the relationship between changes in U.S. rates and foreign rates.

Chapter 6

Duration and Convexity for Mortgage-Backed Securities

Mortgage-backed securities are backed by pools of mortgage loans. There are two types of mortgage-backed securities. The first type are those issued by the Government National Mortgage Association (Ginnie Mae or GNMA), the Federal National Mortgage Association (Fannie Mae or FNMA), and the Federal Home Loan Mortgage Corporation (Freddie Mac or FHLMC). These entities are government agencies. Ginnie Mae is a federally related institution which means that its guarantee to make interest and principal payments carries the full faith and credit of the U.S. government. Fannie Mae and Freddie Mac are government sponsored enterprises. The mortgage-backed securities issued by these three entities are called *agency mortgage-backed securities*. The second type of mortgage-backed securities are those issued by private entities such as banks, finance companies, broker/dealers, and thrifts that do not carry any explicit or implicit government guarantees. These securities expose investors to credit risk and are referred to as *nonagency mortgage-backed securities*.

The basic mortgage security is a *mortgage passthrough security* or, simply, a *passthrough*. This security is backed by a pool of mortgage loans and the cash flows of the underlying mortgages are distributed to certificate holders on a pro rata basis. That is, each certificate holder is entitled to the same proportionate share of the interest payments and all principal repayments. Pools of passthroughs have been used as collateral for the creation of a *collateralized mortgage obligation* (CMO). In a CMO, different bond classes, called *tranches*, are created. There are separate rules for distribution of interest and principal repayment to each tranche. Finally, a mortgage passthrough security can be carved into two certificates such that one class of certificate holders is entitled to only the interest payments generated from the underlying pool of mortgage loans and another class of certificate holders is entitled to only the principal repayments. The former securities are called *interest-only* (*IO*) securities and the latter are called *principal-only* (*PO*) securities. IO and PO securities are referred to as *stripped mortgage-backed securities* or, simply, *mortgage strips*.

Mortgage-backed securities are securities with embedded options. Specifically, the borrower (homeowner) has the option to prepay the loan in whole or in part prior to the scheduled date. Any unscheduled principal repayment is called a *prepayment*. The cash flows from a mortgage-backed security consist of interest payments, regularly scheduled principal payments, and any prepayments. For agency mortgage-backed securities, the uncertainty regarding the cash flows is due to prepayments and the risk associated with uncertain cash flows is called *prepayment risk*. For nonagency mortgage-backed securities, there is both prepayment risk and default risk.

The complication in the valuation of mortgage-backed securities and therefore in the computation of effective duration — which requires price projections for a rate shock up and down — is due to the uncertainty about prepayments. Prepayment risk as well as other assumptions to be discussed later that are made in valuing a mortgage-backed security can lead to measures that do not do an adequate job in projecting prices if rates change, as well as lead to significant differences in the duration and convexity measures reported by dealers and computed by vendors of analytical systems.

We begin this chapter with an explanation of the model used for valuing mortgage-backed securities, Monte Carlo simulation. We then look at how good the effective duration measure is in projecting actual price changes. This will lead us to an investigation of the assumptions underlying the Monte Carlo simulation model and their potential impact on the estimate of effective duration. We will also see the significant differences and the reasons for the differences in the effective durations reported by dealers and vendors. Three approaches for estimating duration based on market data — empirical duration, current coupon duration, and option-implied duration — will then be explained.

MONTE CARLO SIMULATION MODEL

Mortgage-backed securities are commonly valued using a Monte Carlo simulation model (simply Monte Carlo model, hereafter). The binomial model is used to value callable agency debentures and corporate bonds because it accommodates securities in which the decision to exercise a call option is not dependent on how interest rates evolved over time. That is, the decision of an issuer to call a bond will depend on the level of the rate at which the issue can be refunded relative to the issue's coupon rate, and not the path interest rates took to get to that rate. In contrast, mortgage-backed securities are interest rate path-dependent securities. This means that the cash flow received in one month is determined not only by the current interest rate level, but also by the path that interest rates took to get to the current level.

In the case of passthrough securities, prepayments are interest rate path-dependent because this month's prepayment rate depends on whether there have been prior opportunities to refinance since the underlying mortgages were originated — a phenomenon referred to as "prepayment burnout." Pools of passthroughs are used as collateral for the creation of CMOs. Consequently, there are typically two sources of path dependency in a CMO tranche's cash flows. First, the collateral prepayments are path-dependent as discussed above. Second, the cash flow to be received in the current month by a CMO tranche depends on the outstanding balances of the other tranches in the deal. Thus, we need the history of prepayments to calculate these balances.

Conceptually, the valuation of passthroughs using the Monte Carlo model is simple. In practice, however, it is very complex. The simulation involves generating a set of cash flows based on simulated future mortgage refinancing rates, which in turn imply simulated prepayment rates. Valuation modeling for CMOs is similar to valuation modeling for passthroughs, although the difficulties are amplified because the issuer has sliced and diced both the prepayment risk and the interest rate risk into tranches. The sensitivity of the passthroughs comprising the collateral to these two risks is not transmitted equally to every tranche. Some of the tranches wind up more sensitive to prepayment risk and interest rate risk than the collateral, while some of them are much less sensitive.

Below we describe the valuation process. What is critical to understand is the assumptions that are made along the way. The assumptions are sources of risk. Collectively these risks are called *modeling risk* and later in this chapter we will see how various aspects of these modeling risks affect the effective duration computed.

The typical model that dealers and vendors employ to generate random interest rate paths takes as input today's term structure of interest rates and a volatility assumption. The term structure of interest rates is the theoretical spot rate (or zero coupon) curve implied by today's Treasury securities. Some dealers use the on-the-run Treasury issues, while other dealers, such as Lehman Brothers, use off-the-run Treasury issues. The argument for using off-the-run Treasury issues is that the price/yield of on-the-run Treasury issues will not reflect their true economic value because the market price reflects their value for financing purposes (i.e., an issue may be on special in the repo market). Some dealers (such as PaineWebber) and vendors of analytical systems use the LIBOR curve instead of the Treasury curve — or give the user a choice to use the LIBOR curve. The reason is that some investors are interested in spreads that they can earn relative to their funding costs and LIBOR for many investors is a better proxy for that cost than Treasury rates.

The volatility assumption determines the dispersion of future interest rates in the simulation. Today, many vendors do not use one volatility number for the yield of all maturities of the yield curve. Instead, they use either a short/long yield volatility or a term structure of yield volatility. A short/long yield volatility means that volatility is specified for maturities up to a certain number of years (short yield volatility) and a different yield volatility for greater maturities (long yield volatility). The short yield volatility is assumed to be greater than the long yield volatility. A term structure of yield volatilities means that a yield volatility is assumed for each maturity.

The interest rate paths generated must be calibrated to the market. This means that the values generated from the model for on-the-run Treasury issues must equal the current market price for these issues.

Each model has an assumption about how interest rates evolve over time given the yield volatility assumption. Typically, there are no significant differences in the interest rate models of dealers and vendors.

The simulation works by generating many scenarios of future interest rate paths. In each month of the scenario (i.e., path), an interest rate and a mortgage refinancing rate are generated. The monthly interest rates are used to discount the projected cash flows in the scenario. The mortgage refinancing rate is needed to determine the cash flows because it represents the opportunity cost the mortgagor is facing at that time.

If the refinancing rates are high relative to the mortgagor's original coupon rate (i.e., the rate on the mortgagor's loan), the mortgagor will have less incentive to refinance, or even a positive disincentive (i.e., the homeowner will avoid moving in order to avoid paying a higher rate). If the refinancing rate is low relative to the mortgagor's original coupon rate, the mortgagor has an incentive to refinance.

Prepayments are projected by feeding the refinancing rate and loan characteristics into a prepayment model. Given the projected prepayments for each month, the cash flows along an interest rate path can be determined.

To make this more concrete, consider a newly issued mortgage passthrough security with a maturity of 360 months. Exhibit 1 shows *N* simulated interest rate path scenarios. Each scenario consists of a path of 360 simulated 1-month future interest rates. (The number of paths generated is based on a well known principle in simulation which will not be discussed here.) So, our first assumption that we make to get Exhibit 1 is the volatility of interest rates.

Exhibit 2 shows the paths of simulated mortgage refinancing rates corresponding to the scenarios shown in Exhibit 1. In going from Exhibit 1 to Exhibit 2, an assumption must be made about the relationship between the Treasury rates and refinancing rates. The assumption is that there is a constant spread relationship between the mortgage-refinancing rate and the 10-year Treasury yield.

Given the mortgage refinancing rates, the cash flows on each interest rate path can be generated. This requires a prepayment model. So our next assumption is that the prepayment model used to generate prepayments, and therefore the cash flows, is correct. The resulting cash flows are depicted in Exhibit 3.

Exhibit 1: Simulated Paths of 1-Month Future Interest Rates

	Interest Rate Path Number						
Month	1	2	3	...	n	...	N
1	$f_1(1)$	$f_1(2)$	$f_1(3)$	...	$f_1(n)$	...	$f_1(N)$
2	$f_2(1)$	$f_2(2)$	$f_2(3)$	...	$f_2(n)$	...	$f_2(N)$
3	$f_3(1)$	$f_3(2)$	$f_3(3)$	...	$f_3(n)$	...	$f_3(N)$
...	...	...	...	...	...	...	...
t	$f_t(1)$	$f_t(2)$	$f_t(3)$	...	$f_t(n)$	...	$f_t(N)$
...	...	...	...	...	...	...	...
358	$f_{358}(1)$	$f_{358}(2)$	$f_{358}(3)$	...	$f_{358}(n)$	...	$f_{358}(N)$
359	$f_{359}(1)$	$f_{359}(2)$	$f_{359}(3)$	...	$f_{359}(n)$	...	$f_{359}(N)$
360	$f_{360}(1)$	$f_{360}(2)$	$f_{360}(3)$	...	$f_{360}(n)$	...	$f_{360}(N)$

Notation:

$f_t(n)$ = 1-month future interest rate for month t on path n
N = total number of interest rate paths

Exhibit 2: Simulated Paths of Mortgage Refinancing Rates

	Interest Rate Path Number						
Month	1	2	3	...	n	...	N
1	$r_1(1)$	$r_1(2)$	$r_1(3)$	...	$r_1(n)$	...	$r_1(N)$
2	$r_2(1)$	$r_2(2)$	$r_2(3)$	...	$r_2(n)$	...	$r_2(N)$
3	$r_3(1)$	$r_3(2)$	$r_3(3)$	...	$r_3(n)$	...	$r_3(N)$
...	...	...	...	...	...	...	...
t	$r_t(1)$	$r_t(2)$	$r_t(3)$	...	$r_t(n)$	...	$r_t(N)$
...	...	...	...	...	...	...	...
358	$r_{358}(1)$	$r_{358}(2)$	$r_{358}(3)$	...	$r_{358}(n)$	...	$r_{358}(N)$
359	$r_{359}(1)$	$r_{359}(2)$	$r_{359}(3)$	...	$r_{359}(n)$	...	$r_{359}(N)$
360	$r_{360}(1)$	$r_{360}(2)$	$r_{360}(3)$	...	$r_{360}(n)$	...	$r_{360}(N)$

Notation:

$r_t(n)$ = mortgage refinancing rate for month t on path n
N = total number of interest rate paths

Given the cash flows on an interest rate path, the path's present value can be calculated. The discount rate for determining the present value is the simulated spot rate for each month on the interest rate path plus an appropriate spread. It can be shown that these discount rates are related to the simulated rates in Exhibit 1. Thus, a present value for each interest rate path can be calculated. The present value on an interest rate path can be thought of as the theoretical value of the passthrough if that path was actually realized. The theoretical value of the passthrough is then determined by calculating the average of the theoretical values of all the interest rate paths.

Exhibit 3: Simulated Cash Flows on Each of the Interest Rate Paths

	Interest Rate Path Number						
Month	1	2	3	...	n	...	N
1	$C_1(1)$	$C_1(2)$	$C_1(3)$	...	$C_1(n)$	...	$C_1(N)$
2	$C_2(1)$	$C_2(2)$	$C_2(3)$	...	$C_2(n)$	...	$C_2(N)$
3	$C_3(1)$	$C_3(2)$	$C_3(3)$	...	$C_3(n)$	...	$C_3(N)$
...	...	...	...	...	...	...	...
t	$C_t(1)$	$C_t(2)$	$C_t(3)$	...	$C_t(n)$	...	$C_t(N)$
...	...	...	...	...	...	...	...
358	$C_{358}(1)$	$C_{358}(2)$	$C_{358}(3)$	...	$C_{358}(n)$	...	$C_{358}(N)$
359	$C_{359}(1)$	$C_{359}(2)$	$C_{359}(3)$	...	$C_{359}(n)$	...	$C_{359}(N)$
360	$C_{360}(1)$	$C_{360}(2)$	$C_{360}(3)$	...	$C_{360}(n)$	...	$C_{360}(N)$

Notation:

$C_t(n)$ = cash flow for month t on path n

N = total number of interest rate paths

This procedure for valuing a passthrough is also followed for a CMO tranche or a mortgage strip. The cash flow for each month on each interest rate path is found according to the principal repayment and interest distribution rules of the deal.

The *option-adjusted spread* is found as follows. It is the spread that must be added to all of the simulated rates in Exhibit 1 that will make the theoretical value produced by the model equal to the market price.

EFFECTIVE DURATION AND CONVEXITY

To calculate effective duration, the value of the security must be estimated when rates are shocked up and down a given number of basis points. In terms of the Monte Carlo model, the yield curve used (either the Treasury yield curve or LIBOR curve) is shocked up and down and the new curve is used to generate the values to be used in the effective duration and effective convexity formulas.

There are two important aspects of this process of generating the values when the rates are shocked that are critical to understand. First, the assumption is that the relationships assumed do not change when rates are shocked up and down. Specifically, the yield volatility is assumed to be unchanged to derive the new interest rate paths for a given shock (i.e., the new Exhibit 1), the spread between the mortgage rate and the 10-year Treasury rate is assumed to be unchanged in constructing the new Exhibit 2 from the newly constructed Exhibit 1, and the OAS is assumed to be constant. The constancy of the OAS comes into play because when discounting the new cash flows (i.e., the cash flows in the new Exhibit 3), the current OAS that was computed is assumed to be the same and is added to the new rates in the new Exhibit 1.

We'll use an illustration by Lakhbir Hayre and Hubert Chang to explain the calculation of effective duration for a mortgage-backed security, a FNMA 7.5% TBA passthrough on May 1, 1996.[1] On that day, the base mortgage rate was 7.64% and the Treasury yield curve was as follows:

3 mos	6 mos	1 yr	2 yr	3 yr	4 yr	5 yr	7 yr	10 yr	20 yr	30 yr
5.10	5.27	5.57	6.00	6.15	6.27	6.38	6.50	6.68	6.79	6.91

The price of the issue at the time was 98.781 (i.e., 98-25). The OAS was 65 basis points. Based on a shock of 25 basis points, the estimated prices holding the OAS constant at 65 basis points were as follows:

$V_- = 99.949$ for a decrease in the yield curve of 25 basis points
$V_+ = 97.542$ for an increase in the yield curve of 25 basis points

Using equation (1) in Chapter 4, the effective duration based on a Δy of 0.0025 is then

$$\frac{99.949 - 97.542}{2 \times 98.781 \times 0.0025} = 4.87$$

How good was the effective duration for this passthrough in estimating its price change from May 1, 1996 (the date that the effective duration was computed) to the end of the month, May 31, 1996? The 10-year Treasury yield over the month increased 17.5 basis points from 6.675% to 6.85%. Using equation (3) in Chapter 4, the projected decrease in the price of this passthrough based on an effective duration of 4.87 is:

$$4.87 \times 98.781 \times 0.00175 = 0.840 \text{ or } 27 \text{ ticks}$$

[1] Lakhbir Hayre and Hubert Chang, "Effective and Empirical Duration of Mortgage Securities," *The Journal of Fixed Income* (March 1997), pp. 17-33.

Thus, the price of this passthrough is projected to decline by approximately 27 ticks. The actual price on May 31, 1996 was 97-30, 27 ticks lower than at the beginning of the month. Thus, effective duration did an excellent job of projecting the price change, in this case.

A CLOSER LOOK AT EFFECTIVE DURATION AND THE UNDERLYING ASSUMPTIONS

We have just seen how effective duration is computed. There are now two questions we must address. First, will the estimates of the price change using duration always be as good as in the previous example? Second, why are there differences in the effective durations reported by dealers and vendors of analytical services? The questions are not mutually exclusive since, as we shall see, the assumptions employed in the Monte Carlo model will impact how well effective duration predicts price changes when rates change. Moreover, it is the differences in the assumptions that cause differences in effective duration reported by dealers and vendors.

Let's look at the first question. After showing how to calculate the effective duration for the FNMA 7.5s, and how well the computed effective duration predicted price changes for May 1996, Hayre and Chang went on to assess the performance predictability from June 7, 1996 to June 27, 1996 using effective duration. The effective duration on June 7, 1996 was calculated to be 4.95 based on a price of 97-29 (i.e., 97.906). The 10-year Treasury yield at the time was 6.905%. On June 27, 1996, the 10-year Treasury yield decreased by 7.5 basis points to 6.83%. Based on an effective duration of 4.95, the projected increase in price was:

$$4.95 \times 97.906 \times 0.00075 = 0.363 \text{ or } 12 \text{ ticks}$$

The actual price increase on June 27, 1996 was 6 ticks (from 97-29 to 98-03). After adjusting for the cost of carry because the passthroughs are TBA, Hayre and Chang found that the actual change in price was 4 ticks. Thus, the 12 tick change in price as projected based on effective duration did not do as good a job of projecting the actual price change of 4 ticks in comparison to the previous period, May 1 to May 31, 1996. We'll address why shortly.

Exhibit 4: Effective Durations Reported for FNMA 30-Year TBA Passthroughs for Various Dealers and BARRA as of December 29, 1995

Coupon	Old BARRA	New BARRA	Lehman	CSFB Emp	Salomon	DLJ	DLJ Emp	MS	MS RCM
6.0	5.1	4.90	5.20	5.4	0.0	6.0	4.7	5.1	0.0
6.5	5.0	4.66	4.30	4.7	5.0	5.6	4.0	4.8	4.2
7.0	4.7	3.89	3.95	4.3	4.0	4.8	3.5	3.8	3.7
7.5	4.2	3.02	2.80	3.4	2.9	3.5	2.6	2.9	3.0
8.0	3.5	2.25	1.30	2.5	1.7	1.7	1.8	2.2	2.2
8.5	2.7	1.62	0.70	1.6	1.1	0.7	1.3	1.9	1.9
9.0	2.3	1.12	0.26	1.0	0.6	0.5	0.9	1.8	2.0
9.5	2.0	0.77	0.00	0.3	1.0	0.7	0.8	1.6	0.0
10.0	2.9	1.85	1.40	0.0	1.8	1.2	0.6	0.0	0.0
10.5	3.3	1.84	1.50	0.0	0.0	1.2	0.6	0.0	0.0

Notes:

"Emp" denotes empirical duration estimate

"RCM" denotes relative coupon model

Dealers:

Lehman = Lehman Brothers

CSFB = Credit Suisse First Boston

Salomon = Salomon Brothers (now Salomon Smith Barney)

DLJ = Donaldson, Lufkin & Jenrette

MS = Morgan Stanley

Source: Exhibit 5a in Oren Cheyette, Sam Choi, and Elena Blanter, "The New BARRA Fixed Rate Prepayment Model," *BARRA Newsletter* (Spring 1996).

Differences in Reported Effective Durations by Dealers and Vendors

With respect to differences in effective durations reported by dealers and vendors, Exhibits 4 and 5 illustrate this. The exhibits show the differences in the effective durations reported by five dealers (Lehman Brothers, CS First Boston, Salomon, Donaldson Lufkin & Jenrette (DLJ), and Morgan Stanley) and one vendor (BARRA) on December 29, 1995. Exhibit 4 shows the reported effective duration for FNMA 30-year TBA passthroughs for 10 coupons and Exhibit 5 does the same for GNMA I 30-year TBA passthroughs. The duration for CS First Boston and one of the dealers, DLJ, is based on empirical duration, an alternative duration measure that we will describe later in this chapter. One of the reported durations for Morgan Stanley is based on an alternative duration measure discussed later in this chapter, "relative coupon model." Exhibit 6 compares the reported effective durations of another vendor, Capital Management Sciences (CMS), to two dealer estimates (Goldman and Salomon).

Moreover, vendors of analytical systems update their models periodically. The first two columns of Exhibits 4 and 5 show the differences in effective durations by one vendor, BARRA, based on an older prepayment model it developed and a new prepayment model it developed in 1995. There are significant differences in the two effective durations. The new model produces effective durations that are more consistent with those of the dealers.[2]

Exhibit 5: Effective Durations Reported for GNMA I 30-Year TBA Passthroughs for Various Dealers and BARRA as of December 29, 1995

Coupon	Old BARRA	New BARRA	Lehman	CSFB Emp	Salomon	DLJ	DLJ Emp	MS	MS RCM
6.0	5.97	5.48	6.31	4.80	0.0	6.55	4.75	6.10	0.00
6.5	5.60	5.04	5.31	4.60	5.7	6.33	4.19	5.54	4.13
7.0	5.64	4.18	4.73	4.23	4.9	5.42	3.60	4.54	3.73
7.5	5.01	3.29	3.64	3.50	3.6	4.18	2.65	3.51	3.18
8.0	4.30	2.47	2.03	2.50	2.3	2.33	1.74	2.61	2.41
8.5	3.50	2.08	1.09	1.66	1.3	1.09	1.21	1.90	2.03
9.0	2.90	1.94	0.6	0.41	0.6	1.28	0.76	1.41	2.27
9.5	2.40	1.84	0.47	0.34	0.5	1.57	0.45	0.00	0.00
10.0	3.40	3.67	1.28	0.32	1.5	1.60	0.26	0.00	0.00
10.5	3.80	3.85	1.76	-0.10	0.0	1.85	0.18	0.00	0.00

Notes:

"Emp" denotes empirical duration estimate

"RCM" denotes relative coupon model

Dealers:

Lehman = Lehman Brothers

CSFB = Credit Suisse First Boston

Salomon = Salomon Brothers (now Salomon Smith Barney)

DLJ = Donaldson, Lufkin & Jenrette

MS = Morgan Stanley

Source: Exhibit 5b in Oren Cheyette, Sam Choi, and Elena Blanter, "The New BARRA Fixed Rate Prepayment Model," *BARRA Newsletter* (Spring 1996).

[2] Oren Cheyette, Sam Choi, and Elena Blanter, "The New BARRA Fixed Rate Prepayment Model," *BARRA Newsletter* (Spring 1996).

Exhibit 6: Effective Durations Reported for FNMA 30-Year TBA Passthroughs for Two Dealers and Capital Management Sciences as of July 1998

Coupon		CMS BondEdge	Goldman	Salomon
6.5	1997	4.1		3.5
	1996	3.9		3.2
	1995	3.7	3.7	3.1
	1994	3.7		3.1
	1993	3.6	3.6	3.1
7.0	1997	3.1		2.2
	1996	3.0		2.0
	1995	2.9	3.1	1.8
	1994	2.8		2.0
	1993	2.8	2.4	1.9
7.5	1996	2.3		0.9
	1995	2.2	2.1	0.8
	1994	2.2		0.8
	1993	2.3	1.7	0.9
8.0	1996			0.5
	1995		1.4	0.5
	1994		1.0	0.1
	1992		1.2	0.5
8.5	1996			0.6
	1995		1.2	0.9
	1994			0.7
	1992			0.8
	1987		1.5	0.7
9.0	1995		1.3	0.8
	1994			0.8
	1991		1.6	1.0
	1986		1.4	0.8

Source: Capital Management Sciences

Even the providers of bond indexes update their valuation models and change their duration numbers. For example, in 1995 Lehman Brothers updated its prepayment model based on the slower prepayment experience in that year. Lehman Brothers notified the users of Lehman's Mortgage Index that some of the durations would change dramatically. For example, the duration of FNMA 9.5s originated in 1995 more than doubled from 0.8 to 2, while the duration for the FNMA 8.5s of 1991 increased from 2.5 to 3.7.[3]

[3] Gunnar Klinkhammer, "Mortgage Durations: No Two Models Agree," *On the Edge*, Capital Management Sciences (April 1996), p. 3.

Significance of Assumptions

Choi[4] and Hayre and Chang,[5] as well as others, have explained and illustrated why these differences occur. Choi provides the following four reasons for the differences among the reported effective durations of dealers and vendors.

1. differences in the amount of the rate shock used
2. directional bias versus non-directional bias rate shock
3. differences in prepayment models
4. differences in option-adjusted spread

In Chapter 4, we discussed the first reason. As explained, the rate shock is the amount interest rates are increased and decreased to obtain the two values that are inserted into the effective duration formula. If the change is too large, there is the problem with picking up the effect of convexity. If the duration is too small, such as 1 or 10 basis points, the error realized in estimating the new prices is amplified because of the division by a small number.

A directionally biased effective duration is computed by using only the price change resulting from one rate shock (up or down) rather than prices from both an up and down shock. The direction of the bias for the rate will depend on the objective of the user. If the concern is with a rise in rates on a long position, an increase in rates may be used to determine the effective duration. However, in the case of some mortgage-backed securities the motivation for using a directional bias is due to the fact that some mortgage derivatives and certain high coupon passthroughs exhibit a price/yield relationship that is not monotonically increasing or decreasing within a certain range. This is shown in Exhibit 7 for an interest-only (IO) stripped mortgage-backed security. Notice how the effective duration would be different if the prices used were based on (1) either an increase or a decrease in rates only and (2) an average for up and down rates. In the latter case, the duration would show that the price decreased in both the up and down rate change scenarios and, as a result, the computed duration is not meaningful.

---

[4] Sam Choi, "Effective Durations for Mortgage-Backed Securities: Recipes for Improvement," *The Journal of Fixed Income* (March 1996), pp. 24-30.

[5] Hayre and Chang, "Effective and Empirical Duration of Mortgage Securities."

Exhibit 7: Price/Yield Relationship for an Interest-Only Stripped Mortgage Security

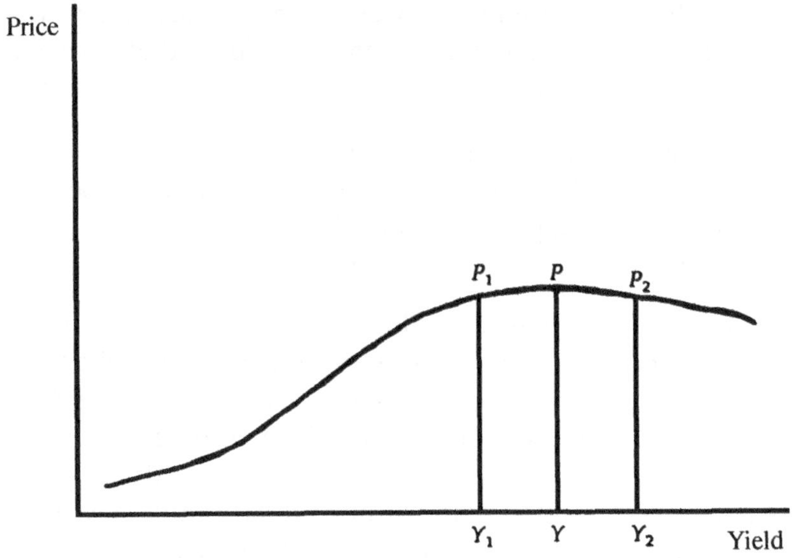

Prepayment models differ across dealers and vendors. Some dealer models consistently forecast slower prepayments relative to other dealer models and others the reverse. If the prepayment speeds that are forecasted are too fast, the effective duration will be lower than if slower speeds are forecasted. The reverse is the situation for prepayment speeds that are too slow — the effective duration will be greater.

Choi illustrates the case of overestimates of prepayments.[6] In the refinancing wave of 1992-1993, dealer models were forecasting slower prepayments than were being experienced. This is because prepayment models are influenced by the long history of prepayment rates and these historical rates are influenced by alternative mortgage instruments and refinancing costs in the past. The refinancing wave of 1992-1993 resulted from not only lower interest rates but also the creativeness of mortgage originators in making it more economic for homeowners to refinance for much smaller drops in interest rates than were required in the past. Yet, the prepayment models were not "recalibrated" to take this into account.

[6] Choi, "Effective Durations for Mortgage-Backed Securities."

Exhibit 8: Overpredicted Duration Resulting from Slower than Actual Prepayments

Bond	Median Broker Estimate	Actual Empirical Duration	Overpredicted Amount	Date
FNMA 8%	5.00	3.70	1.30	92Q3
FNMA 9%	2.60	2.30	0.30	92Q3
FNMA 10%	2.00	1.10	0.90	92Q3
FNMA 8%	4.40	3.30	1.10	93Q1
FNMA 9%	2.00	1.70	0.30	93Q1
FNMA 10%	1.80	0.80	1.00	93Q1
FNMA 8%	2.80	1.20	1.60	93Q3
FNMA 9%	1.90	0.60	1.30	93Q3
FNMA 10%	1.70	0.40	1.30	93Q3

Source: Exhibit 4 in Sam Choi, "Effective Durations for Mortgage-Backed Securities: Recipes for Improvement," *The Journal of Fixed Income* (March 1996), p. 24. Reprinted with permission from Institutional Investor, Inc., *The Journal of Fixed Income*, 488 Madison Avenue, New York, NY 10022.

Exhibit 8 shows for three quarters in 1992-1993 the median duration estimate of dealers for three FNMA coupon passthroughs, the actual empirical duration, and the overpredicted amount of the effective duration. Because of the lag in updating prepayment models, some analysts recommend using short-term prepayments to decrease errors in estimating effective duration.

Finally, the effective duration is dependent on the OAS computed. There are two problems here. First, recall that the calculation of the OAS is a byproduct of the Monte Carlo model. Therefore, the computed value for the OAS depends on all of the assumptions in the Monte Carlo model. Specifically, it depends on the yield volatility assumed and the prepayment model employed. Dealers and vendors make different assumptions regarding yield volatility and use proprietary prepayment models. These can result in differences in OAS. The second problem is that even if the OAS values computed by all dealers and vendors are identical, the effective durations may not do well in predicting future price changes because of the assumption in calculating the projected prices computed from the Monte Carlo model that are used when rates are shocked up and down. Recall that the assumption is that when rates are shocked, the OAS is constant. However, market observers believe that OAS is affected by increased prepayment uncertainty and this is related to changes in rates.

Hayre and Chang focus on the main assumptions in calculating effective duration which are:

1. a parallel shift in the yield curve
2. a constant OAS when rates change
3. a constant current-coupon/Treasury spread
4. a constant term structure of interest rate volatility
5. absence of convexity

We already discussed the constant OAS assumption and the issue related to the absence of convexity.

Hayre and Chang use the prediction error of 6 ticks based on the effective duration for the FNMA 7.5s for the period June 7 to June 27, 1996 to illustrate the impact of these assumptions by looking at what the Monte Carlo model would have projected for the price had the assumptions been consistent with what actually happened by June 27, 1996.

Consider first the assumption that the yield curve shifts in a parallel fashion. The Treasury yield curve actually shifted down between June 7 and June 27. For the 6-month to 5-year sector of the yield curve, rates declined by 12 basis points. At the shorter end and for maturities greater than 5 years, rates declined by less than 12 basis points. If the yield curve that actually occurred on June 27 been assumed on June 7, the predicted price would have been 98-11. Thus, the predicted price would indicate a price increase of 14 ticks (from 97-29 on June 7). Based on a 10-year Treasury yield decline of 7.5 basis points, it was found earlier that there was a 4 tick price increase (after adjusting for the cost of carry). Thus, the reshaping of the yield curve accounts for 2 ticks in the price discrepancy between the 12 ticks based on duration assuming a parallel shift and the 14 ticks due to a nonparallel shift.

The constant OAS assumption when the 10-year Treasury yield changes was investigated by looking at the actual change in the OAS. On June 7, the OAS was computed to be 57 basis points. The OAS increased to 62 basis points on June 27. Had a 62 basis point OAS been assumed in computing duration on June 7 instead of

57 basis points, the projected price change would have been 8 ticks lower. This is a major reason for the 8 tick discrepancy (between 12 ticks using effective duration and the 4 tick actual price change).

In the model used by Hayre and Chang, the Salomon model, a term structure of yield volatility is used. The assumption is then that the term structure of yield volatility is unchanged. A change in the term structure of yield volatility did occur between the two periods.[7] Repricing the FNMA 7.5s on June 7 using the term structure of yield volatility on June 27, the difference in the projected price change was 2 ticks.

In generating the refinancing rates in the Monte Carlo model, it is assumed that there is a constant spread between mortgage rates and the 10-year Treasury rate. Over the period June 7 to June 27, the spread increased by 2 basis points. Using the same methodology, Hayre and Chang found this to cause a 0.5 tick discrepancy.

Finally, as discussed earlier, because of the convexity of mortgage-backed securities, there is an asymmetric change in price when rates change. Hayre and Chang examined the impact of convexity and found that it had only a minimal impact on the price discrepancy, –0.1 ticks.

Let's now look at the impact of all these assumptions. The actual price change after adjusting for carry is +4 ticks. The price change predicted by duration is +8 ticks. Thus, duration overestimated the price change by +4 ticks. The prediction error due to each of the assumptions is as follows:

Nonparallel yield curve shift	+2.0 ticks
Change in OAS	–8.0 ticks
Change in volatility	+2.0 ticks
Change in mortgage/Treasury spread	0.5 ticks
Convexity	–0.1 ticks

The total impact is –3.6 ticks. That is, if all the assumptions were taken into account along with duration, the predicted price change would have been +4.4 ticks (8 ticks – 3.6 ticks). This is close the actual price change of +4 ticks.

---

[7] The term structure of yield volatility is based on the implied yield volatility in the cap market, the volatility for Eurodollar CDs at the short end, and the swap market at the long end.

Risk Measures for Assessing Modeling Risk

A key point here is that because of modeling risk, it is important to have measures that assess the potential impact on price change due to each critical assumption or factor in the valuation process. In Chapter 5, we introduced risk measures that estimate the impact of these factors on the predicted price. Volatility risk (vega) measures the exposure of a security with an embedded option to a change in the term structure of yield volatility holding all other factors constant, and spread duration measures the exposure to a change in the OAS holding all other factors constant. We'll discuss risk measures to assess the impact of a reshaping of the yield curve in Chapter 7.

The exposure to changes in prepayments can be quantified by looking at how higher and lower prepayments from the prepayment model would impact the price. Specifically, in generating the cash flows on each interest rate path, a prepayment model is used. The prepayment model provides a projected prepayment rate for each month. (This rate is called the "single monthly mortality rate.") To quantify the exposure to prepayment uncertainty, the Monte Carlo model is run twice. In one run, the prepayment rate from the model for each month is decreased by a fixed percentage. In a second run, the monthly prepayment rates are increased by the same fixed percentage. In both runs, the OAS and all other factors are held constant. The average change in the two values is then used to estimate the prepayment sensitivity of a mortgage-backed security.

Vendors such as Capital Management Sciences will provide several measures of prepayment sensitivity. The *overall prepayment uncertainty sensitivity* measure is found by changing the monthly prepayment rates up and down 10%. There are two *partial prepayment sensitivity* measures that take into consideration the major factors that affect prepayments. It is well known that prepayments occur due to refinancing and due to relocations. One partial prepayment sensitivity measure adjusts the monthly prepayment rates on the interest rate paths for prepayments due to refinancings and a second for relocations. CMS refers to these measures as the *refinancing partial prepayment uncertainty measure* and *relocation partial prepayment uncertainty measure*, respectively.[8]

---

[8] Klinkhammer, "Mortgage Durations: No Two Models Agree."

EMPIRICAL DURATION

For mortgage-backed securities, several approaches based on observed market prices are used to calculate duration. These market-based approaches are empirical duration, coupon curve duration, and option-implied duration. In this section we discuss empirical duration.

Empirical duration, sometimes referred to as *implied duration*, is the sensitivity of a mortgage-backed security as estimated empirically from historical prices and yields. Regression analysis is used to estimate the relationship. This approach was first suggested in 1986 by Scott Pinkus and Marie Chandoha[9] and then in 1990 by Paul DeRossa, Laurie Goodman, and Mike Zazzarino.[10]

More recently, Laurie Goodman and her colleagues have provided more information on the methodology used at PaineWebber.[11] On a daily basis the following regressions are calculated:

$$\text{Change in mortgage price} = a + b\,(\text{Change in 10-year yield})$$

The empirical duration is then calculated as follows:

$$\text{Empirical duration} = \frac{b(\text{Change in mortgage price}/\text{Change in 10-year yield})}{\text{Full price of the mortgage}}$$

where "mortgage" means mortgage-backed security.

Exhibit 9 compares empirical duration, effective duration (referred to as OAS duration in the exhibit), and cash flow duration (discussed at the end of this chapter) for 30-year GNMAs, 30-year FNMAs, and 15-year FNMAs for each of the actively traded coupons based on prices from July 1, 1993 through May 12, 1998.

---

[9] Scott M. Pinkus and Marie A. Chandoha, "The Relative Price Volatility of Mortgage Securities," *Journal of Portfolio Management* (Summer 1986), pp. 9-22.

[10] Paul DeRossa, Laurie Goodman, and Mike Zazzarino, "Duration Estimates on Mortgage-Backed Securities," *Journal of Portfolio Management* (Winter 1993), pp. 32-37.

[11] See Laurie S. Goodman and Jeffrey Ho, "Mortgage Hedge Ratios: Which One Works Best?" *The Journal of Fixed Income* (December 1997), pp. 23-33, and Laurie S. Goodman and Jeffrey Ho, "An Integrated Approach to Hedging and Relative Value Analysis," Chapter 15 in Frank J. Fabozzi (ed.), *Advances in the Valuation and Management of Mortgage-Backed Securities* (New Hope, PA: Frank J. Fabozzi Associates, 1999).

Exhibit 9: Comparison of Empirical, Effective (OAS), Cash Flow, Option Implied, and Price Model Durations

	5/12/98 Price	Cash flow Dur	OAS Dur	Empirical Dur	Option Implied Dur	Price Model Dur
GNSF 6.0	96:26	6.27	6.57	5.32	5.53	5.75
GNSF 6.5	99:02	5.82	5.98	4.36	4.52	4.97
GNSF 7.0	101:05+	5.59	5.25	3.55	3.62	4.01
GNSF 7.5	102:24+	4.88	4.31	2.20	3.01	2.95
GNSF 8.0	103:28	3.98	3.32	1.41	2.59	1.74
GNSF 8.5	105:18+	3.03	2.54	0.44	0.00	1.03
FNCL 6.0	96:17+	5.55	5.88	5.10	5.22	5.29
FNCL 6.5	98:30+	5.64	5.29	4.19	4.19	4.68
FNCL 7.0	101:02+	5.28	4.55	3.39	3.32	3.79
FNCL 7.5	102:20+	4.35	3.66	2.03	2.69	2.64
FNCL 8.0	103:24	3.72	2.84	1.23	2.32	1.48
FNCL 8.5	104:18	2.90	2.26	0.46	0.00	0.59
FNCI 6.0	98:16	4.33	4.31	3.77	3.85	6.12
FNCI 6.5	100:11	4.11	3.90	2.92	3.03	5.07
FNCI 7.0	101:25	3.66	3.31	2.10	2.46	3.80
FNCI 7.5	102:28+	2.98	2.69	1.10	2.00	2.28
FNCI 8.0	103:03	2.42	2.24	0.55	1.85	0.72

Note: Hedge ratios versus 10-year Treasury for 30-year mortgages. 5-year Treasury for 15-year mortgages.

Source: Exhibit 3 in Laurie S. Goodman and Jeffrey Ho, "An Integrated Approach to Hedging and Relative Value Analysis," Chapter 15 in Frank J. Fabozzi (ed.), *Advances in the Valuation and Management of Mortgage-Backed Securities* (New Hope, PA: Frank J. Fabozzi Associates, 1999).

There are three advantages to the empirical duration approach.[12] First, the duration estimate does not rely on any theoretical formulas or analytical assumptions. Second, the estimation of the required parameters is easy to compute using regression analysis. Finally, the only inputs that are needed are a reliable price series and Treasury yield series.

There are disadvantages.[13] First, a reliable price series for the mortgage security may not be available. For example, there may be no price series available for a thinly traded mortgage derivative security or the prices may be matrix priced or model priced rather

[12] See Bennett W. Golub, "Towards a New Approach to Measuring Mortgage Duration," Chapter 32 in Frank J. Fabozzi (ed.), *The Handbook of Mortgage-Backed Securities* (Chicago: Probus Publishing, 1995), p. 672.

[13] Golub, "Towards a New Approach to Measuring Mortgage Duration."

than actual transaction prices. Second, an empirical relationship does not impose a structure for the options embedded in a mortgage-backed security and this can distort the empirical duration. Third, the price history may lag current market conditions. This may occur after a sharp and sustained shock to interest rates has been realized. Finally, the volatility of the spread to Treasury yields can distort how the price of a mortgage-backed security reacts to yield changes.

Exhibits 4 and 5 show the empirical duration computed by CS First Boston and DLJ. For DLJ, both the effective duration computed using a Monte Carlo model and the empirical duration are shown so that you can see how they differ. The fact that they do differ should be no surprise because the models for computing effective duration give less weight to recent market information and industry trends (e.g., the innovations and strategies of mortgage bankers to encourage refinancing).

Price Model Duration Measure

Goodman and Ho present a more elaborate empirical model from which to derive duration that takes into account the several factors that we have noted impact the price of a mortgage-backed security: level of rates, shape of the yield curve, and expected interest rate volatility.[14] The price model that they present allows not only an estimate of the sensitivity of the price to changes in the level of rates, but also to the other factors.

In their price model, the 10-year Treasury yield is used as a proxy for the level of rates, the spread between the 10-year and 2-year Treasury yields is used as a proxy for the shape of the yield curve, and the implied 3-month yield volatility on the 10-year Treasury note is used as a proxy for expected interest rate volatility. The price model involves estimating the following regression:

$$\begin{aligned}\text{Price} = {} & a + b\,(\text{10-year yield}) + c\,(\ln[\text{10-year yield}]) \\ & + d\,(\text{10-year/2-year spread}) + e\,(\text{volatility})\end{aligned}$$

where ln[10-year yield] means the natural logarithm of the 10-year Treasury yield.

[14] Goodman and Ho, "An Integrated Approach to Mortgage Hedging and Relative Value Analysis."

For the passthroughs whose durations are reported in Exhibit 9, the coefficient of determination (popularly referred to as the "R-squared") of the regression relationship exceeded 97.5%.[15] This means that at least 97.5% of the variation in daily prices was explained by the factors in the regression.

Given the estimates for the parameters above, duration (called by Goodman and Ho *price model duration* or *hedging duration*) is found as follows:

$$\text{Price model duration} = -[b + c/(\text{10-year Treasury yield})]$$

For example, for the FNMA 7% price model regression, the regression estimate for b was -11.89 and the regression estimate for c was 45.87. On the close of May 12, 1998, the 10-year Treasury yield was 5.70%. Therefore, the price model duration is:

$$\text{Price model duration} = -[-11.89 + (45.87/5.7)] = 3.84.$$

Exhibit 9 shows the price model duration for the securities.

Relative Performance of Empirical Duration versus Effective Duration

Several studies have examined the relative performance of effective duration and empirical duration. Typically, the analysis is based on hedging performance. Specifically, from duration estimates, hedge ratios can be constructed. The tests of relative performance look at how the duration derived hedge ratios have performed historically.

In their study, Hayre and Chang conclude the following. First, in most months effective duration outperformed empirical duration in estimating price changes. However, there were enough months where the reverse was true, suggesting that a portfolio manager should not automatically discard the information contained in empirical duration. Because of this, Hayre and Chang recommend combining effective duration and empirical duration. They do not offer any specific procedure for obtaining a combined measure; it could be simply a weighted average of the two durations. They label

---

[15] See Exhibit 1 in Goodman and Ho, "An Integrated Approach to Mortgage Hedging and Relative Value Analysis."

the duration measure that combines effective duration and empirical duration as the *updated empirical duration.*[16]

The second major conclusion involves the constant OAS and attempts to incorporate the correlation between OAS and yield changes into a model for effective duration. Hayre and Chang found that there is little relationship between this correlation and the relative performance of the two duration measures.

Goodman and Ho looked at the hedging performance of duration-derived hedge ratios using effective duration, empirical duration, and their price model duration (a type of empirical duration). In contrast to the findings of Hayre and Chang, they find that effective duration does not perform as well as empirical duration measures.[17]

COUPON CURVE DURATION

The *coupon curve duration* uses market prices to estimate the duration of a mortgage-backed security. It is an easier approach to duration estimation than empirical duration. This approach, first suggested by Douglas Breeden,[18] starts with the coupon curve of prices for similar mortgage-backed securities. By rolling up and down the coupon curve of prices, the duration can be obtained. Because of the way it is estimated, this approach to duration estimation was referred to by Breeden as the "roll-up, roll-down approach." The prices obtained from rolling up and rolling down the coupon curve of prices are substituted into the duration formula given by equation (1) in Chapter 4.

To illustrate this approach, let's use the coupon curve of prices for Ginnie Maes in June 1994. A portion of the coupon curve of prices for that month was as follows:

---

[16] Douglas Breeden comes to the same conclusion regarding combining effective duration by dealers and empirical duration. (See "Complexities of Hedging Mortgages," *The Journal of Fixed Income* (December 1994), pp. 6-41.)

[17] Goodman and Ho, "Mortgage Hedge Ratios: Which One Works Best," p. 28.

[18] Douglas Breeden, "Risk, Return, and Hedging of Fixed-Rate Mortgages," *The Journal of Fixed Income* (September 1991), pp. 85-107.

Coupon	Price
6%	85.19
7%	92.06
8%	98.38
9%	103.34
10%	107.28
11%	111.19

Suppose that the coupon curve duration for the 8s is sought. If the yield declines by 100 basis points, the assumption is that the price of the 8s will increase to the price of the 9s. Thus, the price will increase from 98.38 to 103.34. Similarly, if the yield increases by 100 basis points, the assumption is that the price of the 8s will decline to the price of the 7s (92.06). Using the duration formula given by equation (1) in Chapter 4, the corresponding values are:

$$V_0 = 98.38$$
$$V_- = 103.34$$
$$V_+ = 92.06$$
$$\Delta y = 0.01$$

The estimated duration based on the coupon curve is then:

$$\text{Duration} = \frac{103.34 - 92.06}{2(98.38)(0.01)} = 5.73$$

Breeden tested the coupon curve durations and found them to be relatively accurate.[19] Bennett Golub reports a similar finding.[20]

While the advantages of the coupon curve duration are the simplicity of its calculation and the fact that current prices embody market expectations, there are disadvantages. The approach is limited to generic mortgage-backed securities and difficult to use for mortgage derivatives.

OPTION-IMPLIED DURATION

In the over-the-counter option market, dealers buy and sell put and call options on mortgage passthroughs and Treasury securities.

[19] Breeden, "Risk, Return, and Hedging of Fixed-Rate Mortgages."
[20] Golub, "Towards a New Approach to Measuring Mortgage Duration," p. 673.

Goodman and Ho argue that the information contained in the prices of these options provides valuable information in estimating duration. Specifically, they argue that the ratio of the option fee (price) of an at-the-money forward option for a given passthrough to the option fee (price) of an at-the-money forward Treasury is a good proxy for the option market's expectations of the relative price volatility of the two securities. Using this ratio a duration measure can be computed. Goodman and Ho call the resulting duration *option-implied duration.*

Exhibit 9 shows the option-implied duration for the passthroughs analyzed. Tests of the option-implied duration by Goodman and Ho find that they tend to perform slightly better than empirical measures.[21]

CASH FLOW DURATION

We saved the *worst* for last. Some market participants calculate (but hopefully do not use) a measure called *cash flow duration.* This duration measure has been computed in two ways.

The first way is to assume that when interest rates change the prepayments do not change. So, the value for the security changes because a new discount rate (resulting from the rate shock) is used and not a change in the cash flows. Computed in this way, the cash flow duration is equivalent to modified duration. The PaineWebber Mortgage Group, for example, refers to the cash flow duration interchangeably with modified duration. Obviously, this measure suffers from all of the problems associated with using modified duration for a security with an embedded option.

The second way cash flow duration is used is to change rates and allow for the cash flows to change by changing the prepayment speed. For example, assume that the current prepayment speed is 120 PSA[22] for a security and the cash flow yield for the security is 7%. To get the two values to use in the duration formula given by

[21] Goodman and Ho, "Mortgage Hedge Ratios: Which One Works Best," p. 28.
[22] It is assumed that the reader is familiar with the Public Securities Association (PSA) prepayment convention.

equation (1) in Chapter 4, suppose the cash flow yield is shocked by 25 basis points. If the cash flow yield is increased to 7.25%, then a prepayment model is used to determine the new cash flows at the higher yield level. Suppose that a prepayment model indicates that at a 7.25% yield the prepayment speed will decline to 105 PSA. Then the cash flows for this security are generated based on 105 PSA and discounted at the 7.25% yield. This gives the value of V_+. Suppose that if the cash flow yield declines to 6.75% the prepayment model indicates that the prepayment speed will increase to 135 PSA. Then the new cash flows for this security will be generated based on 135 PSA and discounted at 6.75%. The resulting value for the security is V_-.

This second way that cash flow duration may be calculated is superior to the first in that it at least recognizes that the cash flows may change when rates change. However, it still suffers from the problem that in computing the V_+ and V_- it only recognizes one possible cash flow stream (i.e., not a large number of interest rate paths) and that all cash flows are discounted at the one rate resulting from the shock.

SUMMARY

There are various approaches to estimating the duration of mortgage-backed securities — effective duration (also called option-adjusted duration), empirical duration, coupon curve duration, option-implied duration, and cash flow duration. Effective durations reported by dealers and vendors vary widely because of modeling risk in the Monte Carlo simulation model used to value mortgage-backed securities. The factors that cause differences in effective duration estimates include differences in prepayment models and yield volatility assumptions. The factors that cause effective duration to perform poorly in predicting price changes when interest rates change are assumptions regarding a parallel shift in the yield curve, a constant OAS when rates change, and a constant interest rate volatility.

There are three measures that use market data to estimate duration. These include empirical duration (including price model duration), coupon curve duration, and option-implied duration. The last measure uses observed prices on over-the-counter options for a mortgage passthrough and 10-year Treasury.

Cash flow duration is a term that has been used in the industry in two ways. One definition is that it measures the sensitivity to changes in interest rates assuming that when rates change, cash flows do not change. Effectively, this definition of cash flow duration is equivalent to modified duration. A second definition of cash flow duration is that when rates change, the cash flows are changed based on a change in the prepayment assumption. While superior to the first definition, it is a simple approach to how prepayments may change and although it is acceptable to use in limited circumstances, it is best to avoid using it.

Evidence on the relative performance of effective duration and empirical duration is mixed. One study that compared effective duration and empirical duration suggests that the former is superior but the latter does contain information. Therefore, the best strategy might be to use a combination of the two duration measures. Evidence from a second study suggests that empirical duration is superior to effective duration and option-implied duration performs slightly better than empirical duration.

Probably the best one line conclusion to this chapter is the one expressed by Hayre and Chang: "No single duration measure will consistently work well for mortgage securities."[23] To that it should be added that there are some measures that don't work at all.

---

[23] Hayre and Chang, "Effective and Empirical Duration of Mortgage Securities," p. 29.

Chapter 7

Yield Curve Risk Measures

As explained in Chapter 2, the change in the price of a bond and a bond portfolio will be affected by how the term structure of interest rates changes. While technically the term structure of interest rates is represented by the term structure of spot rates, it is common to refer to the term structure of interest rates in terms of the "yield curve." Thus, we refer to the exposure of a portfolio to a change in the term structure of interest rates as exposure to a change in the yield curve.

In this chapter, we will see that duration and convexity may be an inadequate measure of interest rate risk when the yield curve does not change in a parallel manner. As a result, it is necessary to be able to measure the exposure of a portfolio and certain types of securities to shifts in the yield curve. Three approaches for measuring this exposure are described in this chapter — yield curve reshaping duration, key rate duration, and yield curve specific duration.

DURATION, CONVEXITY, AND NONPARALLEL YIELD CURVE SHIFTS

To illustrate the limitations of duration and convexity, let's first look at how two portfolios consisting of hypothetical Treasury securities with the same portfolio duration will perform if the yield curve does not shift in a parallel fashion. Consider the three hypothetical Treasury securities shown in Exhibit 1. Security A is the short-term Treasury, security B is the long-term Treasury, and security C is the intermediate-term Treasury. Each Treasury security is selling at par, and it is assumed that the next coupon payment is six months from now. The duration and convexity for each security are calculated in the exhibit. Since all the securities are trading at par value, the durations and convexities are then the dollar duration and dollar convexity per $100 of par value.

Exhibit 1: Three Hypothetical Treasury Securities to Illustrate the Limitations of Duration and Convexity

Information on three Treasury securities:

Treasury issue	Coupon rate (%)	Price	Yield to maturity (%)	Maturity (years)
A	6.5	100	6.5	5
B	8.0	100	8.0	20
C	7.5	100	7.5	10

Calculation of duration and convexity (shock rates by 10 basis points):

Treasury issue	Value if rate changes by		Duration	Convexity
	+10 bp	−10 bp		
A	99.5799	100.4222	4.21122	10.67912
B	99.0177	100.9970	9.89681	73.63737
C	99.3083	100.6979	6.49821	31.09724

Suppose that the following two Treasury portfolios are constructed. The first portfolio consists of only security C, the 10-year issue, and shall be referred to as the "bullet portfolio." The second portfolio consists of 51.86% of security A and 48.14% of security B, and this portfolio shall be referred to as the "barbell portfolio."

The dollar duration of the bullet portfolio is 6.49821. Recall that dollar duration is a measure of the dollar price sensitivity of a security or a portfolio. The dollar duration of the barbell is the weighted average of the dollar duration of the two Treasury securities in the portfolio and is computed below:

$$0.5186\,(4.21122) + 0.4814\,(9.89681) = 6.94821$$

The dollar duration of the barbell is equal to the dollar duration of the bullet. In fact, the barbell portfolio was designed to produce this result.

Duration is just a first approximation of the change in price resulting from a change in interest rates. The convexity measure provides a second approximation. The dollar convexity measure of the two portfolios is not equal. The dollar convexity measure of the bullet portfolio is 31.09724. The dollar convexity measure of the barbell is a weighted average of the dollar convexity measure of the two Treasury securities in the portfolio. That is,

$$0.5186\,(10.67912) + 0.4814\,(73.63737) = 40.98658$$

Thus, the bullet has a dollar convexity measure that is less than that of the barbell portfolio. Below is a summary of the dollar duration and dollar convexity of the two portfolios:

	Treasury Portfolio	
Parameter	Bullet	Barbell
Dollar duration	6.49821	6.49821
Dollar convexity	31.09724	40.98658

Which is the better Treasury portfolio in which to invest? The answer depends on the portfolio manager's investment objectives and investment horizon. Let's assume a 6-month investment horizon. The last column of Exhibit 2 shows the difference in the total return over a 6-month investment horizon for the two Treasury portfolios, assuming that the yield curve shifts in a "parallel" fashion.[1] By parallel it is meant that the yield for the short-term security (A), the intermediate-term security (C), and the long-term security (B) changes by the same number of basis points, shown in the first column of the exhibit. The total return reported in the second column of Exhibit 2 is:

Bullet portfolio's total return – Barbell portfolio's total return

Thus a positive value in the last column means that the bullet portfolio outperformed the barbell portfolio while a negative sign means that the barbell portfolio outperformed the bullet portfolio.

Which portfolio is the better investment alternative if the yield curve shifts in a parallel fashion *and* the investment horizon is six months? The answer depends on the amount by which yields change. Notice in the last column that if yields change by less than 100 basis points, the bullet portfolio will outperform the barbell portfolio. The reverse is true if yields change by more than 100 basis points.

Now let's look at what happens if the yield curve does not shift in a parallel fashion. The last column of Exhibits 3 and 4 show the relative performance of the two Treasury portfolios for a nonpar-

---

[1] Note that no assumption is needed for the reinvestment rate since the three securities shown in Exhibit 1 are assumed to be trading right after a coupon payment has been made and therefore there is no accrued interest.

allel shift of the yield curve. Specifically, in Exhibit 3 it is assumed that if the yield on C (the intermediate-term security) changes by the amount shown in the first column, A (the short-term security) will change by the same amount plus 30 basis points, whereas B (the long-term security) will change by the same amount shown in the first column less 30 basis points. That is, the nonparallel shift assumed is a flattening of the yield curve. For this yield curve shift, the barbell will outperform the bullet for the yield changes assumed in the first column. While not shown in the exhibit, for changes greater than 300 basis points for C, the opposite would be true.

In Exhibit 4, the nonparallel shift assumes that for a change in C's yield, the yield on A will change by the same amount less 30 basis points, whereas the yield on B will change by the same amount plus 30 basis points. That is, it assumes that the yield curve will steepen. In this case, the bullet portfolio would outperform the barbell portfolio for all but a change in yield greater than 250 basis points for C.

Exhibit 2: Performance of Bullet and Barbell Treasury Portfolios Over a 6-Month Horizon Assuming a Parallel Yield Curve Shift: Scenario Analysis

Yield change (in b.p.)	Price plus coupon ($)			Total return (%)		
	A	B	C	Bullet	Barbell	Difference*
−300	115.6407	141.0955	126.7343	53.47	55.79	−2.32
−250	113.4528	133.6753	122.4736	44.95	46.38	−1.43
−200	111.3157	126.8082	118.3960	36.79	37.55	−0.76
−150	109.2281	120.4477	114.4928	28.99	29.26	−0.27
−100	107.1888	114.5512	110.7559	21.51	21.47	0.05
−50	105.1965	109.0804	107.1775	14.35	14.13	0.22
−25	104.2176	106.4935	105.4453	10.89	10.63	0.26
0	103.2500	104.0000	103.7500	7.50	7.22	0.28
25	102.2935	101.5961	102.0907	4.18	3.92	0.27
50	101.3481	99.2780	100.4665	0.93	0.70	0.23
100	99.4896	94.8852	97.3203	−5.36	−5.45	0.09
150	97.6735	90.7949	94.3050	−11.39	−11.28	−0.11
200	95.8987	86.9830	91.4146	−17.17	−16.79	−0.38
250	94.1640	83.4271	88.6433	−22.71	−22.01	−0.70
300	92.4686	80.1070	85.9857	−28.03	−26.96	−1.06

* A positive sign indicates that the bullet portfolio outperformed the barbell portfolio; a negative sign indicates that the barbell portfolio outperformed the bullet portfolio.

Exhibit 3: Performance of Bullet and Barbell Treasury Portfolios Over a 6-Month Horizon Assuming a Flattening of the Yield Curve: Scenario Analysis

Yield change for C (in bp)	Price plus coupon ($)			Total return (%)		
	A	B	C	Bullet	Barbell	Difference*
−300	114.3218	145.8342	126.7343	53.47	58.98	−5.51
−250	112.1645	138.0579	122.4736	44.95	49.26	−4.31
−200	110.0573	130.8648	118.3960	36.79	40.15	−3.36
−150	107.9989	124.2057	114.4928	28.99	31.60	−2.62
−100	105.9879	118.0356	110.7559	21.51	23.58	−2.06
−50	104.0232	112.3139	107.1775	14.35	16.03	−1.67
−25	103.0578	109.6094	105.4453	10.89	12.42	−1.53
0	102.1036	107.0033	103.7500	7.50	8.92	−1.42
25	101.1603	104.4914	102.0907	4.18	5.53	−1.35
50	100.2279	102.0699	100.4665	0.93	2.23	−1.30
100	98.3949	97.4829	97.3203	−5.36	−4.09	−1.27
150	96.6037	93.2142	94.3050	−11.39	−10.06	−1.33
200	94.8531	89.2380	91.4146	−17.17	−15.70	−1.47
250	93.1421	85.5311	88.6433	−22.71	−21.04	−1.67
300	91.4697	82.0718	85.9857	−28.03	−26.11	−1.92

Assumptions:
Change in yield of security C results in a change in the yield of security A plus 30 basis points.
Change in yield of security C results in a change in the yield of security B minus 30 basis points.
* A positive sign indicates that the bullet portfolio outperformed the barbell portfolio; a negative sign indicates that the barbell portfolio outperformed the bullet portfolio.

The key point here is that looking at duration or convexity tells us little about performance over some investment horizon because performance depends on the magnitude of the change in yields and how the yield curve shifts.

YIELD CURVE RESHAPING DURATIONS

It should be clear from our illustrations that neither the duration nor the convexity of a portfolio or position measures the exposure to yield curve risk. The sensitivity of a portfolio to changes in the shape of the yield curve can be approximated. In this section and the two that follow we describe three approaches to measuring yield curve risk.

Exhibit 4: Performance of Bullet and Barbell Treasury Portfolios Over a 6-Month Horizon Assuming a Steepening of the Yield Curve: Scenario Analysis

Yield change	Price plus coupon ($)			Total return (%)		
for C (in bp)	A	B	C	Bullet	Barbell	Difference*
−300	116.9785	136.5743	126.7343	53.47	52.82	0.65
−250	114.7594	129.4918	122.4736	44.95	43.70	1.24
−200	112.5919	122.9339	118.3960	36.79	35.14	1.65
−150	110.4748	116.8567	114.4928	28.99	27.09	1.89
−100	108.4067	111.2200	110.7559	21.51	19.52	1.99
−50	106.3863	105.9874	107.1775	14.35	12.39	1.97
−25	105.3937	103.5122	105.4453	10.89	8.98	1.91
0	104.4125	101.1257	103.7500	7.50	5.66	1.84
25	103.4426	98.8243	102.0907	4.18	2.44	1.74
50	102.4839	96.6046	100.4665	0.93	−0.69	1.63
100	100.5995	92.3963	97.3203	−5.36	−6.70	1.34
150	98.7582	88.4758	94.3050	−11.39	−12.38	0.99
200	96.9587	84.8200	91.4146	−17.17	−17.77	0.60
250	95.2000	81.4080	88.6433	−22.71	−22.88	0.17
300	93.4812	78.2204	85.9857	−28.03	−27.73	−0.30

Assumptions:

Change in yield of security C results in a change in the yield of security A minus 30 basis points.

Change in yield of security C results in a change in the yield of security B plus 30 basis points.

* A positive sign indicates that the bullet portfolio outperformed the barbell portfolio; a negative sign indicates that the barbell portfolio outperformed the bullet portfolio.

The first approach looks at the sensitivity of a portfolio to a change in the slope of the yield curve. The first issue is to define what is meant by the slope of the yield curve. There are several definitions that have been used to describe the slope of the yield curve. Some market participants define yield curve slope as the difference in the Treasury yield curve at two maturity levels. For instance, the yield curve slope can be defined as the difference between the yield on the 30-year on-the-run Treasury and the 2-year on-the-run Treasury.

The *yield curve reshaping duration* introduced by Klaffky, Ma, and Nozari focuses on three points on the yield curve: 2-year, 10-year, and 30-year, and the spread between the 10-year and 2-year issues and the spread between the 30-year and 10-year issues.[2] The

[2] Thomas E. Klaffky, Y.Y. Ma, and Ardavan Nozari, "Managing Yield Curve Exposure: Introducing Reshaping Durations," *The Journal of Fixed Income* (December 1992), pp. 5-15

former spread is referred to as the short end of the yield curve, and the latter spread the long end of the yield curve. Klaffky, Ma, and Nozari refer to the sensitivity of a portfolio to changes in the short end of the yield curve as *short-end duration* (SEDUR) and to changes in the long-end of the yield curve as *long-end duration* (LEDUR). These concepts, however, are applicable to other points on the yield curve.[3]

To calculate the SEDUR of each security in the portfolio, the percentage change in the security's price is calculated for (1) a steepening of the yield curve at the short end by 50 basis points, and (2) a flattening of the yield curve at the short end of the yield curve by 50 basis points. Then the security's SEDUR is computed as follows:

$$\text{SEDUR} = \frac{V_s - V_f}{2V_0 \Delta y}$$

where

V_s = security's price if the short-end of the yield curve steepens by 50 basis points
V_f = security's price if the short-end of the yield curve flattens by 50 basis points
V_0 = security's current market price
Δy = number of basis points the yield curve is changed by

To calculate the LEDUR, the same procedure is used for each security in the portfolio: calculate the price for (1) a flattening of the yield curve at the long end by 50 basis points, and (2) a steepening of the yield curve at the long end of the yield curve by 50 basis points. Then the security's LEDUR is computed in the following manner:

$$\text{LEDUR} = \frac{V_f - V_s}{2V_0 \, \Delta y}$$

The formulas for SEDUR and LEDUR are equivalent to the formula for calculating duration given by equation (1) in Chapter 4.

[3] Some vendors of analytical systems have developed proprietary models for measuring slope changes. See, for example, Wesley Phoa, "Dissecting Yield Curve Risk," in Frank J. Fabozzi (ed), *Managing Fixed Income Portfolios* (New Hope, PA: Frank J. Fabozzi Associates, 1997). The model described is the one developed by Capital Management Sciences.

Exhibit 5: Bonds and Portfolios Used to Illustrate the Calculation of SEDUR and LEDUR

Security	Coupon rate (%)	Price ($)	Yield (%)	Maturity (years)
U	6.0	100	6.0	2
V	8.0	100	8.0	30
W	7.0	100	7.0	10

Portfolios

	Percentage of bond in portfolio	
Security	Portfolio 1	Portfolio 2
U	42.5	22.0
V	47.5	22.0
W	10.0	56.0

Dollar Duration and Convexity

	Dollar duration	Dollar convexity
Security U	1.85855	2.22220
Security V	11.31258	107.12569
Security W	7.10631	32.15018
Portfolio 1	6.87718	55.07957
Portfolio 2	6.87718	42.06064

We will use the three securities in Exhibit 5, securities U, V, and W, to demonstrate how to calculate SEDUR and LEDUR. From these three securities two portfolios are constructed as shown in the second panel of the exhibit. Portfolio 1 is concentrated in the 10-year maturity sector, while portfolio 2 is more heavily distributed in the 2-year and 30-year maturity sectors. Both portfolios, however, have the same dollar duration of 6.87718.

The SEDUR for the 2-year issue, U, is found by steepening the yield curve by 50 basis points and flattening it by 50 basis points. These values can be found by decreasing the yield on the 2-year by 50 basis points and increasing it by 50 basis points. The resulting values are $V_s = 99.0763$ and $V_f = 100.9349$. Using the formula for SEDUR:

$$\frac{100.9349 - 99.0763}{2(100)(0.005)} = 1.85860$$

The SEDUR for the 30-year issue is zero. Since the analysis proceeds from the shifting of the yield curve holding the 10-year yield constant, the SEDUR for the 10-year issue is zero.

Similarly, for the 2-year issue and the 10-year issue the LEDUR is zero. For the 30-year issue, the LEDUR is found by steepening the yield curve by 50 basis points and flattening it by 50 basis points. This means increasing and decreasing the yield on the 30-year issue by 50 basis points. The resulting values are V_s = 96.5259 and V_f = 103.6348. Using the formula for LEDUR:

$$\frac{103.6348 - 96.5259}{2(100)(0.005)} = 7.10889$$

The portfolio SEDUR and LEDUR are the weighted averages of the corresponding durations for each security in the portfolio. The SEDUR for the two portfolios is calculated as follows:

Portfolio 1: 0.425 (1.85860) + 0.475 (0) + 0.10 (0) = 0.789
Portfolio 2: 0.220 (1.85860) + 0.220 (0) + 0.56 (0) = 0.409

The LEDUR for the two portfolios is calculated as follows:

Portfolio 1: 0.425 (0) + 0.475 (0) + 0.10 (7.10889) = 0.711
Portfolio 2: 0.220 (0) + 0.220 (0) + 0.56 (7.10889) = 3.981

The various duration measures for the two portfolios are summarized below:

	Duration	SEDUR	LEDUR
Portfolio 1	6.88	0.789	0.711
Portfolio 2	6.88	0.409	3.981

These measures indicate that while both portfolios are exposed to the same risk for a small parallel shift in the level of interest rates, for a nonparallel shift, portfolio 1's exposure at the short end of the yield curve is about twice that of portfolio 2's. That is, if the short end of the yield curve shifts by 50 basis points, portfolio 1's value will change by 0.39% while portfolio 2's will change by about 0.20%. Portfolio 2's exposure to a shift in the long end of the yield curve, however, is considerably greater than portfolio 1's. A shift of 50 basis points at the long end will change portfolio 2's value by approximately 2% but portfolio 1's value by about only 0.36%. As emphasized earlier in the chapter, just focusing on duration would have masked the yield curve exposure.

So far, we have looked at only bonds with maturities at the three points on the yield curve that are used to define the short end and long end. The methodology can be generalized to other maturities as follows:

1. The shift in yields begins with the 10-year Treasury.
2. At the short end, the steepening or flattening of the yield curve for any maturity other than two years is proportionate to the change in the 10-year to 2-year spread.
3. At the long end, the steepening or flattening for any security with a maturity greater than 10 years is assumed to be proportionate to the change in the 30-year to 10-year spread.

KEY RATE DURATIONS

The second approach to measure yield curve risk is to change the yield for a particular maturity of the yield curve and determine the sensitivity of a security or portfolio to this change holding all other yields constant. The sensitivity of the change in value to a particular change in yield is called *rate duration*. There is a rate duration for every point on the yield curve. Consequently, there is not one rate duration, but a vector of durations representing each maturity on the yield curve. The total change in value if all rates change by the same number of basis points is simply the duration of a security or portfolio to a parallel shift in rates.

This approach was first suggested by Donald Chambers and Willard Carleton in 1988[4] who called it "duration vectors." Robert Reitano suggested a similar approach in a series of papers and referred to these durations as "partial durations."[5] The most popular version of this approach is that developed by Thomas Ho in 1992.[6]

[4] Donald Chambers and Willard Carleton, "A Generalized Approach to Duration," *Research in Finance* 7(1988).

[5] See, for example, Robert R. Reitano, "Non-Parallel Yield Curve Shifts and Durational Leverage," *Journal of Portfolio Management* (Summer 1990), pp. 62-67, and "A Multivariate Approach to Duration Analysis," *ARCH* 2(1989).

[6] Thomas S.Y. Ho, "Key Rate Durations: Measures of Interest Rate Risk," *The Journal of Fixed Income* (September 1992), pp. 29-44.

Ho's approach focuses on 11 key maturities of the spot rate curve. These rate durations are called *key rate durations*. The specific maturities on the spot rate curve for which a key rate duration is measured are 3 months, 1 year, 2 years, 3 years, 5 years, 7 years, 10 years, 15 years, 20 years, 25 years, and 30 years. Changes in rates between any two key rates are calculated using a linear approximation.

The impact of any type of yield curve shift can be quantified using key rate durations. A level shift can be quantified by changing all key rates by the same number of basis points and determining, based on the corresponding key rate durations, the effect on the value of a portfolio. The impact of a steepening of the yield curve can be found by (1) decreasing the key rates at the short end of the yield curve and determining the change in the portfolio's value using the corresponding key rate durations, and (2) increasing the key rates at the long end of the yield curve and determining the change in the portfolio's value using the corresponding key rate durations.

The key rate durations are superior to the yield curve reshaping durations for assessing yield curve risk. To illustrate the key rate duration methodology, suppose that instead of a set of 11 key rates, there are only three key rates — 2 years, 16 years, and 30 years.[7] The effective duration of a zero-coupon security is the number of years to maturity. Thus, the three key rate durations are 2, 16, and 30. Consider the following two $100 portfolios comprised of 2-year, 16-year, and 30-year issues:

Portfolio	2-year issue	16-year issue	30-year issue
I	$50	$0	$50
II	$0	$100	$0

The key rate durations, denoted $D(i)$, for the three issues and the effective duration are as follows:

Issue	$D(1)$	$D(2)$	$D(3)$	Effective Duration
2-year	2	0	0	2
16-year	0	16	0	16
30-year	0	0	30	30

A portfolio's key rate duration is the weighted average of the key rate durations of the securities in the portfolio. The key rate

[7] This is the numerical example used by Ho, "Key Rate Durations," p. 33.

duration and the effective duration for each portfolio are calculated below:

Portfolio I

$D(1) = (50/100) \times 2 + (0/100) \times 0 + (50/100) \times 0 = 1$

$D(2) = (50/100) \times 0 + (0/100) \times 16 + (50/100) \times 0 = 0$

$D(3) = (50/100) \times 0 + (0/100) \times 0 + (50/100) \times 30 = 15$

Effective duration

$= (50/100) \times 2 + (0/100) \times 16 + (50/100) \times 30 = 16$

Portfolio II

$D(1) = (0/100) \times 0 + (100/100) \times 0 + (0/100) \times 0 = 0$

$D(2) = (0/100) \times 0 + (100/100) \times 16 + (0/100) \times 0 = 16$

$D(3) = (0/100) \times 0 + (100/100) \times 0 + (0/100) \times 0 = 0$

Effective duration

$= (0/100) \times 2 + (100/100) \times 16 + (0/100) \times 30 = 16$

Thus, the key rate durations differ for the two portfolios. However, the effective duration for each portfolio is the same. Despite the same effective duration, the performance of the two portfolios will not be the same for a nonparallel shift in the spot rates. Consider the following three scenarios:

Scenario 1: All spot rates shift down 10 basis points.
Scenario 2: The 2-year key rate shifts up 10 basis points and the 30-year rate shifts down 10 basis points.
Scenario 3: The 2-year key rate shifts down 10 basis points and the 30-year rate shifts up 10 basis points.

The total return (%) for the two portfolios for each of these scenarios is as follows:

Portfolio	Scenario 1	Scenario 2	Scenario 3
I	1.6	1.4	−1.4
II	1.6	0	0

Thus, only for the parallel yield curve shift (scenario 1) do the two portfolios have identical performance based on their effective durations.

Exhibit 6: Key Rate Durations of Non-Callable Treasury Bonds

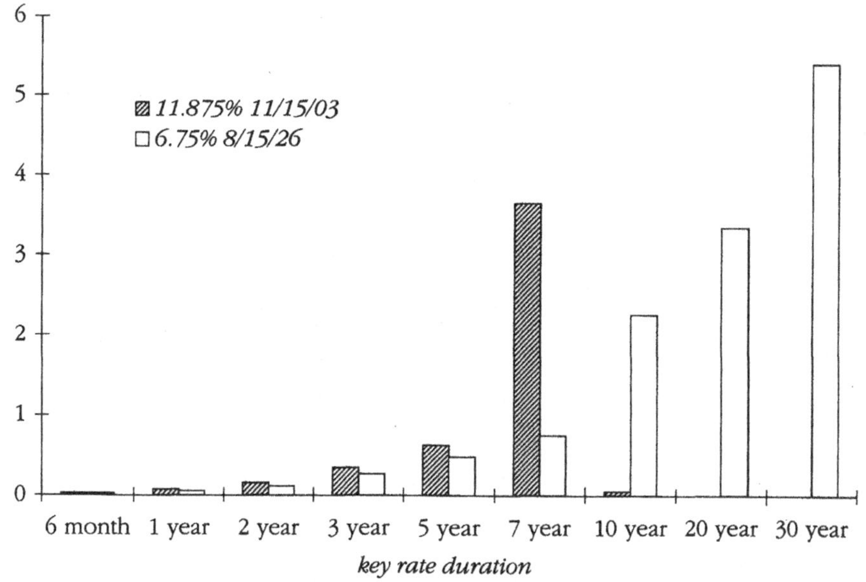

Source: Exhibit 1-15 in Wesley Phoa, *Advanced Fixed Income Analytics* (New Hope, PA: Frank J. Fabozzi Associates, 1997), p. 24.

The key rate durations can be computed for an individual security or for a portfolio. Exhibit 6 shows the key rate duration profile of two noncallable Treasury bonds (11.875% 11/5/03 and 6.75% 8/15/26) as computed by Wesley Phoa of Capital Management Sciences (CMS).[8] Here it can be seen how the key rate duration profile identifies the yield curve risk exposure generated from the coupon payments and final principal payment of a Treasury bond. Notice the substantial exposure for the 30-year bond to changes in long rates.

The key rate duration profile of a callable Treasury (7.875% 11/15/07) is shown in Exhibit 7. For this bond the yield curve risk exposure is spread out across maturities rather than concentrated around the call date or the maturity date. The key rate durations of a callable bond depend on the yield volatility assumption. Phoa notes that changing the yield volatility assumption has little impact on the key rate durations for this type of security.[9]

[8] Wesley Phoa, *Advanced Fixed Income Analytics* (New Hope, PA: Frank J. Fabozzi Associates, 1997), p. 24.

[9] Phoa, *Advanced Fixed Income Analytics*, p. 26.

Exhibit 7: Key Rate Durations of a Callable Treasury Bond

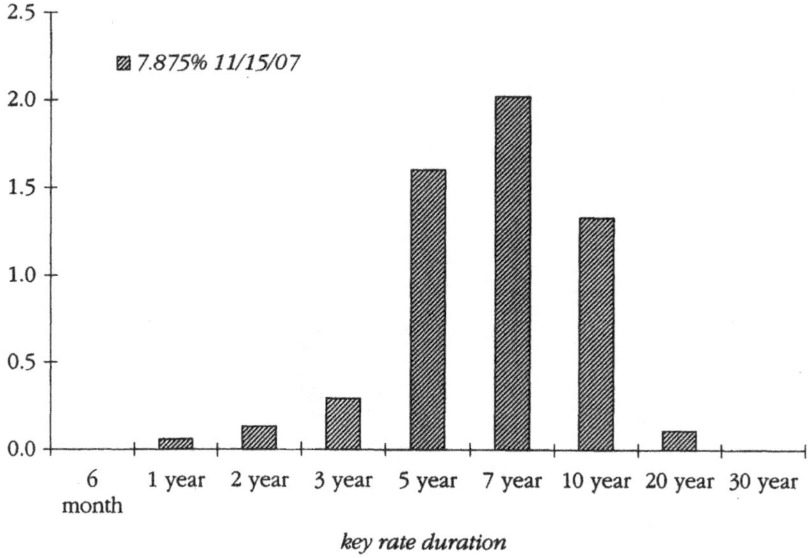

Source: Exhibit 1-16 in Wesley Phoa, *Advanced Fixed Income Analytics* (New Hope, PA: Frank J. Fabozzi Associates, 1997), p. 24.

Exhibits 8 and 9 show the key rate duration profiles for mortgage-backed securities as computed by Thomas Ho of BARRA.[10] Exhibit 8 shows the key rate durations for a Ginnie Mae 30-year 10% passthrough. At the time of the analysis, the Ginnie Mae passthrough was a new issue. From the exhibit it can be seen that the new issue passthrough's key rate duration profile exhibits a bell-shaped curve with the peak of the curve between 5 and 15 years. Adding up the key rate durations from 5 to 15 years (i.e., the 5-year, 7-year, 10-year, and 15-year key rate durations) indicates that of the total interest rate exposure, about 70% is within this maturity range. That is, the effective duration alone masks the fact that the interest rate exposure for this passthrough is due to changes in the 5-year to 15-year maturity range.

The key rate duration profile of a PO and an IO created from the Ginnie Mae passthrough are shown in Exhibit 9. Let's look at the PO. A PO will have a high positive duration. From the key rate duration profile for the PO shown in Exhibit 9 it can be seen that the

[10] Ho, "Key Rate Durations."

key rate durations are negative up to year 7. Thereafter, the key rate durations are positive and have a high value. While the total risk exposure (i.e., effective duration) may be positive, there is yield curve risk. For example, the key rate durations suggest that if the long end of the yield curve is unchanged, but the short end of the yield curve (up to year 7) decreases, the PO's value will decline despite an effective duration that is positive. IO's have a high negative duration. However, from the key rate duration profile in Exhibit 9 it can be seen that the key rate durations are positive up to year 10 and then they take on high negative values. As with the PO, this security is highly susceptible to how the yield curve changes.

Let's look at three actual Treasury portfolios to make the concept of key rate duration more concrete. Exhibit 10 shows three Treasury portfolios as of April 23, 1997. The first portfolio has 11 Treasury securities with approximately equal dollar amounts in each maturity. This portfolio is a ladder portfolio. The second portfolio is a barbell portfolio and the third a bullet portfolio. The effective duration for each Treasury portfolio is 4.7. Exhibit 10 shows the key rate durations for each security and the key rate durations for each portfolio. The key rate duration profile for each portfolio is graphed in Exhibit 11.

Exhibit 8: Key Rate Duration Profile for a 10% 30-Year Ginnie Mae Passthrough

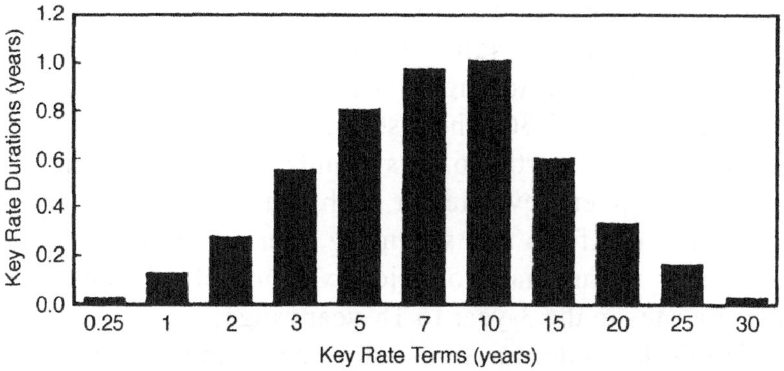

Source: Exhibit 12 in Thomas S.Y. Ho, "Key Rate Durations: Measures of Interest Rate Risks," *The Journal of Fixed Income* (September 1992), p. 38.
This copyrighted material is reprinted with permission from Institutional Investor, Inc. *The Journal of Fixed Income*, 488 Madison Avenue, New York, NY 10022.

Exhibit 9: Key Rate Duration Profiles for a PO and an IO for Current Coupon Ginnie Mae

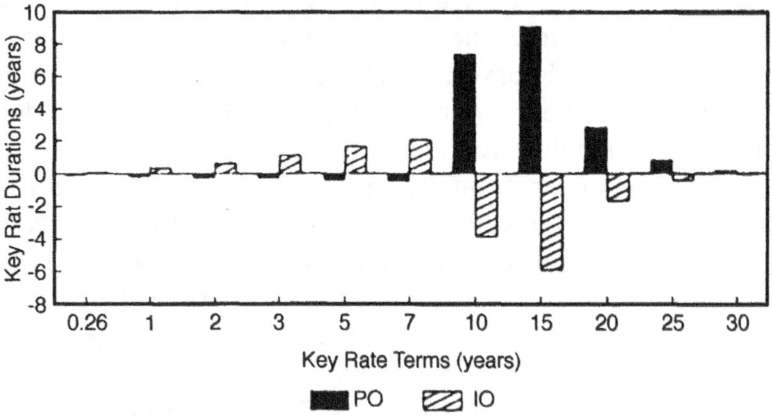

Source: Exhibit 13 in Thomas S.Y. Ho, "Key Rate Durations: Measures of Interest Rate Risks," *The Journal of Fixed Income* (September 1992), p. 38.
This copyrighted material is reprinted with permission from Institutional Investor, Inc. *The Journal of Fixed Income*, 488 Madison Avenue, New York, NY 10022.

As a second illustration, consider the portfolio of corporate bonds shown in Exhibit 12. There are 25 issues in the portfolio, each with a par value of \$5 million. The information is based on market values on May 4, 1998. Look at the first issue — AT&T 7.5s of 9/1/2009. The effective duration for this issue is 2.36. Look at the 5-year key rate duration. The value is 0.46. This means that if the 5-year rate changes by 100 basis points while all other rates along the yield curve remain the same, this issue's value will change by approximately 0.46%. Adding up the 11 key rate durations gives the effective duration of 2.36. The last line of Exhibit 12 shows the key rate duration for the portfolio. It is found by multiplying the key rate duration for a given key rate for each issue by its relative market weight in the portfolio and summing over all the issues. The key rate durations tell us that the major exposure of this portfolio is to changes in rates in the 3-year to 15-year range.

While key rate duration is by far the most commonly used measure of yield curve risk, Phoa makes the following observations about key rate duration:

Exhibit 10: Key Rate and Effective Durations for Three Treasury Portfolios (April 23, 1997): Ladder, Barbell, and Bullet

LADDER PORTFOLIO — KEY RATE DURATIONS

Bond	Code	Cusip	Coupon	Maturity	Description	Size	3Mo	1yr	2yr	3yr	5yr	7yr	10yr	15yr	20yr	25Yr	30yr	Eff Dur
1	TB	912810EW	6.000	2/15/26	TB 2/26 6.000	4,057,595	0.02	0.06	0.12	0.26	0.47	0.73	1.33	1.69	1.57	1.45	4.60	12.31
2	TN	912827X4	6.375	3/31/01	TN 3/01 6.375	11,679,547	0.01	0.06	0.11	1.79	1.45	0.00	0.00	0.00	0.00	0.00	0.00	3.42
3	TB	912810ET	7.625	2/15/25	TB 2/25 7.625	11,124,914	0.02	0.06	0.12	0.27	0.49	0.76	1.38	1.76	1.62	2.32	2.81	11.63
4	TC	912810BR	8.500	5/15/99	TC 599 8.500	2,987,478	0.06	0.00	0.00	0.00	0.00	0.00	0.00	0.00	0.00	0.00	0.00	0.06
5	TB	912810EG	8.750	8/15/20	TB 8/20 8.750	5,348,333	0.02	0.06	0.12	0.28	0.50	0.78	1.42	1.81	2.80	2.74	0.00	10.56
6	TB	912810DS	10.625	8/15/15	TB 8/15 10.625	1,944,533	0.02	0.07	0.13	0.30	0.53	0.83	1.50	3.01	2.77	0.00	0.00	9.16
7	TC	912810CM	11.750	2/15/10	TC 2/10 11.750	7,323,250	0.02	0.08	0.15	0.36	0.62	3.10	1.03	0.01	0.00	0.00	0.00	5.36
8	TC	912810DL	12.500	8/15/14	TC 8/14 12.500	1,212,780	0.02	0.07	0.14	0.33	0.59	0.91	3.19	1.86	0.01	0.00	0.00	7.13
9	TN	912820AQ	0.000	5/15/99	TN 599 0.000	37,154,780	0.00	0.66	0.86	0.00	0.00	0.00	0.00	0.00	0.00	0.00	0.00	1.52
10	TN	912820AT	0.000	5/15/99	TN 5/99 0.000	10,840,357	0.00	0.00	1.54	0.70	0.00	0.00	0.00	0.00	0.00	0.00	0.00	2.24
11	TN	912820BA	0.000	5/15/99	TN 5/99 0.000	8,472,702	0.00	0.00	0.00	1.84	2.09	0.00	0.00	0.00	0.00	0.00	0.00	3.93
Total Portfolio							0.01	0.25	0.49	0.50	0.49	0.50	0.50	0.50	0.50	0.50	0.50	4.75

BARBELL PORTFOLIO — KEY RATE DURATIONS

Bond	Code	Cusip	Coupon	Maturity	Description	Size	3Mo	1yr	2yr	3yr	5yr	7yr	10yr	15yr	20yr	25Yr	30yr	Eff Dur
1	TN	9128272P	6.625	3/31/02	TN 3/02 6.625	86,528,320	0.12	0.06	0.12	0.34	3.62	0.00	0.00	0.00	0.00	0.00	0.00	4.14
2	TC	912810BR	8.500	5/15/99	TC 5/99 8.500	69,853,088	0.07	0.00	0.00	0.00	0.00	0.00	0.00	0.00	0.00	0.00	0.00	0.07
3	TB	912810DY	8.750	5/15/17	TB 5/17 8.750	63,761,372	0.01	0.06	0.12	0.28	0.50	0.78	1.41	1.80	4.69	0.06	0.00	9.73
Total Portfolio							0.03	0.04	0.08	0.22	1.49	0.25	0.46	0.59	1.53	0.02	0.00	4.71

BULLET PORTFOLIO — KEY RATE DURATIONS

Bond	Code	Cusip	Coupon	Maturity	Description	Size	3Mo	1yr	2yr	3yr	5yr	7yr	10yr	15yr	20yr	25Yr	30yr	Eff Dur
1	TN	9128272H	5.875	2/15/00	TN 2/00 5.875	2,388,518	0.01	0.05	0.52	1.94	0.00	0.00	0.00	0.00	0.00	0.00	0.00	2.53
2	TN	912827V4	6.125	9/30/00	TN 9/00 6.125	3,949,212	0.01	0.05	0.11	2.26	0.61	0.00	0.00	0.00	0.00	0.00	0.00	3.04
3	TN	9128272J	6.250	2/15/07	TN 2/07 6.250	26,670,542	0.02	0.06	0.11	0.25	0.45	1.00	5.20	0.00	0.00	0.00	0.00	7.08
4	TB	912810BQ	6.250	8/15/23	TB 8/23 6.250	7,015,242	0.02	0.06	0.12	0.27	0.48	0.74	1.34	1.71	1.58	3.99	1.51	11.82
5	TN	9128272J	7.125	9/30/99	TN 9/99 7.125	1,146,557	0.01	0.06	1.23	0.90	0.00	0.00	0.00	0.00	0.00	0.00	0.00	2.20
6	TB	912810EM	7.250	8/15/22	TB 8/22 7.250	1,059,479	0.02	0.06	0.12	0.27	0.49	0.76	1.37	1.75	1.62	4.51	0.32	11.30
7	TB	912810DX	7.500	11/15/16	TB 11/16 7.500	2,360,381	0.01	0.06	0.12	0.27	0.48	0.75	1.36	2.12	4.74	0.00	0.00	9.93
8	TC	912810BR	8.500	5/15/99	TC 5/99 8.500	33,761,656	0.06	0.00	0.00	0.00	0.00	0.00	0.00	0.00	0.00	0.00	0.00	0.06
9	TB	222655P9	8.750	11/15/08	TB 11/08 8.750	18,540,286	0.01	0.06	0.13	0.29	0.51	0.80	3.98	1.45	0.00	0.00	0.00	7.24
Total Portfolio							0.03	0.04	0.10	0.30	0.30	0.51	2.34	0.50	0.24	0.30	0.10	4.75

Source: BARRA

Exhibit 11: Key Rate Duration Profile for Three Treasury Portfolios (April 23, 1997): Ladder, Barbell, and Bullet

(a) Ladder Portfolio

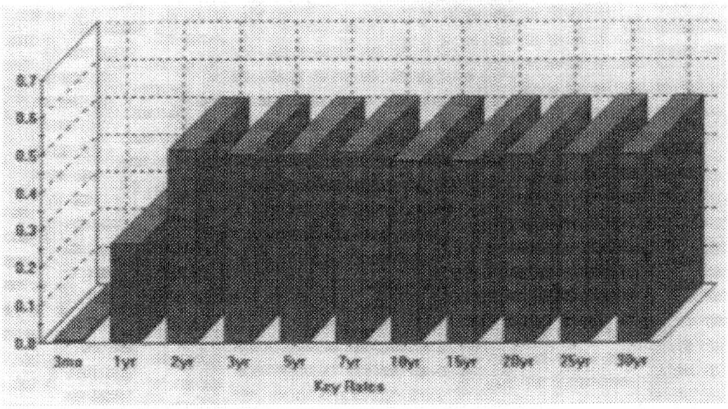

(b) Barbell Portfolio

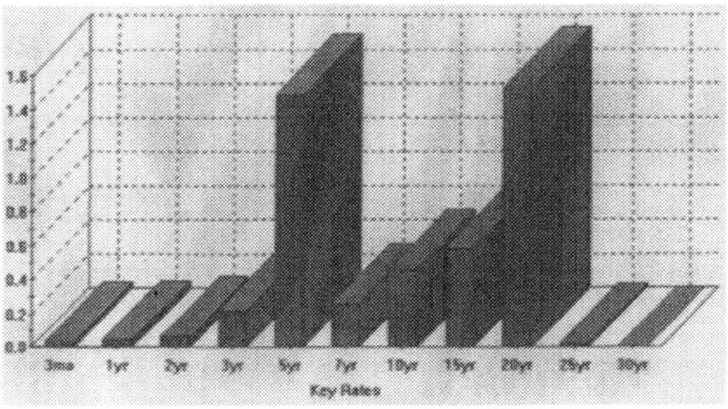

(c) Bullet Portfolio

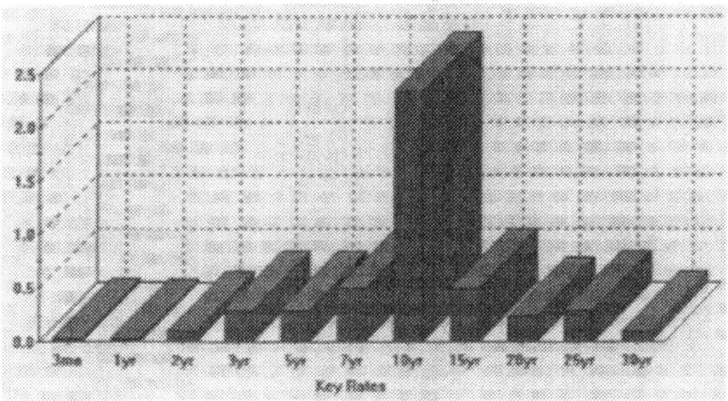

Source: BARRA

Exhibit 12: Key Rate Duration Profile for a 25-Issue Corporate Portfolio

						Key Rate Duration for										
Issuer	Coupon (%)	Maturity Date	Market Value ($)	Percent of Market Value	Effective Duration	3-Mos	1-Year	2-Year	3-Year	5-Year	7-Year	10-Year	15-Year	20-Year	25-Year	30-Year
AT&T Corp	7.50	09/01/09	5,027,300	3.89	2.36	0.05	0.22	0.31	0.42	0.46	0.38	0.44	0.07	0.0	0.00	0.00
Aetna Services	8.00	01/15/17	4,973,600	3.85	5.77	0.03	0.12	0.27	0.50	0.67	0.78	1.01	1.27	1.12	0.00	0.00
Tenet Healthcare	9.50	11/15/01	5,156,600	3.99	2.02	0.05	0.25	0.30	1.11	0.32	0.00	0.00	0.00	0.00	0.00	0.00
Bank of New York	7.00	03/15/11	4,666,900	3.61	5.97	0.02	0.06	0.27	0.48	0.71	0.83	2.00	1.60	0.00	0.00	0.00
CMS Energy Corp	8.00	06/15/04	4,750,400	3.68	4.02	0.02	0.07	0.30	0.53	1.66	1.43	0.00	0.00	0.00	0.00	0.00
Caterpillar Fin	7.68	04/15/99	5,048,900	3.91	0.87	0.11	0.76	0.00	0.00	0.00	0.00	0.00	0.00	0.00	0.00	0.00
Chase Manhattan	9.05	02/01/02	5,124,100	3.97	0.76	0.11	0.19	−0.02	0.31	0.16	0.0	0.00	0.00	0.00	0.00	0.00
Citicorp	7.50	06/17/12	4,793,100	3.71	5.53	0.02	0.07	0.38	0.51	0.67	0.77	1.29	1.83	0.00	0.00	0.00
Coca-Coal Enter	8.50	02/01/12	5,447,300	4.22	8.11	0.02	0.07	0.13	0.30	0.52	0.80	2.47	3.80	0.00	0.00	0.00
Delta Airlines	10.00	05/17/09	6,018,400	4.66	6.75	0.01	0.07	0.14	0.31	0.55	0.84	3.97	0.85	0.00	0.00	0.00
Walt Disney Com	7.50	06/27/11	4,793,800	3.71	5.40	0.02	0.06	0.38	0.58	0.66	0.75	1.59	1.35	0.00	0.00	0.00
Dow Chemical	7.75	09/15/20	5,038,900	3.90	10.34	0.02	0.06	0.13	0.29	0.51	0.79	1.41	1.75	3.40	1.99	0.00
Eastman Kodak	9.75	10/01/04	5,628,300	4.36	4.83	0.02	0.07	0.15	0.33	1.59	2.67	0.00	0.00	0.00	0.00	0.00
GMAC	7.50	05/02/03	5,032,300	3.90	4.11	0.02	0.06	0.12	0.29	3.62	0.00	0.00	0.00	0.00	0.00	0.00
GTE South Inc	9.38	04/01/00	5,077,500	3.93	0.01	−0.03	0.01	0.02	0.00	0.00	0.00	0.00	0.00	0.00	0.00	0.00
Dow Chemical	9.00	05/15/10	5,800,700	4.49	6.07	0.01	0.07	0.18	0.45	0.76	1.05	2.51	1.03	0.00	0.00	0.00
Equitable of IO	9.30	06/01/98	5,012,800	3.88	0.08	0.08	0.00	0.00	0.00	0.00	0.00	0.00	0.00	0.00	0.00	0.00
Federal Realty	8.75	05/15/10	5,122,500	3.97	0.03	−0.06	0.00	0.00	0.00	0.00	0.21	−0.11	0.00	0.00	0.00	0.00
First Chicago	9.88	08/15/00	5,358,600	4.15	2.01	0.02	0.08	1.39	0.52	0.00	0.00	0.00	0.00	0.00	0.00	0.00
Firemans Fund	8.88	10/15/01	5,140,500	3.98	2.95	0.02	0.07	0.04	2.04	0.58	0.00	0.00	0.00	0.00	0.00	0.00
First Brands Co	9.12	04/01/99	5,061,800	3.92	0.08	0.08	0.00	0.00	0.00	0.00	0.00	0.00	0.00	0.00	0.00	0.00
Wells Fargo	9.38	11/15/98	5,272,500	4.08	0.50	0.31	0.18	0.00	0.00	0.00	0.00	0.00	0.00	0.00	0.00	0.00
Fleet Financial	8.62	01/15/07	5,423,300	4.20	6.04	0.02	0.07	0.13	0.30	0.53	2.50	2.50	0.00	0.00	0.00	0.00
Goldman Sachs	8.12	02/01/99	5,132,900	3.97	0.71	0.25	0.46	0.00	0.00	0.00	0.00	0.00	0.00	0.00	0.00	0.00
Honeywell Inc.	9.38	06/15/09	5,252,400	4.07	0.33	−0.13	0.00	0.00	0.34	0.00	0.05	0.09	−0.02	0.00	0.00	0.00
Total Portfolio			$129,155,400		3.45	0.04	0.12	0.19	0.39	0.56	0.57	0.80	0.54	018	0.08	0.00

For each issue, $5 million of par value is purchased.

Source: BARRA

- The yield curve shifts used in the definition of key rate duration are not economically meaningful; in fact, they are highly unrealistic. Therefore, single key rate durations do not have any economic interpretation, and are purely tools: "building blocks" of yield curve risk.
- The definition of a specific key rate duration may depend on the set of yield curve grid points chosen. For example, the value and meaning of the 10-year key rate duration will differ depending on whether the adjacent grid points are at 7 and 30 years, or at 7 and 20 years.
- The definition of a specific key rate duration also depends on how zero coupon yields are interpolated between grid points...
- Care must be taken when computing key rate durations for securities with interest-rate sensitive cashflows, particularly ARMs with reset caps or floors. Using 100 bp shifts can give unrealistic results because of the violently sawtoothed displacement to the forward curve, and it may be better to use, say, 10 bp shifts.[11]

LEVEL, SLOPE, AND CURVATURE DURATION

Ram Willner has suggested another approach to yield curve risk measures.[12] The approach involves representing the yield curve by a mathematical function that is described in terms of level, slope, curvature, and location of the yield curve hump (i.e., the maximum point of curvature). Given the estimated yield curve, exposure to changes in the parameters — level, slope, and curvature — can be calculated.

Mathematical Representation of the Yield Curve

The mathematical representation of the yield curve used by Willner is:[13]

---

[11] Phoa, *Advanced Fixed Income Analytics*, p. 24.

[12] Ram Willner, "A New Tool for Portfolio Managers: Level, Slope, and Curvature Durations," *The Journal of Fixed Income* (June 1996), pp. 48-59.

[13] This mathematical representation was developed by Nelson and Siegel and is the solution to differential equations describing rational interest rate behavior. See, C. Nelson and A. Siegel, "Parsimonious Modeling of Yield Curves," *Journal of Business* 60 (1987).

$$Y = L + (S + C)\frac{(1 - e^{-M/H})}{M/H} - C(e^{-M/H})$$

where

Y = yield to maturity
H = constant associated with curve hump positioning
M = maturity of security (in years)
e = 2.71828

and L, S, and C are the parameters that must be estimated.

The properties of this yield curve function are as follows. First, as maturity increases, holding all other factors constant, the yield to maturity approaches L. The implication is that the estimated parameter L represents the long-run rate and therefore provides the level of the yield curve.

Second, as maturity decreases, the yield approaches $L + S$. Therefore, $L + S$ represents the short rate. It then follows that the spread between the long rate and short rate is $-S$ and for some constant long maturity, M, the slope of the yield curve is $-S/M$.

Third, for either very short-term maturities or very long-term maturities, the parameter C does not appear. It does appear for intermediate maturities. Therefore, the parameter C represents the curvature of the yield curve over intermediate maturities.

To summarize:

- L represents the level of rates
- $-S$ represents the spread between the long-term and short-term rates
- $-S/M$ represents the slope of the yield curve
- C represents the curvature of the yield curve

Application to international bond portfolios

In Chapter 5, we discussed the problem of estimating the duration contribution of foreign bonds to a U.S. portfolio. A methodology for estimating the contribution was suggested by Lee Thomas and Ram Willner.[14] Recall that the procedure is to estimate the following regression for a country's bonds:

---

[14] Lee R. Thomas and Ram Willner, "Measuring the Duration of an Internationally Diversified Portfolio," *Journal of Portfolio Management* (Fall 1997), pp. 93-99.

$$\Delta y_{f,t} = \alpha + \beta \Delta y_{\text{US},t}$$

where

$\Delta y_{f,t}$ = change in a foreign bond's yield in month t
$\Delta y_{\text{US},t}$ = change in U.S. yield in month time t

and α and β are the parameters to be estimated for the countries whose bonds are candidates for inclusion in the portfolio. The parameter β_i is called the *country beta*. The duration that is attributed to a foreign bond in a U.S. portfolio is found by multiplying the country duration beta by the U.S. duration.

We illustrated the application of this methodology in Chapter 5. For example, suppose that the duration for a Canadian bond is 7.20 and Canada's beta is 0.89. Then the contribution to duration is 6.41, found by multiplying 7.20 by 0.89.

In subsequent research, Willner showed how to link the Thomas-Willner methodology to the level, slope, and curvature durations discussed above.[15] Specifically, the following regression equation must first be estimated using monthly data

$$R_{f,t} = \alpha + \beta_L^* [d_{L,t} \Delta L_{\text{US},t}] + \beta_S^* [d_{S,t} \Delta S_{\text{US},t}] + \beta_C^* [d_{C,t} \Delta C_{\text{US},t}]$$

where

$R_{f,t}$ = return in month t on the foreign bond
$d_{L,t}$, $d_{S,t}$, and $d_{C,t}$ = level, slope, and curvature durations in month t, respectively
$L_{\text{US},t}$, $S_{\text{US},t}$, $C_{\text{US},t}$ = change in the U.S. level, slope, and curvature in month t, respectively
β_L^*, β_S^*, and β_C^* = parameters to be estimated

Assuming that the level, slope, and curvature durations are virtually constant over the estimation period, a country's level beta, slope beta, and curvature beta, denoted by β_L, β_S, and β_C, can be

---

[15] Ram Willner, "Improved Measurement of Duration Contributions to Foreign Bonds in Domestic Portfolios," Chapter 9 in Frank J. Fabozzi (ed.), *Perspectives on Interest Rate Risk Management for Money Managers and Traders* (New Hope, PA: Frank J. Fabozzi Associates, 1998).

estimated by dividing the estimates of β_L^*, β_S^*, and β_C^* each by the corresponding average duration value.

To illustrate the use of the estimated values in assessing the risk contribution of foreign bonds to a U.S. portfolio, we'll use the example presented by Willner. Exhibit 13 shows the country level, slope, and curvature betas for 15 countries. The parameters are estimated for the period July 1992 to July 1997. Other information reported in the exhibit are measures of the statistical significance for each estimated beta (the t-value is reported in parentheses below the corresponding estimated beta) and the coefficient of determination (R-squared). In the next-to-the last column of the exhibit, the country beta just based on yield changes (i.e., ignoring changes in the yield curve) is reported.

Let's use the betas in Exhibit 13 to estimate the contribution of a foreign bond's various durations to the corresponding duration of a U.S. portfolio. Suppose the yield curve durations have been estimated for a Canadian bond:

Duration	Canada
level	7.34
slope	2.13
curvature	1.87

Given the Canadian level, slope, and curvature betas in Exhibit 13, the contribution to each yield curve risk of a U.S. bond portfolio is:

contribution to level duration:	$0.95 \times 7.34 = 6.98$
contribution to slope duration	$0.97 \times 2.13 = 2.07$
contribution to curvature duration:	$0.94 \times 1.87 = 1.76$

Now let's look at how well these duration estimates did in predicting the price change for the month July 1997 for a Canadian bond. In that month, the yield on that bond dropped by 55 basis points resulting in a gain per \$100 of par value of \$4 (ignoring any currency effects). Earlier we noted that the duration for a Canadian bond ignoring yield curve risk is 7.20 and the contribution due to duration based on the adjustment as provided by the country beta is 6.41. The yield on a U.S. bond with a similar duration declined by 50 basis points. So for a 50 basis point decline in U.S. rates, the estimated change in value for this Canadian bond is approximately 3.2% or \$3.20 ($0.5 \times 0.89 \times 7.20$) per \$100 par value.

Exhibit 13: Betas for 15 Countries (July 1992-July 1997)

Country	β_L (t-stat)	β_S	β_C	R^2	β	R^2
Australia	1.08	1.14	1.20	0.47	1.04	0.49
	(5.97)	(3.00)	(5.77)		(8.68)	
Austria	0.35	0.54	0.07	0.16	0.23	0.13
	(3.87)	(2.90)	(0.71)		(3.61)	
Belgium	0.48	0.82	0.04	0.13	0.29	0.09
	(3.58)	(2.91)	(0.24)		(3.00)	
Canada	0.95	0.97	0.94	0.47	0.89	0.49
	(6.30)	(3.07)	(5.44)		(8.67)	
Denmark	0.74	1.04	0.18	0.16	0.48	0.14
	(3.99)	(2.65)	(0.83)		(3.68)	
France	0.73	0.99	0.24	0.26	0.51	0.23
	(5.13)	(3.32)	(1.48)		(4.95)	
Germany	0.64	1.04	0.11	0.35	0.42	0.26
	(6.17)	(4.81)	(0.93)		(5.32)	
Holland	0.62	0.93	0.19	0.32	0.45	0.27
	(5.74)	(4.09)	(1.56)		(5.51)	
Ireland	0.72	0.84	0.40	0.20	0.55	0.21
	(4.18)	(2.33)	(2.02)		(4.65)	
Italy	0.83	0.74	0.16	0.07	0.43	0.06
	(2.92)	(1.24)	(0.48)		(2.53)	
Japan	0.22	0.03	0.36	0.07	0.30	0.08
	(1.66)	(0.12)	(2.38)		(2.75)	
Spain	0.79	0.70	0.26	0.08	0.47	0.08
	(2.99)	(1.26)	(0.86)		(2.82)	
Sweden	0.91	0.81	0.12	0.12	0.49	0.09
	(3.64)	(1.54)	(0.43)		(2.95)	
Switzerland	0.31	0.14	0.17	0.06	0.25	0.07
	(2.51)	(0.54)	(1.19)		(2.59)	
UK	0.77	1.00	0.24	0.20	0.51	0.18
	(4.49)	(2.77)	(1.23)		(4.30)	

Source: Exhibit 3 in Ram Willner, "Improved Measurement of Duration Contributions to Foreign Bonds in Domestic Portfolios," Chapter 9 in Frank J. Fabozzi (ed.), *Perspectives on Interest Rate Risk Management for Money Managers and Traders* (New Hope, PA: Frank J. Fabozzi Associates, 1998).

For the month of July 1997, the change in the U.S. level, slope, and curvature was –0.43, 0.29, and –0.61, respectively. Given the contribution to each yield curve duration computed above, the dollar price change attributed to each is shown below:

Dollar price change due to:	Dollar price change:
level	0.43 × 6.98 = 3.00
slope	–0.29 × 2.07 = –0.60
curvature	0.61 × 1.76 = 1.07
	Total $3.47

Thus, ignoring yield curve duration, the estimated price change is $3.20 of the $4 actual price change while using yield curve duration measures the estimate is $3.47.

SUMMARY

When using a portfolio's duration and convexity to measure the exposure to interest rates, it is assumed that the yield curve shifts in a parallel fashion. For a nonparallel shift in the yield curve, duration and convexity may not provide adequate information about the risk exposure to changes in interest rates. Exposure of a portfolio to a shift in the yield curve is called yield curve risk.

One method to measure yield curve risk is to calculate a portfolio's yield curve reshaping duration. Yield curve reshaping duration decomposes the yield curve into a short end and a long end. The sensitivity of a portfolio to changes in the short end of the yield curve is called short-end duration (SEDUR) and to changes in the long end of the yield curve is called long-end duration (LEDUR).

An alternative approach to measuring yield curve risk is to change the yield for a particular maturity of the yield curve and determine the sensitivity of a security or portfolio to this change holding all other yields constant. Key rate duration is the sensitivity of the change in a bond or a portfolio's value to a particular key rate. The most popular version of key rate duration uses 11 key maturities of the spot rate curve (3 months, 1, 2, 3, 5, 7, 10, 15, 20, 25, and 30 years).

A third approach to measuring a portfolio's yield curve risk is by estimating the yield curve by a mathematical function that describes the yield curve in terms of level, slope, curvature, and location of the yield curve hump (i.e., the maximum point of curvature). From the mathematical function, the exposure to a change in level, slope, curvature, and location of the hump can be determined, thereby summarizing the total price change in a bond's price.

Chapter 8

Risk Measures for Interest Rate Derivatives

A portfolio manager or trader will seek to control the interest rate risk of a portfolio using the most effective means possible. By effective, it is meant that changes in the risk exposure of a portfolio can be done quickly and at minimal transaction costs (where transaction costs include market impact costs). Typically, altering the risk exposure can be done most effectively using derivative instruments.

While there may be an understanding of how a particular derivative instrument can impact the risk exposure of a portfolio to changes in interest rates, that is not enough. Risk control requires that this be quantified, in terms of either duration or dollar duration. In Chapter 4, we explained how this is done. In that chapter we showed that a portfolio's dollar duration can be viewed as the sum of the current dollar duration without a controlling position and the dollar duration of the controlling position. It is the dollar duration of the controlling position that can be changed quickly using derivative instruments to rebalance the portfolio so as to achieve the target duration or target dollar duration.

In this chapter we will look at how to measure the dollar duration and duration of three interest rate derivative instruments: futures/forward contracts, swaps, and options. We describe the instruments briefly and the effective economic position of an investor who takes a position in one of these instruments. Once we understand the economic equivalence of a derivative instrument, we can compute its dollar duration or duration. All of these instruments are leveraged instruments so their exposure to changes in interest rates is a multiple of the bond underlying the contract.

FUTURES AND FORWARD CONTRACTS

Futures and forward contracts are agreements that require a party to the agreement either to buy or sell something at a designated future date at a predetermined price. That is, one party is agreeing to make delivery and the other is agreeing to take delivery. The price at which the parties agree to transact in the case of a futures contract is called the *futures price*, and in the case of a *forward contract*, the forward price. The designated date on which the parties must transact is called the *settlement* or *delivery date*.

Futures contracts are standardized agreements as to the delivery date (or month) and quality of the deliverable, and are traded on organized exchanges. The clearinghouse associated with the exchange where the contract is traded guarantees the performance of each party to a futures contract. Thus, counterparty risk is minimal. Unlike a futures contract, a forward contract is an over-the-counter (OTC) instrument. As a result, forward contracts are usually non-standardized (that is, the terms of each contract are negotiated individually between buyer and seller), there is no clearinghouse, and secondary markets are often non-existent or extremely thin. Since there is no clearinghouse, both parties to a forward contract are exposed to counterparty risk.

When a position is first taken in a futures contract, the investor must deposit a minimum dollar amount per contract as specified by the exchange. This amount is called *initial margin* and is required as deposit for the contract. As the price of the futures contract fluctuates, the value of the investor's equity in the position changes. At the end of each trading day, the exchange determines the day's settlement price for the futures contract. This price is used to mark to market the investor's position, so that any gain or loss from the position is reflected in the investor's equity account. *Maintenance margin* is the minimum level (specified by the exchange) to which an investor's equity position may fall as a result of an unfavorable price movement before the investor is required to deposit additional margin. The additional margin deposited is called *variation margin*, and it is an amount necessary to bring the equity in the account back to its initial margin level. Any excess margin in the account may be withdrawn by the investor.

Exhibit 1: Effect of Rate Changes on Parties to a Futures Contract

	Interest rates	
Party	Decrease	Increase
Buyer (long)	Gains	Loses
Seller (short)	Loses	Gains

Forward contracts may or may not be marked to market, depending on the wishes of the two parties. For a forward contract that is not marked to market, there are no interim cash flow effects because no additional margin is required.

Risk and Return Characteristics of Futures Contracts

When an investor takes a position in the market by buying a futures contract, the investor is said to be in a *long position* or to be *long futures*. If, instead, the investor's opening position is the sale of a futures contract, the investor is said to be in a *short position* or *short futures*. The buyer of a futures contract will realize a profit if the futures price increases; the seller of a futures contract will realize a profit if the futures price decreases.

When the underlying to a futures or forward contract is a bond, the gain or loss to a party depends on how interest rates change. A decline in rates increases the underlying bond's price and, as we shall see later, increases the futures price. Thus, a decline in interest rates results in a gain for the party long futures and a loss for the party short futures. Since a rise in interest rates decreases the price of the underlying bond and thereby the futures price, the party short futures realizes a gain while the party long futures realizes a loss.

The effect of changes in interest rates on the parties to a futures contract is summarized in Exhibit 1.

Economics of a Futures Position and Dollar Duration

When a position is taken in a futures contract in which the underlying is a bond, the party need not pay for the entire amount of the dollar investment in the underlying bonds. Instead, only initial margin must be put up. Consequently, an investor can create a leveraged position in the underlying bonds by using futures.

Exhibit 2: Summary of the Impact of a Futures Position on the Dollar Duration of a Portfolio

Position	Dollar Duration	Impact on Dollar Duration of Portfolio
Long	Positive	Increases dollar duration
Short	Negative	Decreases dollar duration

At first, the leverage available in the futures market may suggest that the market benefits only those who want to speculate on price movements. This is not true. Futures markets can be used to control risk. Without the leverage possible in futures transactions, the cost of controlling risk using futures would be too high for many market participants.

When the underlying of a futures contract is a bond, what is the effect of this leverage on the sensitivity of the value of a futures contract when interest rates change? That is, what can we expect a futures position's duration to be (once we finally explain how to compute it)? When talking about futures contracts, it is easier to understand sensitivity to rate changes in terms of dollar duration. A long position in a futures contract in which the underlying is a bond is equivalent to buying that bond on a leveraged basis. So, whatever the dollar duration of the underlying bond is, the dollar duration of the futures position will be a multiple of that. Thus, buying a futures contract for a portfolio will increase the dollar duration of the portfolio. Selling a futures contract in which a bond is the underlying is equivalent to shorting bonds. A short bond position has a negative duration. So, when a short position is added to a portfolio, this is equivalent to reducing the portfolio's dollar duration.

Exhibit 2 provides a summary of the impact of a long and short position on the dollar duration of a portfolio.

Now, to quantify how much dollar duration is added or subtracted from a portfolio when one or more futures positions are taken, it is necessary to understand (1) the nuances of the futures contracts used by managers (Treasury bond and note futures) and (2) the relationship between the cash market price and the futures price.

Treasury Bond and Note Futures Contracts

Interest rate futures contracts can be classified by the maturity of their underlying security. Short-term interest rate futures contracts have an underlying security that matures in less than one year. The maturity of the underlying security of long-term futures contracts exceeds one year. Our focus below is on the commonly used futures contracts in which the underlying security's maturity exceeds one year. The underlying for such contracts traded in the United States are Treasury bonds and notes.

Treasury Bond Futures Contracts

The Treasury bond futures contract is traded on the Chicago Board of Trade (CBT). The underlying instrument for a Treasury bond futures contract is $100,000 par value of a hypothetical 20-year 8% coupon bond. However, no such Treasury bond exists. Instead, the CBT delivery rules allow one of several Treasury bond issues to be delivered. The choice of which Treasury bond issue to deliver from among those that may be delivered is given to the seller of the futures contract. The CBT has established criteria that a Treasury bond issue must satisfy in order to be acceptable for delivery. Exhibit 3 shows the 30 Treasury bond issues that the seller can select from to deliver to the buyer of the June 1997 futures contract. The futures price is quoted in terms of par value being 100.

Conversion Factor and Converted Price The delivery process for the Treasury bond futures contract makes the contract interesting. At the settlement date, the seller of a futures contract (the short) is required to deliver to the buyer (the long) $100,000 par value of an 8% 20-year Treasury bond. Since no such bond exists, the seller must choose from one of the acceptable deliverable Treasury bonds that the CBT has specified.

To make delivery equitable to both parties, the CBT introduced *conversion factors* for determining the price of each acceptable deliverable Treasury issue that may be delivered. The conversion factor is determined by the CBT before a contract with a specific settlement date begins trading. Exhibit 3 shows for each of the acceptable Treasury issues the corresponding conversion factor. The conversion factor is based on the price that a deliverable bond would sell for at the beginning of the delivery month if it were to yield 8%. The conversion factor is constant throughout the trading period of the futures contract.

Exhibit 3: Treasury Bond Issues Acceptable for Delivery to Satisfy the June 1997 Futures Contract

Issue Coupon (%)	Issue Maturity	Conversion Factor	Issue Coupon (%)	Issue Maturity	Conversion Factor
6.625	2/15/27	0.8451	8.750	8/15/20	1.0783
6.500	11/15/26	0.8312	8.750	5/15/20	1.0778
6.750	8/15/26	0.8598	8.500	2/15/20	1.0518
6.000	2/15/26	0.7767	8.125	8/15/19	1.0128
6.875	8/15/25	0.8750	8.875	2/15/19	1.0891
7.625	2/15/25	0.9585	9.000	11/15/19	1.1012
7.500	11/15/24	0.9447	9.125	5/15/18	1.1128
6.250	8/15/23	0.8097	8.875	8/15/17	1.0866
7.125	2/15/23	0.9054	8.750	5/15/17	1.0736
7.625	11/15/22	0.9594	7.500	11/15/16	0.9511
7.250	8/15/22	0.9194	7.250	5/15/16	0.9276
8.000	11/15/22	0.9998	9.250	2/15/16	1.1196
8.125	8/15/21	1.0132	9.875	11/15/15	1.1781
8.125	5/15/21	1.0130	10.625	8/15/15	1.2482
7.875	2/15/21	0.9868	11.250	2/15/15	1.3033

The product of the settlement price and the conversion factor for a deliverable issue is called the *converted price*. The amount that the buyer must pay the seller when a Treasury bond is delivered is called the *invoice price*. The invoice price is the settlement futures price plus accrued interest. However, as just noted, the seller can deliver one of several acceptable Treasury issues. The invoice price is adjusted based on the actual Treasury issue delivered. It is the conversion factor that is used to adjust the invoice price. The invoice price is:

$$\text{Invoice price} = \text{Contract size} \times \text{Futures contract settlement price} \times \text{Conversion factor} + \text{Accrued interest}$$

Suppose that the June 1997 Treasury bond futures contract settles at 108-16 and that the issue delivered is the 11.25s of 2/15/15. The futures contract settlement price of 108-16 means 108.5% of par value or 1.085 times par value. As indicated in Exhibit 3, the conversion factor for this issue is 1.3033. Since the contract size is \$100,000, the invoice price the buyer pays the seller is:

$$\$100{,}000 \times 1.085 \times 1.3033 + \text{Accrued interest} = \$141{,}408.05 + \text{Accrued interest}$$

Cheapest-to-Deliver Issue In selecting the issue to be delivered, the short will select from among all the deliverable issues the one that will give the largest rate of return from a *cash and carry trade*. A cash and carry trade is one in which a cash bond that is acceptable for delivery is purchased and simultaneously the Treasury bond futures contract is sold. The bond purchased can be delivered to satisfy the short futures position. Thus, by buying the Treasury bond issue that is acceptable for delivery and selling the futures, an investor has effectively sold the bond at the delivery price (i.e., converted price).

A rate of return can be calculated for this trade. The rate of return is determined by: (1) the price plus accrued interest of the Treasury bond that could be purchased; (2) the converted price plus the accrued interest that will be received upon delivery of that Treasury bond issue to satisfy the short futures position; (3) the coupon payments that will be received between the purchase date and the delivery date; and, (4) the reinvestment income that will be realized on the coupon payments between the time received and the delivery date. The annual rate of return calculated for an acceptable Treasury issue is called the *implied repo rate*.

Market participants will select the acceptable Treasury issue that gives the largest implied repo rate in the cash and carry trade as the one to deliver. The issue that satisfies this criterion is referred to as the *cheapest-to-deliver issue*. As explained later, it plays a key role in the pricing of this futures contract.

Delivery Options In addition to the choice of which acceptable Treasury issue to deliver — sometimes referred to as the *quality option* or *swap option* — the short position has three more options granted under CBT delivery guidelines. The first is related to the quality option. If a Treasury bond is auctioned prior to the settlement date, then the short can select this new issue to deliver. This option is referred to as the *new auction option*. The second option grants the short the right to decide when in the delivery month delivery actually will take place. This is called the *timing option*. The third option is the right of the short to give notice of intent to deliver up to 8:00 p.m. Chicago time after the closing of the exchange (3:15 p.m. Chicago time) on the date when the futures settlement price has been fixed. This option is referred to as the *wild card option*. Because of the quality option, the new auction option, the timing option, and the wild card option — in sum referred to as the *delivery options* — the long can never be sure which Treasury bond will be delivered or when it will be delivered.

Treasury Note Futures

There are three Treasury note futures contracts: 10-year, 5-year, and 2-year. All three contracts are modeled after the Treasury bond futures contract and are traded on the CBT. The underlying instrument for the 10-year Treasury note futures contract is $100,000 par value of a hypothetical 10-year 8% Treasury note. There are several acceptable Treasury issues that may be delivered by the short. An issue is acceptable if the maturity is not less than 6.5 years and not greater than 10 years from the first day of the delivery month. The delivery options granted to the short position are the same as for the Treasury bond futures contract.

For the 5-year Treasury note futures contract, the underlying is $100,000 par value of a U.S. Treasury note that satisfies the following conditions: (1) an original maturity of not more than five years and three months and (2) a remaining maturity not less than four years and three months.

The underlying for the 2-year Treasury note futures contract is $200,000 par value of a U.S. Treasury note with a remaining maturity of not more than two years and not less than one year and nine months. Moreover, the original maturity of the note delivered to satisfy the 2-year futures cannot be more than five years and three months.

Theoretical Futures/Forward Price

Since our objective is to understand how the value of futures or forward contracts change when interest rates change, we must understand how the price of a futures/forward contract is determined. Using arbitrage arguments, it can be shown that the theoretical futures price can be determined on the basis of the following information:

1. The price of the bond in the cash market.
2. The coupon rate on the bond.

3. The interest rate for borrowing and lending until the settlement date.

The borrowing and lending rate is referred to as the *financing rate*.

We will use the following notation:

r = annualized financing rate (%)
c = annualized current yield, or annual coupon rate divided by the cash market price (%)
P = cash market price
F = futures price
t = time, in years, to the futures delivery date

The theoretical futures price is then:

$$F = P + Pt(r - c) \tag{1}$$

For example, assume the following values:

$$r = 0.08,\ c = 0.12,\ P = 100,\ t = 0.25$$

Then the theoretical futures price is

$$F = 100 + 100 \times 0.25(0.08 - 0.12) = 100 - 1 = 99$$

The theoretical price may be at a premium to the cash market price (higher than the cash market price) or at a discount from the cash market price (lower than the cash market price), depending on $(r - c)$. The term $r - c$ is called the *net financing cost* because it adjusts the financing rate for the coupon interest earned. The net financing cost is more commonly called the *cost of carry*, or simply *carry*. *Positive carry* means that the current yield earned is greater than the financing cost; *negative carry* means that the financing cost exceeds the current yield earned.

Adjustments to the Theoretical Pricing Model

While we have not derived the theoretical price for a futures contract and merely stated the results, it is important to understand that there are several assumptions made to derive equation (1). First, no interim cash flows due to variation margin or coupon interest payments are assumed in the model. However, we know that interim cash flows can occur for both of these reasons.[1] Incorporating interim coupon payments into the pricing model is not difficult. However, the value of the coupon payments at the settlement date will depend on the interest rate at which they can be reinvested. The shorter the maturity of the contract and the lower the coupon rate, the less important the reinvestment income is in determining the theoretical futures price.

The second assumption in deriving the theoretical futures price is that the borrowing and lending rates are equal. Typically, however, the borrowing rate is higher than the lending rate. As a result, there is not one theoretical futures price but rather there are lower and upper boundaries for the theoretical futures price.

The third assumption made to derive equation (1) is that only one instrument is deliverable. But as explained earlier, the futures contracts on Treasury bonds and Treasury notes are designed to allow the short the choice of delivering one of a number of deliverable issues (the quality or swap option). Because there may be more than one deliverable, market participants track the price of each deliverable bond and determine which bond is the cheapest to deliver. The theoretical futures price will then trade in relation to the cheapest-to-deliver issue.

There is the risk that while an issue may be the cheapest to deliver at the time a position in the futures contract is taken, it may not be the cheapest to deliver after that time. A change in the cheapest to deliver can dramatically alter the futures price. Because the swap option is an option granted by the long to the short, the long will want to pay less for the futures contract than indicated by equa-

---

[1] Consider first variation margin. If interest rates rise, the short position in futures will receive margin as the futures price decreases; the margin can then be reinvested at a higher interest rate. If interest rates fall, there will be variation margin that must be financed by the short position; however, because interest rates have declined, financing will be possible at a lower cost. The same is true for a forward contract that is marked to market. Thus, whichever way rates move, those who are short futures or forwards that are marked to market gain relative to those who are short forwards that are not marked to market. Conversely, those who are long futures or forwards that are not marked to market lose relative to those who are long forwards that are marked to market. These facts account for the difference between futures prices and forward prices for non-marked-to-market contracts.

tion (1). Therefore, as a result of the quality option, the theoretical futures price as given by equation (1) must be adjusted as follows:

$$F = P + Pt(r - c) - \text{Value of quality option} \quad (2)$$

Market participants have employed theoretical models in attempting to estimate the fair value of the quality option.

Finally, in deriving equation (1) a known delivery date is assumed. For Treasury bond and note futures contracts, the short has a timing and wild card option, so the long does not know when the security will be delivered. The effect of the timing and wild card options on the theoretical futures price is the same as with the quality option. These delivery options result in a theoretical futures price that is lower than the one suggested in equation (1), as shown below:

$$\begin{aligned} F = P + Pt(r - c) &- \text{Value of quality option} \\ &- \text{Value of new auction option} - \text{Value of timing option} \\ &- \text{Value of wild card option} \quad (3) \end{aligned}$$

or alternatively,

$$F = P + Pt(r - c) - \text{Delivery options}$$

Market participants attempt to value the delivery options in order to apply equation (3).

Duration and Dollar Duration

Now we turn to how to measure the dollar duration and duration of a bond futures position. Keep in mind what the goal is: it is to measure the sensitivity of a bond futures position to changes in rates.

The general methodology for computing the dollar duration is as follows for a given Treasury futures contract position:

Step 1: Determine the current dollar value of the Treasury futures position.

Step 2: Determine the new *price* of the cheapest-to-deliver issue due to an increase in rates.

Step 3: Determine the theoretical futures price based on the new price of the cheapest-to-deliver issue resulting from an increase in rates and adjusting for the conversion factor.

Step 4: Compute the dollar value of the bond futures position based on the new theoretical futures price found in Step 3.

Step 5: Compute the dollar duration of the bond futures position resulting from an increase in rates by subtracting the amount computed in Step 4 from the amount determined in Step 1.

Step 6: Determine the new *price* of the cheapest-to-deliver issue resulting from a decrease in rates.

Step 7: Determine the theoretical futures price based on the new price of the cheapest-to-deliver issue resulting from a decrease in rates and adjusting for the conversion factor.

Step 8: Compute the dollar value of the bond futures position based on the new theoretical futures price found in Step 7.

Step 9: Compute the dollar duration of the bond futures position resulting from a decrease in rates by subtracting the amount computed in Step 9 from the amount determined in Step 1.

Step 10: Compute the average dollar duration for the futures position by taking the average of the amounts found in Step 5 and Step 9.

Step 10 gives the average dollar duration for the futures position for the number of basis points used to shock rates in Steps 2 and 6.

Let's discuss Steps 2 and 6. The new price of the underlying won't be difficult to compute when rates are shocked for Treasury bond and note futures contracts. This is because the underlying bonds and notes are option-free. But there is a complication. If we know the cheapest-to-deliver issue for the particular Treasury bond or note futures contract, we can easily calculate the new price if rates are shocked. However, recognition must be given to the fact that with the Treasury bond and note futures contracts, changes in rates can change the cheapest-to-deliver issue. In fact, how much rates are shocked in Steps 2 and 6 may affect whether the cheapest-to-deliver issue changes from the current one. This is particularly true when rates are around 8% (the coupon rate on the underlying bonds and notes). Therefore, in Step 2 and Step 6, it is important when shocking rates to determine if the cheapest-to-deliver issue will change and, if it does, to use the new cheapest-to-deliver issue in the subsequent computation.

Why did we focus on dollar duration rather than duration? Recall that duration is the approximate percentage change in price. But what is the price of this leveraged instrument? The investor does not put up the full price of the position in order to acquire the position. Only the initial margin need be made in cash or a cash equivalent. Consequently, what is the base investment made by the investor? Rather than debate what should be used as the base investment in order to compute duration, let's simply ask why we are interested in calculating the exposure to changes in rates. As we have emphasized, it is to determine how a futures position will alter the exposure of a portfolio to changes in rates. Once we know how a futures position changes the dollar duration of a portfolio, we can determine for a portfolio its dollar duration. Given the funds invested by the investor in the portfolio, the portfolio's duration can be computed.

INTEREST RATE SWAP

In a plain vanilla interest rate swap, one party agrees to pay the other party fixed interest payments at designated dates for the life of the contract. This party is referred to as the *fixed-rate payer.* The other party agrees to make interest rate payments that float based on some reference rate. This party is referred to as the *floating-rate payer.*

The reference rates that have been used for the floating rate in an interest rate swap are those on various money market instruments: Treasury bills, the London interbank offered rate (LIBOR), commercial paper, bankers acceptances, certificates of deposit, the federal funds rate, and the prime rate. The most common reference rate is LIBOR. The date that the swap stops accruing interest is called the maturity date. The frequency with which the floating-rate is determined for the floating-rate payer is called the reset frequency. The rate that the fixed-rate payer agrees to pay and the floating-rate payer agrees to accept in exchange for the reference rate is called the *swap rate*.

To illustrate a generic interest rate swap, suppose that for the next five years party X agrees to pay party Y 10% per year (the swap rate), while party Y agrees to pay party X 6-month LIBOR (the reference rate). Party X is the fixed-rate payer, while party Y is the floating-rate payer. Assume that the notional principal amount is $50 million, and that payments are exchanged every six months for the next five years. This means that every six months, party X (the fixed-rate payer) will pay party Y $2.5 million (10% times $50 million divided by 2). The amount that party Y (the floating-rate payer) will pay party X will be 6-month LIBOR times $50 million divided by 2. If 6-month LIBOR is 7%, party Y will pay party X $1.75 million (7% times $50 million divided by 2). Note that we divide by two because one-half year's interest is being paid.

Interest rate swaps are over-the-counter instruments. This means that they are not traded on an exchange. The risk that each party takes on when it enters into a swap is that the other party will fail to fulfill its obligations as set forth in the swap agreement. That is, each party faces counterparty risk.

Risk/Return Characteristics of an Interest Rate Swap

The value of an interest rate swap will fluctuate with market interest rates. To see how, let's consider our hypothetical swap. Suppose that interest rates change immediately after parties X and Y enter into the swap. First, consider what would happen if the market demanded that in any 5-year swap the fixed-rate payer must pay 11% in order to receive 6-month LIBOR. If party X (the fixed-rate payer) wants to sell its position to party A, then party A will benefit by having to pay only 10% (the original swap rate agreed upon) rather than 11% (the current swap rate) to receive 6-month LIBOR. Party X will want compensation for this benefit. Consequently, the value of party X's position has increased. Thus, if interest rates increase, the fixed-rate payer will gain and the floating-rate payer will lose.

Next, consider what would happen if interest rates decline to, say, 6%. Now a 5-year swap would require a new fixed-rate payer to pay 6% rather than 10% to receive 6-month LIBOR. If party X wants to sell its position to party B, the latter would demand compensation to take over the position. In other words, if interest rates decline, the fixed-rate payer will lose, while the floating-rate payer will gain.

Exhibit 4: Effect of Rate Changes on Interest Rate Swap Counterparties

	Interest Rates	
Counterparty	Decrease	Increase
Floating-rate payer	Gains	Loses
Fixed-rate payer	Loses	Gains

The effect on the counterparites when interest rates change is summarized in Exhibit 4.

Economic Interpretation of a Swap Position

Looking at the economics of a swap makes it easier to understand the price sensitivity of a swap's value when interest rates change. There are two ways that a swap position can be viewed: (1) a package of forward/futures contracts, and (2) a package of cash flows from buying and selling cash market instruments.

Package of Forward Contracts

The fixed-rate payer in a swap can be viewed as entering into a package of forward contracts in which it pays a fixed amount periodically and receives the reference rate. One can think of the reference rate as any commodity. The value of that commodity in the market changes over time. But the fixed-rate payer is paying a fixed amount for the commodity determined at the time the swap is entered into.

Consider what happens if interest rates increase. The fixed-rate payer realizes a gain. Look at Exhibit 1. There we see that the party to a futures/forward contract that realizes a gain if interest rates increase is the party that is short a futures or forward contract. Thus, the fixed-rate payer has effectively the position of an investor who has sold a package of futures or forward contracts. Since the sale of futures contracts reduces the dollar duration of a portfolio (see Exhibit 2), the party who pays a fixed rate in a swap reduces the dollar duration of a portfolio. But by how much does the dollar duration decrease? We'll see how to determine that once we get to our next economic interpretation of a swap.

Exhibit 5: Effect of Rate Changes on Interest Rate Swap Counterparties and Bond Futures Counterparties

Counterparties to:		Interest Rates	
Swap	Bond Futures/Forward	Decrease	Increase
Floating-rate payer	Buyer	Gains	Loses
Fixed-rate payer	Seller	Loses	Gains

Now let's look at the floating-rate payer. This party can be viewed as entering into a package of forward contracts in which it sells the reference rate (i.e., a commodity) at a fixed price. If interest rates increase, Exhibit 4 shows that the value of a floating-rate payer's swap position declines. As can be seen from Exhibit 1, the buyer of a futures contract realizes a decline in his or her position if interest rates rise. Thus, the floating-rate payer's position can be viewed as a package of long futures positions. Since a long futures position when added to a portfolio increases the portfolio's dollar duration, entering into a swap in which the manager pays floating and receives fixed adds dollar duration to a portfolio.

Exhibit 5 summarizes for the counterparties to a swap and a futures/forward contract how the value of the position changes when interest rates change.

We now turn to an economic interpretation of a swap that will help us understand how to compute its dollar duration.

Package of Cash Market Instruments

To understand why a swap can also be viewed as a package of cash market instruments, consider an investor who enters into the transaction below:

- buy \$50 million par value of a 5-year floating-rate bond that pays 6-month LIBOR every six months
- finance the purchase by borrowing \$50 million for five years on terms requiring a 10% annual interest rate paid every six months.

The cash flows for this transaction are set forth in Exhibit 6. The second column of the exhibit shows the cash flows from purchasing the 5-year floating-rate bond. There is a \$50 million cash outlay and then ten cash inflows. The amount of the cash inflows is uncertain because they depend on future LIBOR. The next column shows the cash flows from borrowing $50 million on a fixed-rate basis. The last column shows the net cash flows from the entire transaction. As the last column indicates, there is no initial cash flow (no cash inflow or cash outlay). In all ten 6-month periods, the net position results in a cash inflow of LIBOR and a cash outlay of $2.5 million. This net position, however, is identical to the position of a fixed-rate payer in a swap.

It can be seen from the net cash flow in Exhibit 6 that a fixed-rate payer has a cash market position that is equivalent to a long position in a floating-rate bond and a short position in a fixed-rate bond — the short position being the equivalent of borrowing by issuing a fixed-rate bond. This is equivalent to a leveraged position in a floating-rate bond with a $50 million value that is financed at the swap rate.

Exhibit 6: Cash Flow For the Purchase of a 5-Year Floating-Rate Bond Financed by Borrowing on a Fixed-Rate Basis

Transaction:

- Purchase $50 million of a 5-year floating-rate bond:
  floating rate = LIBOR, semiannual pay
- Borrow $50 million for five years:
  fixed rate = 10%, semiannual payments

Six Month Period	Cash Flow (In Millions of Dollars) From:		
	Floating-Rate Bond*	Borrowing Cost	Net
0	−$50	+$50.0	$0
1	$+(LIBOR_1/2) \times 50$	−2.5	$+(LIBOR_1/2) \times 50 - 2.5$
2	$+(LIBOR_2/2) \times 50$	−2.5	$+(LIBOR_2/2) \times 50 - 2.5$
3	$+(LIBOR_3/2) \times 50$	−2.5	$+(LIBOR_3/2) \times 50 - 2.5$
4	$+(LIBOR_4/2) \times 50$	−2.5	$+(LIBOR_4/2) \times 50 - 2.5$
5	$+(LIBOR_5/2) \times 50$	−2.5	$+(LIBOR_5/2) \times 50 - 2.5$
6	$+(LIBOR_6/2) \times 50$	−2.5	$+(LIBOR_6/2) \times 50 - 2.5$
7	$+(LIBOR_7/2) \times 50$	−2.5	$+(LIBOR_7/2) \times 50 - 2.5$
8	$+(LIBOR_8/2) \times 50$	−2.5	$+(LIBOR_8/2) \times 50 - 2.5$
9	$+(LIBOR_9/2) \times 50$	−2.5	$+(LIBOR_9/2) \times 50 - 2.5$
10	$+(LIBOR_{10}/2) \times 50 + 50$	−52.5	$+(LIBOR_{10}/2) \times 50 - 2.5$

* The subscript for LIBOR indicates the 6-month LIBOR as per the terms of the floating-rate bond at time *t*.

What about the position of a floating-rate payer? It can be easily demonstrated that the position of a floating-rate payer is equivalent to purchasing a fixed-rate bond and financing that purchase at a floating rate, where the floating rate is the reference rate for the swap. That is, the floating-rate payer has created a leveraged position in the fixed-rate bond with a value of $50 million and financed the position on a floating-rate basis.

Dollar Duration of a Swap

Effectively, a position in an interest rate swap is a leveraged position. This agrees with both of our economic interpretations of an interest rate swap. In the case of a package of futures/forward contracts, we know that futures/forwards are leveraged instruments. In the case of a package of cash instruments, it is a leveraged position involving either buying a fixed-rate bond and financing on a floating-rate basis (i.e., floating-rate payer position) or buying a floating-rate bond on a fixed-rate basis (i.e., fixed-rate payer position). So, we would expect that the dollar duration of a swap is a multiple of the bond that effectively underlies the swap.

To see how to calculate the dollar duration, let's work with the second economic interpretation of a swap — a package of cash flows from buying and selling cash market instruments. From the perspective of the *floating-rate payer*, the position can be viewed as follows:

Long a fixed-rate bond + Short a floating-rate bond

This means that the dollar duration of an interest rate swap from the perspective of a floating-rate payer is just the difference between the dollar duration of the two bond positions that comprise the swap. That is,

Dollar duration of a swap for a floating-rate payer
= Dollar duration of a fixed-rate bond
– Dollar duration of a floating-rate bond

Most of the interest rate sensitivity of a swap will result from the dollar duration of the fixed-rate bond since, as explained in earlier chapters, the dollar duration of the floating-rate bond will be small. The dollar duration of a floating-rate bond is smaller the closer the swap is to its reset date. If the dollar duration of the floating-rate bond is close to zero then:

Dollar duration of a swap for a floating-rate payer
= Dollar duration of a fixed-rate bond

Thus, adding an interest rate swap to a portfolio in which the manager pays a floating-rate and receives a fixed-rate increases the dollar duration of the portfolio by roughly the dollar duration of the underlying fixed-rate bond. This is because it effectively involves buying a fixed-rate bond on a leveraged basis.

We can use the cash market instrument economic interpretation to compute the dollar duration of a swap for the fixed-rate payer. The dollar duration is:

Dollar duration of a swap for a fixed-rate payer
= Dollar duration of a floating-rate bond
– Dollar duration of a fixed-rate bond

Again, assuming that the dollar duration of the floater is small, we have

Dollar duration of a swap for a fixed-rate payer
= –Dollar duration of a fixed-rate bond

Consequently, a manager who adds a swap to a portfolio involving paying fixed and receiving floating decreases the dollar duration of the portfolio by an amount roughly equal to the dollar duration of the fixed-rate bond.

OPTIONS

An option is a contract in which the writer of the option grants the buyer of the option the right, but not the obligation, to purchase from or sell to the writer something at a specified price within a specified period of time (or at a specified date). The writer, also referred to as the seller, grants this right to the buyer in exchange for a certain sum of money, which is called the *option price* or *option premium*. The price at which the underlying may be bought or sold is called the *strike* or *exercise price*. The date after which an option is void is called the *expiration date*. Our focus in this chapter is on options where the "something" underlying the option is an interest rate instrument.

When an option grants the buyer the right to purchase the designated instrument from the writer (seller), it is referred to as a *call option*, or call. When the option buyer has the right to sell the designated instrument to the writer, the option is called a *put option*, or put.

An option is also categorized according to when the option buyer may exercise the option. There are options that may be exercised at any time up to and including the expiration date. Such an option is referred to as an *American option*. There are options that may be exercised only at the expiration date. An option with this feature is called a *European option*.

The maximum amount that an option buyer can lose is the option price. The maximum profit that the option writer can realize is the option price. The option buyer has substantial upside return potential, while the option writer faces substantial downside risk. Buying calls or selling puts allows the investor to gain if the price of the underlying's value rises. Selling calls and buying puts allows the investor to gain if the price of the underlying's value falls.

There are exchange-traded options and OTC options. The latter are used in the many situations where an institutional investor needs to have a tailor-made option because the standardized exchange-traded option does not satisfy its investment objectives. Investment banking firms and commercial banks act as principals as well as brokers in the OTC options market.

Futures Options

The underlying for an interest rate option can be a bond or an interest rate futures contract. The former options are called *options on physicals*. In the United States, there are no actively traded exchange-traded options on physicals. Options on interest rate futures are called *futures options*. The actively traded interest rate options on exchanges are futures options. Options on Treasury bond and note futures are traded on the CBT. All futures options are of the American type.

A futures option gives the buyer the right to buy from or sell to the writer a designated futures contract at the strike price at any time during the life of the option. If the futures option is a call option, the buyer has the right to purchase one designated futures contract at the strike price. That is, the buyer has the right to acquire a long futures position in the designated futures contract. If the buyer exercises the call option, the writer acquires the corresponding short position in the futures contract.

A put option on a futures contract grants the buyer the right to sell a designated futures contract to the writer at the strike price. That is, the option buyer has the right to acquire a short position in the designated futures contract. If the put option is exercised, the writer acquires the corresponding long position in the designated futures contract.

As the parties to the futures option will realize a position in a futures contract when the option is exercised, the question is: what will the futures price be? Upon exercise, the futures price for the futures contract will be set equal to the strike price. The position of the two parties is then immediately marked-to-market in terms of the then-current futures price. Thus, the futures position of the two parties will be at the prevailing futures price. At the same time, the option buyer will receive from the option seller the economic benefit from exercising. In the case of a call futures option, the option writer must pay the difference between the current futures price and the strike price to the buyer of the option. In the case of a put futures option, the option writer must pay the option buyer the difference between the strike price and the current futures price.

Valuation of Options

The value of an option is a reflection of the option's *intrinsic value* and any additional amount over its intrinsic value. The premium over intrinsic value is often referred to as the *time value*.

The intrinsic value of an option is its economic value if it is exercised immediately. If no positive economic value would result from exercising the option immediately, then the intrinsic value is zero. When an option has intrinsic value, it is said to be "in the money." When the strike price of a call option exceeds the current price of the underlying, the call option is said to be "out of the money;" it has no intrinsic value. A put option is "out of the money" and has no intrinsic value when the current price of the underlying exceeds the strike price. An option for which the strike price is equal to the current price of the underlying is said to be "at the money." An at-the-money option has an intrinsic value of zero.

There are six factors that influence the value of an option in which the underlying is a bond. These factors are listed in Exhibit 7. The impact of each of these factors may depend on whether (1) the option is a call or a put, and (2) the option is an American option or a European option. A summary of the effects of each factor on put and call option prices is presented in Exhibit 7. There are five factors that influence the value of an option in which the underlying is a futures contract. These factors are shown in Exhibit 8. As can be seen in the exhibit, these are the same factors that affect the value of an option on a bond. The factor not included is the coupon payment since the underlying is a futures contract. Exhibit 8 summarizes how each factor affects the value of a futures option. The primary difference between factors that influence the price of a futures option and an option on a bond is the short-term risk-free rate. For both a call and a put futures option, the option price decreases when the short-term risk-free rate increases.

Exhibit 7: Summary of Factors that Affect the Price of an Option on a Bond

Increase in factor with all other factors held constant	Effect on call option	Effect on put option
Current price of underlying security	increase	decrease
Strike price	decrease	increase
Time to expiration (American options)	increase	increase
Expected yield volatility	increase	increase
Short-term risk-free rate	increase	decrease
Coupon interest payments	decrease	increase

Exhibit 8: Summary of Factors that Affect the Price of a Futures Option

Increase in factor with all other factors held constant	Effect on call option	Effect on put option
Current futures price	increase	decrease
Strike price	decrease	increase
Time to expiration	increase	increase
Expected yield volatility	increase	increase
Short-term risk-free rate	decrease	decrease

As we have stressed throughout this book, valuation of a bond is absolutely critical in assessing that bond's sensitivity to changes in interest rates. So, too, is the valuation of an option in determining an option price's sensitivity to changes in interest rates. At any time, the intrinsic value of an option can be determined. The question is, what is the time value of an option worth? To answer this question, option pricing models have been developed.

The most popular model for the pricing of equity options is the Black-Scholes option pricing model.[2] By imposing certain assumptions and using arbitrage arguments, the Black-Scholes option pricing model computes the fair (or theoretical) price of a European call option on a non-dividend-paying stock. There are three assumptions underlying the Black-Scholes model that limit its use in pricing options on bonds.

First, the probability distribution for the prices assumed by the Black-Scholes option pricing model permits some probability — no matter how small — that the price can take on any positive value. For a bond, however, we know that the price cannot exceed the sum of the coupon payments plus the maturity value. Thus, unlike stock prices, bond prices have a maximum value. The only way that a bond's price can exceed the maximum value is if negative interest rates are permitted. The second assumption of the Black-Scholes option pricing model is that the short-term interest rate is constant over the life of the option. Yet the price of an interest rate option will change as interest rates change. A change in the short-term interest rate changes the rates along the yield curve. Therefore, to assume that the short-term rate will be constant is inappropriate for interest rate options. The third assumption is that the variance of prices is constant over the life of the option. As a bond moves closer to maturity its price volatility declines. Therefore, the assumption that price variance is constant over the life of the option is inappropriate.

The more commonly used model for valuing futures options is the Black model. The model was developed to value European options on futures contracts.[3] There are two problems with this

---

[2] Fischer Black and Myron Scholes, "The Pricing of Corporate Liabilities," *Journal of Political Economy* (May-June 1973), pp. 637-659.

[3] Fischer Black, "The Pricing of Commodity Contracts," *Journal of Financial Economics* (March 1976), pp. 161-179.

model. First, the Black model does not overcome the problems cited earlier for the Black-Scholes model. Failing to recognize the yield curve means that there will not be a consistency between pricing bond futures and options on bond futures. Second, the Black model was developed for pricing European options on futures contracts. Futures options, however, are American options. The second problem can be overcome. The Black model was extended by Barone-Adesi and Whaley to American options on futures contracts.[4] However, this model was also developed for equities and is subject to the first problem noted above.

The proper way to value options on a bond is to use an arbitrage-free model that takes into account the yield curve. In Chapter 5, an arbitrage-free binomial model was introduced and used to value a bond. The same model can be used to value an option on a bond. Thus, there will be consistency in the pricing of cash market instruments and options on those instruments. The most popular model employed by dealer firms is the Black-Derman-Toy model.[5] We have already discussed the basic principles for employing this model. In Chapter 5, we used the interest rate tree to value bonds (both option-free and bonds with embedded options). But the same tree can be used to value a stand-alone option on a bond.

Sensitivity of Option Price to Change in Factors

To use options to control risk, a manager needs to know how sensitive the price of an option is to a change in every factor that affects its price. Here we look at the sensitivity of a call option's price to changes in the price of the underlying bond, the time to expiration, and expected yield volatility.

The Call Option Price and the Price of the Underlying Bond

Exhibit 9 shows the theoretical price of a call option based on the price of the underlying bond. The horizontal axis is the price of the underly-

[4] Giovanni Barone-Adesi and Robert E. Whaley, "Efficient Analytic Approximation of American Option Values," *Journal of Finance* (June 1987), pp. 301-320.

[5] Fischer Black, Emanuel Derman, and William Toy, "A One-Factor Model of Interest Rates and Its Application to Treasury Bond Options," *Financial Analysts Journal* (January-February 1990), pp. 24-32.

ing bond at any point in time. The vertical axis is the theoretical call option price. The shape of the curve representing the theoretical price of a call option, given the price of the underlying bond, would be the same regardless of the actual option pricing model used. In particular, the relationship between the price of the underlying bond and the theoretical call option price is convex. Thus, option prices exhibit convexity.

The line from the origin to the strike price on the horizontal axis in Exhibit 9 is the intrinsic value of the call option when the price of the underlying bond is less than the strike price, since the intrinsic value is zero. The 45-degree line extending from the horizontal axis is the intrinsic value of the call option once the price of the underlying bond exceeds the strike price. The reason is that the intrinsic value of the call option will increase by the same dollar amount as the increase in the price of the underlying bond.

For example, if the strike price is \$100 and the price of the underlying bond increases from \$100 to \$101, the intrinsic value will increase by \$1. If the price of the bond increases from \$101 to \$110, the intrinsic value of the option will increase from \$1 to \$10. Thus, the slope of the line representing the intrinsic value after the strike price is reached is 1. Since the theoretical call option price is shown by the convex curve, the difference between the theoretical call option price and the intrinsic value at any given price for the underlying bond is the time value of the option.

Exhibit 9: Theoretical Call Price and Price of Underlying Bond

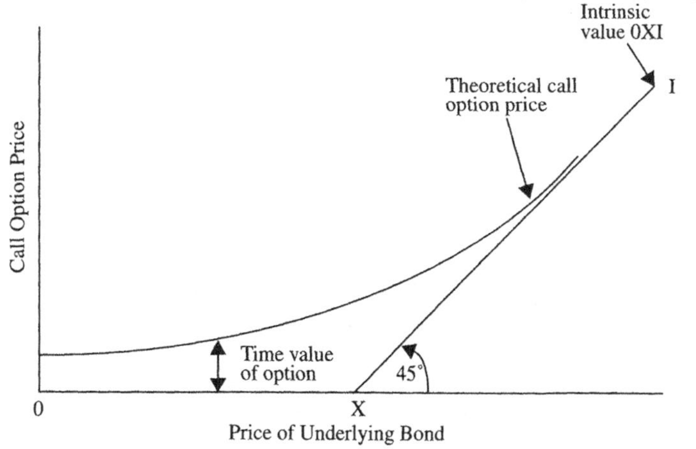

X= Strike price

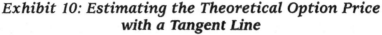

Exhibit 10: Estimating the Theoretical Option Price with a Tangent Line

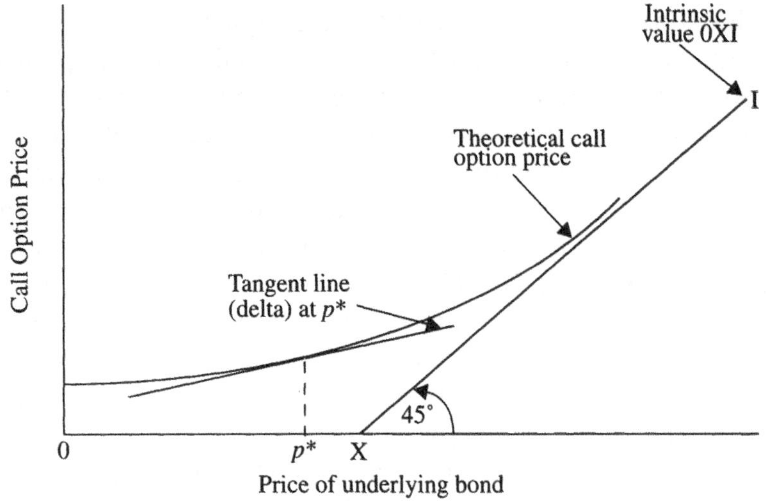

X = Strike price

Exhibit 10 shows the theoretical call option price, but with a tangent line drawn at the price of p^*. The tangent line in the exhibit can be used to estimate what the option price will be (and therefore what the change in the option price will be) if the price of the underlying bond changes. Because of the convexity of the relationship between the option price and the price of the underlying bond, the tangent line closely approximates the new option price for a small change in the price of the underlying bond. For large changes, however, the tangent line does not provide as good an approximation of the option price.

The slope of the tangent line shows how the theoretical call option price will change for small changes in the price of the underlying bond. The slope is popularly referred to as the option's *delta*. Specifically,

$$\text{Delta} = \frac{\text{Change in price of call option}}{\text{Change in price of underlying bond}}$$

For example, a delta of 0.4 means that a \$1 change in the price of the underlying bond will change the price of the call option by approximately \$0.40.

Exhibit 11: Theoretical Option Price with Three Tangents

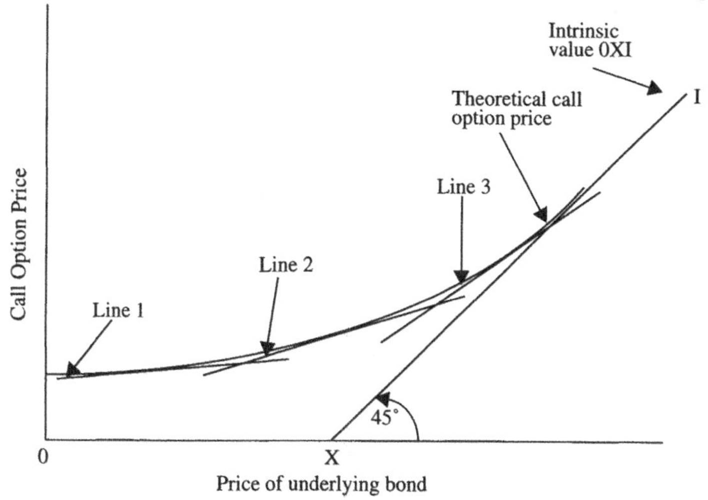

X = Strike price

Exhibit 11 shows the curve of the theoretical call option price with three tangent lines drawn. The steeper the slope of the tangent line, the greater the delta. When an option is deep out of the money (that is, the price of the underlying bond is substantially below the strike price), the tangent line is nearly flat (see Line 1 in Exhibit 11). This means that delta is close to zero. To understand why, consider a call option with a strike price of $100 and two months to expiration. If the price of the underlying bond is $20, the call option's price would not increase by much, if anything, should the price of the underlying bond increase by $1, from $20 to $21.

For a call option that is deep in the money, the delta will be close to one. That is, the call option price will increase almost dollar for dollar with an increase in the price of the underlying bond. In terms of Exhibit 11, the slope of the tangent line approaches the slope of the intrinsic value line after the strike price. As we stated earlier, the slope of that line is 1.

Thus, the delta for a call option varies from zero (for call options deep out of the money) to one (for call options deep in the money). The delta for a call option at the money is approximately 0.5. For a put option, the delta varies from −1 for a deep-in-the-money put option to zero for a deep-out-of-the-money put option.

As we discussed in Chapter 4, when a convex relationship is approximated by a tangent line, the estimate is only a first approximation. The first approximation can be improved. In the case of a bond, duration is the first approximation and the convexity measure combined with the convexity adjustment provides the second approximation. In the case of an option, delta is the first approximation of how the option's price will change. For an option, the equivalence of a bond's convexity measure is the option's *gamma* and is measured as follows:

$$\text{Gamma} = \frac{\text{Change in delta}}{\text{Change in price of underlying bond}}$$

The Option Price and Time to Expiration

All other factors remaining constant, the longer the time to expiration, the greater the option price. Since each day the option moves closer to the expiration date, the time to expiration decreases. The *theta* of an option measures the change in the option price as the time to expiration decreases, or equivalently, it is a measure of time decay. Theta is measured as follows:

$$\text{Theta} = \frac{\text{Change in price of option}}{\text{Decrease in time to expiration}}$$

Assuming that the price of the underlying bond does not change (which means that the intrinsic value of the option does not change), theta measures how quickly the time value of the option changes as the option moves towards expiration.

Buyers of options prefer a low theta so that the option price does not decline quickly as it moves toward the expiration date. An option writer benefits from an option that has a high theta.

The Option Price and Expected Yield Volatility

All other factors being constant, a change in the expected yield volatility will change the option price. The *kappa* or *vega* of an option measures the change in the price of the option for a 1% change in expected yield volatility.[6] That is,

---

[6] Recall in Chapter 5 when we discussed factors that affect the value of a bond with an embedded option, we introduced the vega or volatility duration.

$$\text{Kappa} = \frac{\text{Change in option price}}{1\%\ \text{change in expected yield volatility}}$$

Duration of an Option

The duration of an option measures the price sensitivity of the option to changes in interest rates and can be shown to be equal to:

$$\text{Duration for an option} = \text{Duration of underlying bond} \times \text{Delta} \times \frac{\text{Price of underlying bond}}{\text{Price of option}}$$

As expected, the duration of an option depends on the duration of the underlying bond. It also depends on the price responsiveness of the option to a change in the underlying bond, as measured by the option's delta. The leverage created by a position in an option comes from the last ratio in the formula. The higher the price of the underlying bond relative to the price of the option, the greater the leverage (i.e., the more exposure to changes in interest rates for a given dollar investment).

It is the interaction of all three factors that affects the duration of an option. For example, a deep out-of-the-money option offers higher leverage than a deep-in-the-money option, but the delta of the former is less than that of the latter.

Since the delta of a call option on a bond is positive, the duration of a call option will be positive. Thus, when interest rates decline, the value of a call option will rise. A put option on a bond, however, has a delta that is negative. Thus, duration is negative for a put option. Consequently, when interest rates rise, the value of a put option on a bond rises.

Market participants who think of duration in temporal terms are confused by option durations. For example, what does a duration of 60 mean for an option? It means that if rates change by 100 basis points, the price of the option will change by approximately 60%. Alternatively, it means that the option has the price sensitivity to rate changes of a 60-year zero-coupon bond.

SUMMARY

The role of derivatives in controlling the interest rate risk exposure of a portfolio is to adjust the dollar duration and thereby duration to the target exposure sought by the manager. Interest rate futures/forwards, swaps, and options are leveraged instruments that provide an effective means for quickly and inexpensively altering exposure.

A long futures position is equivalent to buying bonds on a leveraged basis and therefore when added to a portfolio increases the portfolio's dollar duration. A short futures position is equivalent to shorting on a leveraged basis and the addition of this position to a portfolio reduces the portfolio's dollar duration. The calculation of the dollar duration of a Treasury bond or note futures position involves determining how changes in interest rates will affect the value of the cheapest-to-deliver issue and then how a change in the value of the cheapest-to-deliver issue will affect the value of the futures position.

An interest rate swap is economically equivalent to a package of forward contracts or a position in a package of cash market instruments. A floating-rate payer has the equivalent economic position of purchasing a fixed-rate bond (with a value equal to the notional amount) and financing the purchase with a floating-rate loan (the funding rate being equal to the reference rate). Consequently, the dollar duration of a swap for the floating-rate payer is approximately equal to the dollar duration of the underlying bond that is financed. For a fixed-rate payer, the position is equivalent to buying a floating-rate bond and financing it on a fixed-rate basis (the funding rate being equal to the swap rate). So, the dollar duration of a swap for the fixed-rate payer has a negative dollar duration equal to roughly the dollar duration of the underlying bond. Thus, adding a swap to a portfolio in which the manager pays a fixed rate and receives a floating rate decreases the dollar duration of the portfolio.

There are options on bonds and options on bond futures contracts. The value of these contracts is affected by several factors. One key factor is how changes in interest rates change the underlying bond for the option and underlying bond futures contract for a futures option. Option pricing models have been used to determine the fair value of an option. From an option pricing model, the sensitivity of the option to changes in the price of the underlying bond (the delta and gamma of an option), changes in expected volatility (the kappa or vega of an option), and changes in time remaining to the option's expiration date (the theta of an option) can be computed. The duration of an option is determined by the delta of an option, the duration of the underlying bond, and the leverage embedded in the option.

Chapter 9

Other Risk Measures

Thus far in this book, our focus has been on the measurement of the *potential* change in the value of a bond or a portfolio if interest rates change. Duration and convexity are the measures used to quantify this exposure. In this chapter, we look at other measures of risk. At the end of this chapter, we will see where measures of interest rate risk such as duration fit into a risk framework.

The dictionary defines "risk" as "hazard, peril, exposure to loss or injury." With respect to investments, investors have used a variety of definitions to describe risk. Harry Markowitz changed how the investment community thought about risk by quantifying the concept of risk. He defined risk in terms of a statistical measure known as the *standard deviation*. Specifically, Markowitz quantified risk as the standard deviation about an asset's expected return.[1]

To understand the concept of the standard deviation and its appropriateness as a measure of risk, we must introduce some preliminary concepts from statistical theory. We then define alternative risk measures. We will see the difficulties of using historical data to estimate a bond portfolio's standard deviation. The solution is to use a factor model.

Our focus in this chapter is on the concepts, not the calculations. For all of the measures described in this chapter, calculations can be performed using an electronic spreadsheet. So, we won't dwell on the calculations.

THE STANDARD DEVIATION

A *random variable* is a variable for which a probability can be assigned to each possible value that can be taken by the variable. A *probability*

[1] Harry M. Markowitz, "Portfolio Selection," *Journal of Finance* (March 1952), pp. 71-91.

distribution or *probability function* describes all the values that the random variable can take on and the probability associated with each.

In applications to portfolio management, probability distributions are typically obtained from historical observations of the random variable. For example, if the random variable is the 1-year rate of return on a 5-year Treasury strip, then observations on the 1-year rate of return for 5-year Treasury strips are used.

Various measures are used to summarize the probability distribution of a random variable. The two most often used measures are the average value and the standard deviation. The *average value* or *mean value* is simply found by adding up the observed values for the random variable and dividing the sum by the number of observations. For example, let r denote the 1-year rate of return and T denote the number of observations, then the average value, denoted by r_{avg}, is:

$$r_{\text{avg}} = \frac{1}{T}\sum_{t=1}^{T} r_t \tag{1}$$

where r_t is the *t-th* observed rate of return.

The average value is also referred to as the *expected value* of the probability distribution. We will use the term expected value in the discussion below and denote the expected value of the return as r_{EV} rather than r_{avg}.

A portfolio manager is interested not only in the expected value of a probability distribution, but also in the dispersion of the possible outcomes for the random variable around the expected value. A measure of dispersion of the probability distribution is the *variance* of the distribution, denoted Var(r). It is calculated as follows:

$$\text{Var}(r) = \frac{1}{T-1}\sum_{t=1}^{T} (r_t - r_{\text{EV}})^2 \tag{2}$$

Notice that the variance is measuring the deviations of each observed value from the expected value. The greater the variance, the greater the dispersion of the observations for the random variable. The reason that the deviations from the expected value are squared in equation (2) is to avoid observations above and below the expected value from canceling each other out.

Exhibit 1: Quarterly Returns (%) for the Lehman Brothers Treasury Index and Lehman Brothers High Yield Index: First Quarter 1984 to Third Quarter 1997

Year	Qtr	Treasury Index	High Yield Index	Year	Qtr	Treasury Index	High Yield Index
1984	1	0.51	1.69	1991	1	2.12	20.7
	2	-1.23	-3.57		2	1.32	7.37
	3	7.63	7.43		3	5.69	7.04
	4	7.13	4.14		4	5.42	5.37
1985	1	2.13	5.56	1992	1	-1.81	7.39
	2	7.95	7.49		2	3.96	2.75
	3	2.09	3.85		3	5.05	3.89
	4	7.43	6.62		4	0	0.97
1986	1	9.16	9.26	1993	1	4.54	6.07
	2	1.24	3.85		2	2.91	4.21
	3	1.88	1.73		3	3.23	2.08
	4	2.68	1.75		4	-0.34	3.78
1987	1	1.16	7.08	1994	1	-3.02	-1.95
	2	-1.81	-1.54		2	-1.13	-0.32
	3	-2.87	-2.29		3	0.42	1.58
	4	5.72	1.91		4	0.35	-0.3
1988	1	3.25	5.58	1995	1	4.68	5.97
	2	0.95	2.38		2	6.24	6.12
	3	1.67	1.78		3	1.75	2.82
	4	0.96	2.29		4	4.6	2.8
1989	1	1.07	1.19	1996	1	-2.28	1.77
	2	8.16	3.64		2	0.46	1.66
	3	0.8	-1.47		3	1.67	3.77
	4	3.8	2.41		4	2.9	3.5
1990	1	-1.35	-1.65	1997	1	-0.86	1.05
	2	3.48	4.22		2	3.45	4.62
	3	0.77	-10.22		3	3.37	4.54
	4	5.52	-1.75				

The problem with using the variance as a measure of dispersion is that it is in terms of squared units of the random variable. Consequently, the square root of the variance, which is called the *standard deviation,* is used as a more understandable measure of the degree of dispersion. Mathematically this can be expressed as follows:

$$\text{Std}(r) = \sqrt{\text{Var}(r)}$$

where Std(r) denotes the standard deviation of the random variable r.

Exhibit 1 shows quarterly returns for the Lehman Brothers Treasury Index and the Lehman Brothers High Yield Index for the first quarter of 1984 to the third quarter of 1997. There are 55 observations. The expected value (average value), variance, and standard deviation for the quarterly returns are reported in Exhibit 2.

When the random variable is the rate of return over some investment horizon, it can be used to measure the risk associated with an investment. There are some important qualifications of using the standard deviation as a risk measure, and we will address these below. Before doing so, it will make it easier to understand these qualifications if we first introduce a probability distribution called the normal probability distribution.

NORMAL PROBABILITY DISTRIBUTION

In many applications of probability theory, it is assumed that the underlying probability distribution is a *normal distribution*. As explained below, for this probability distribution, given the expected value and the standard deviation, the probability of realizing a value or values can be obtained. An example of a normal distribution is shown in Exhibit 3.

Exhibit 2: Summary of Alternative Risk Measures for the Lehman Brothers Treasury Index and High Yield Index Based on Quarterly Returns: First Quarter 1984 to Third Quarter 1997

	Treasury Index	High Yield Index
Expected value	2.45%	3.14%
Risk Measures:		
Variance	8.9268	17.3930
Std. deviation	2.99%	4.17%
Target semivariance assuming 3% target return		
Target semivariance	5.5583	7.4707
Target semi-std deviation	2.36%	2.73%
Target semivariance assuming 0% target return		
Target semivariance	0.6403	2.5324
Target semi-std deviation	0.80%	1.59%
Semivariance (returns below the expected value)		
Semivariance	4.0175	7.8622
Semi-standard deviation	2.00%	2.80%

Exhibit 3: Normal Distribution

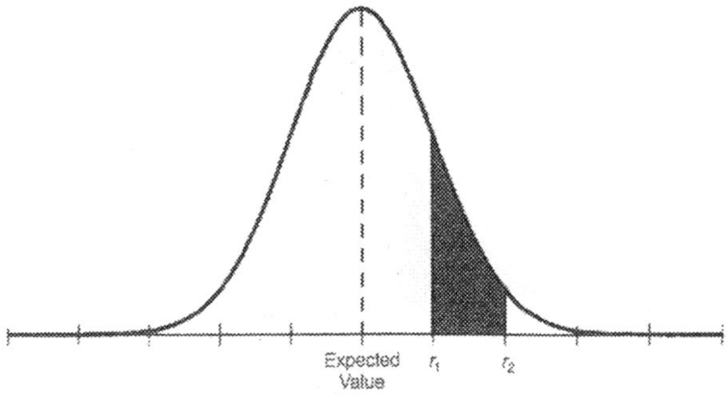

Probability of realizing a value between r_1 and r_2 is shaded area.

The area under the normal distribution or normal curve between any two points on the horizontal axis is the probability of obtaining a value between those two values. For example, the probability of realizing a value for the random variable r that is between r_1 and r_2 in Exhibit 3 is shown by the shaded area. The entire area under the normal curve is equal to 1, which means the sum of the probabilities is 1.

Properties of the Normal Distribution

The normal distribution has the following properties:

1. The point in the middle of the normal curve is the expected value for the distribution.
2. The distribution is *symmetric* around the expected value. That is, half of the distribution is to the left of the expected value and the other half is to the right. Thus, the probability of obtaining a value less than the expected value is 50%. The probability of obtaining a value greater than the expected value is also 50%.
3. The probability that the actual outcome will be within a range of one standard deviation above the expected value and one standard deviation below the expected value is 68.3%.
4. The probability that the actual outcome will be within a range of two standard deviations above the expected value and two standard deviations below the expected value is 95.5%.

Exhibit 4: Properties of a Normal Distribution

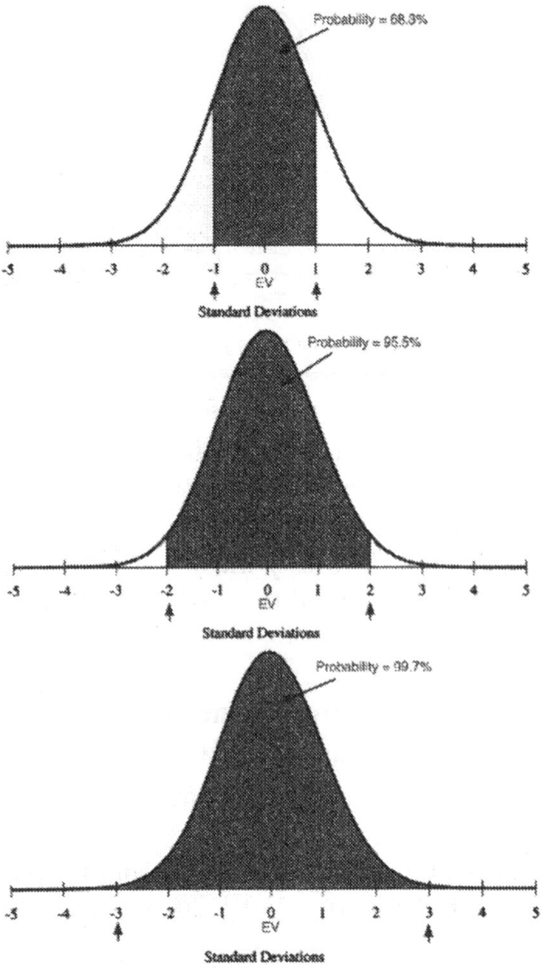

5. The probability that the actual outcome will be within a range of three standard deviations above the expected value and three standard deviations below the expected value is 99.7%.

Exhibit 4 graphically presents these properties.

Normal Distribution Tables and Standardized Values

Tables are available that give the probability of obtaining a value between any two values of a normal distribution. All that must be known in order to determine the probability is the expected value and the standard deviation.

The normal distribution table is constructed for a normal distribution that has an expected value of 0 and a standard deviation of 1. In order to use the table it is necessary to convert the normal distribution under consideration into a distribution that has an expected value of 0 and a standard deviation of 1. This is done by standardizing the values of the distribution under consideration.

The procedure is as follows. Suppose that a normal distribution for some random variable X has an expected value $E(X)$ and a standard deviation denoted by Std(X). To standardize any particular value, say X_1, the following is computed:

$$z_1 = \frac{X_1 - E(X)}{\text{Std}(X)}$$

where z_1 is the *standardized value* for X_1. The standardized value is also called the *normal deviate*.

Exhibit 5 is an abridged table that shows the area under the normal curve, which, as stated before, represents a probability. This particular table shows the probability of obtaining a value greater than some specified value in standardized form in the right-hand tail of the distribution. This is the shaded area shown in the normal curve at the top of Exhibit 5.

The standardized value is nothing more than the number of standard deviations above the expected value since the expected value of z is zero. From an examination of Exhibit 5, we can see the properties of a normal distribution that we discussed earlier. For example, look at the value in the table for a standardized value equal to 2. The probability is 2.28%. This is the probability of realizing a value in each of the tails of the normal distribution. Doubling this probability gives 4.56%, which is the probability of realizing a value in either of the two tails. This means that the probability of getting a value between the two tails is 95.44%. This agrees with the third property of the normal probability distribution that we stated above — there is a 95.5% probability of getting a value between two standard deviations below and above the expected value.

Exhibit 5: Normal Distribution Table

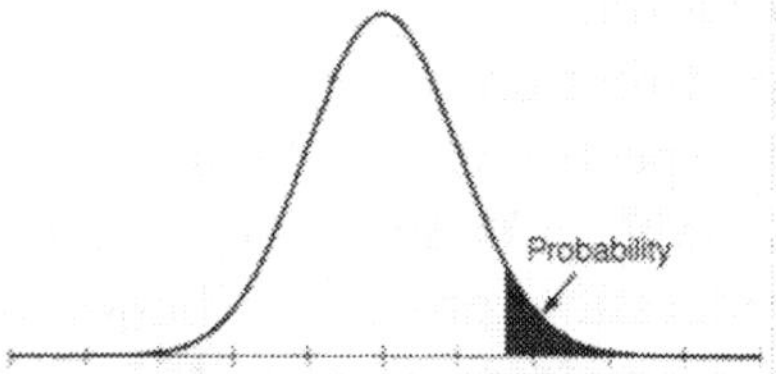

z	0.00	0.01	0.02	0.03	0.04	0.05	0.06	0.07	0.08	0.09
0.0	0.5000	0.4960	0.4920	0.4880	0.4840	0.4801	0.4761	0.4721	0.4681	0.4641
0.1	0.4602	0.4562	0.4522	0.4483	0.4443	0.4404	0.4364	0.4325	0.4286	0.4247
0.2	0.4207	0.4168	0.4129	0.4090	0.4052	0.4013	0.3974	0.3936	0.3897	0.3859
0.3	0.3821	0.3783	0.3745	0.3707	0.3669	0.3632	0.3594	0.3557	0.3520	0.3483
0.4	0.3446	0.3409	0.3372	0.3336	0.3300	0.3264	0.3228	0.3192	0.3156	0.3121
0.5	0.3085	0.3050	0.3015	0.2981	0.2946	0.2912	0.2877	0.2843	0.2810	0.2776
0.6	0.2743	0.2709	0.2676	0.2643	0.2611	0.2578	0.2546	0.2514	0.2483	0.2451
0.7	0.2420	0.2389	0.2358	0.2327	0.2296	0.2266	0.2236	0.2206	0.2177	0.2148
0.8	0.2110	0.2090	0.2061	0.2033	0.2005	0.1977	0.1949	0.1922	0.1894	0.1867
0.9	0.1841	0.1814	0.1788	0.1762	0.1736	0.1711	0.1685	0.1660	0.1635	0.1611
1.0	0.1587	0.1562	0.1539	0.1515	0.1492	0.1469	0.1449	0.1423	0.1401	0.1379
1.1	0.1357	0.1335	0.1314	0.1292	0.1271	0.1251	0.1230	0.1210	0.1190	0.1170
1.2	0.1151	0.1131	0.1112	0.1093	0.1075	0.1056	0.1038	0.1020	0.1003	0.0985
1.3	0.0968	0.0951	0.0934	0.0918	0.0901	0.0885	0.0869	0.0853	0.0838	0.0823
1.4	0.0808	0.0793	0.0778	0.0764	0.0749	0.0735	0.0721	0.0708	0.0694	0.0681
1.5	.0668	0.0655	0.0643	0.0630	0.0618	0.0606	0.0594	0.0582	0.0571	0.0559
1.6	.0548	0.0537	0.0526	0.0516	0.0505	0.0495	0.0485	0.0475	0.0465	0.0455
1.7	.0446	0.0436	0.0427	0.0418	0.0409	0.0401	0.0392	0.0384	0.0375	0.0367
1.8	.0359	0.0351	0.0344	0.0336	0.0329	0.0322	0.0314	0.0307	0.0301	0.0294
1.9	.0287	0.0281	0.0274	0.0268	0.0262	0.0256	0.0250	0.0244	0.0239	0.0233
2.0	0.0228	0.0222	0.0217	0.0212	0.0207	0.0202	0.0197	0.0192	0.0188	0.0183
2.1	0.0179	0.0174	0.0170	0.0166	0.0162	0.0158	0.0154	0.0150	0.0146	0.0143
2.2	0.0139	0.0136	0.0132	0.0129	0.0125	0.0122	0.0119	0.0116	0.0113	0.0110
2.3	0.0107	0.0104	0.0102	0.0099	0.0096	0.0094	0.0091	0.0089	0.0087	0.0084
2.4	0.0082	0.0080	0.0078	0.0075	0.0073	0.0071	0.0069	0.0068	0.0066	0.0064
2.5	0.0062	0.0060	0.0059	0.0057	0.0055	0.0054	0.0052	0.0051	0.0049	0.0048
2.6	0.0047	0.0045	0.0044	0.0043	0.0041	0.0040	0.0039	0.0038	0.0037	0.0036
2.7	0.0035	0.0034	0.0033	0.0032	0.0031	0.0030	0.0029	0.0028	0.0027	0.0026
2.8	0.0026	0.0025	0.0024	0.0023	0.0023	0.0022	0.0021	0.0021	0.0020	0.0019
2.9	0.0019	0.0018	0.0018	0.0017	0.0016	0.0016	0.0015	0.0015	0.0014	0.0014
3.0	0.0013	0.0013	0.0013	0.0012	0.0012	0.0011	0.0011	0.0011	0.0010	0.0010

Exhibit 6: Skewed Distribution

(a) Distribution Skewed to the Right (Positively Skewed)

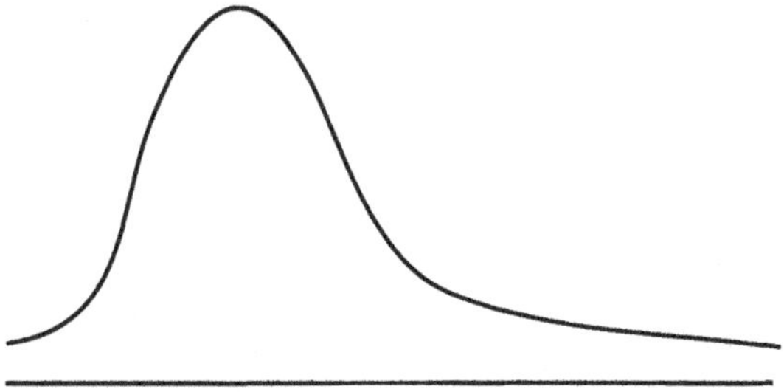

(b) Distribution Skewed to the Left (Negatively Skewed)

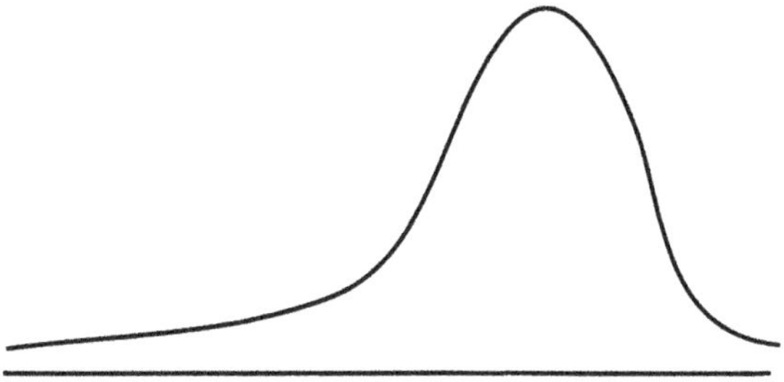

The Appropriateness of Using a Normal Distribution

In a normal distribution, the expected value (mean) and the standard deviation are all the information needed to make statements about the probabilities of outcomes. In order to apply the normal distribution to make statements about probabilities, it is necessary to assess whether a historical distribution (i.e., a distribution created from the observed data) is normally distributed.

For example, as noted earlier, a property of the normal distribution is that the distribution is symmetric around the expected value. However, a probability distribution might be best characterized like those shown in Exhibits 6a and 6b. Such distributions are referred to as *skewed distributions*. The skewed distribution shown in Exhibit 6a is one which has a long tail on the right hand side of the distribution. Such a distribution is referred to as a *positively skewed distribution*. Exhibit 6b shows a skewed distribution that has a long tail on the left hand side of the distribution and is called a *negatively skewed distribution*.

Exhibit 7: Fat Tails

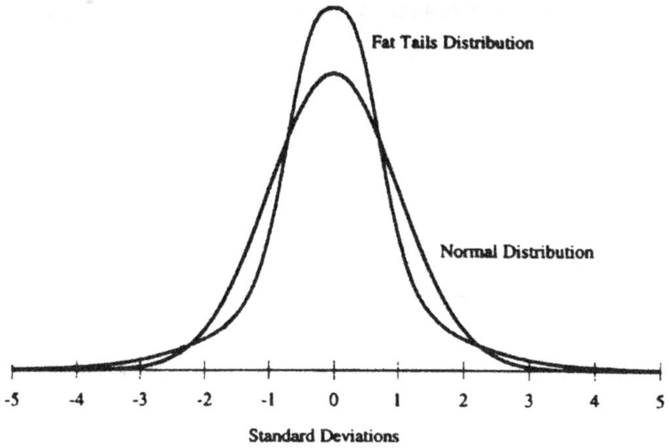

In addition to skewness, a historical distribution may have more outliers (i.e., observations in the "tails") than the normal distribution predicts. Distributions with this characteristic are said to have *fat tails*. This is depicted in Exhibit 7. Notice that if a distribution does indeed have fat tails but is assumed to be normally distributed, the probability of getting a value in a tail will be assumed to be less than the actual probability.

The following two questions must be addressed to determine whether a historical distribution can be characterized as a normal distribution:

1. Does the data fit the values predicted by the normal distribution?
2. Are the returns today independent of the returns of the prior periods?

Most introductory courses in statistics explain how to test if the data for some random variable can be characterized by a normal distribution. Basically the test involves breaking the historical observations into intervals. For each interval, the number of expected (or predicted) observations based on the normal probability distribution are determined. Then the number predicted for the interval and the number actually observed are compared. This is done for all intervals. Statistical tests can then be used to determine if the observed distribution differs significantly from a normal distribution.

Let's look at the evidence on bond returns. For bonds, there is a lower limit on the loss. For Treasury securities, the limit depends on how high rates can rise. Since Treasury rates have never exceeded 16%, this places a lower bound on a negative return from holding a bond. However, there is maximum return. Assuming that negative interest rates are not possible, the maximum price for a bond is the undiscounted value of the cash flows (i.e., the sum of the interest payments and maturity value). In turn, this determines the maximum return. On balance, government bond return distributions are negatively skewed. JP Morgan reports that this occurs for government bonds.[2] Moreover, government bond returns exhibit fat tails and a peakedness greater than predicted by the normal distribution.

One way to overcome the problem of negative skewedness of bond returns is to convert returns into the logarithm of returns. The transformation to logarithm of returns tends to pull in the outlier negative returns resulting in a distribution that is approximately normal. The resulting probability distribution of logarithmic returns is said to be *lognormally distributed.*

Now let's look at the independence of returns. For any probability distribution, it is important to assess whether or not the value of a random variable in one period is affected by the value that the random variable took on in a prior period. Casting this in terms of returns, it is important to know whether the return that can be realized today is affected by the return realized in a prior period. The terms *serial correlation* and *autocorrelation* are used to describe the correlation between the returns in different periods. JP Morgan's analysis suggests that there is only a small positive serial correlation for government bond returns.[3]

DOWNSIDE RISK MEASURES

Now that you understand why the standard deviation can be used as a measure of risk and the limitations of that measure if a distribution is not normally distributed or symmetric, let's look at other measures of risk that have been proposed.

---

[2] *RiskMetrics™ — Technical Document,* JP Morgan, May 26, 1995, New York, p. 48.
[3] *RiskMetrics™ — Technical Document,* p. 48.

Other measures of risk focus on only that portion of the return distribution for an investment that is below a specified level. These measures of risk are referred to as *downside risk measures* and they include target semivariance, shortfall probability, and value at risk. We will discuss each below.

For the different downside risk measures, the portfolio manager must define the *target return*. Returns less than the target return represent adverse consequences. In the case of the standard deviation, it is assumed that the target return is the expected return. However, in practice, this need not be the case. For example, in managing money against a market index, the target return may be X basis points over the market index return. Outcomes that are less than the market index return plus X basis points would represent downside risk. In managing money against liabilities, the target return may be the funding rate on liabilities plus a spread of S basis points. Returns with an outcome of less than the funding rate on liabilities plus S basis points would then represent downside risk.

It is important to understand that the notion of defining the risk of an investment in terms of only adverse consequences has been around a lot longer than the notion of using standard deviation as a measure of risk. In fact, when Professor Markowitz wrote his seminal work on investment risk, he argued that a downside risk measure would be more appropriate, but would be more complicated to deal with mathematically. He actually devoted an entire chapter in his classic book to one of the downside risk measures discussed below as a candidate for risk. Today, while vendors have employed downside risk measures in asset allocation models, not a great deal has been done in using some of these measures in bond portfolio management. The focus has been on the standard deviation as a measure of risk.

Target Semivariance

The *target semivariance* is a measure of the dispersion of the outcomes below the target return specified by the portfolio manager. Mathematically, the target semivariance can be expressed as:

$$\text{Target semivariance} = \frac{1}{T-1} \sum_{\text{for } r_t < r_{\text{target}}} (r_t - r_{\text{target}})^2 \qquad (3)$$

where r_{target} is the target return and T is the number of observations. The summation in equation (3) means the observations used in the calculations are those with a return less than the target return.

For example, suppose that the quarterly target return is 3%. Then for all of the quarterly return observations in Exhibit 1, only the returns of less than 3% represent downside risk and are used in the target semivariance given by equation (3). The results for the target semivariance for the Treasury Index and the High Yield Index are reported in Exhibit 2. Also reported in Exhibit 2 is the target semivariance if the target return is zero.

A special case of the target semivariance is where the target return is the expected value. The resulting value is called the *semivariance*. The equation for the semivariance is:

$$\text{Semivariance} = \frac{1}{t-1} \sum_{\text{for } r_t < r_{\text{EV}}} (r_t - r_{\text{EV}})^2 \qquad (4)$$

The summation in equation (4) means that only returns below the expected value are used. Exhibit 2 reports the semivariance and corresponding standard deviation.

When a probability distribution is symmetric around the expected value, then using the semivariance as a risk measure will give the same ranking of risk for securities as using the variance.

While theoretically the semivariance is superior to the variance (standard deviation) as a risk measure (and, in fact, this is the measure Professor Markowitz considered) it is not used in bond portfolio management to any significant extent. Ronald Kahn gave the following reasons why semivariance (which he defines as downside risk) is not used:[4]

> First, its definition is not as unambiguous as standard deviation or variance, nor are its statistical properties as well known, so it isn't an ideal choice for a universal risk definition. We need a definition which managers, plan sponsors, and beneficiaries can all use.

---

[4] Ronald N. Kahn, "Fixed Income Risk," Chapter 1 in Frank J. Fabozzi (ed.), *Managing Fixed Income Portfolios* (New Hope, PA: Frank J. Fabozzi Associates, 1997), pp. 2-3.

Second, it is computationally challenging for large portfolio construction problems. In fact, while we can aggregate individual bond standard deviations into a portfolio standard deviation, for other measures of risk we must rely much more on historical extrapolation of portfolio return patterns.

Third, to the extent that investment returns are reasonably symmetric, most definitions of downside risk are simply proportional to standard deviation or variance and so contain no additional information. To the extent that investment returns may not be symmetric, there are problems forecasting downside risk. Return asymmetries are not stable over time, and so are very difficult to forecast. Realized downside risk may not be a good forecast of future downside risk. Moreover, we estimate downside risk with only half the data, losing statistical accuracy.

Later in this chapter we look at how individual bond standard deviations of return are combined to determine a bond portfolio's standard deviation. In addition, we will address the problem of using historical return patterns for individual bonds.

Shortfall Risk

Shortfall risk is the probability that the outcome will have a value less than the target return. From a historical distribution of returns, shortfall risk is the ratio of the number of observations below the target return to the total number of observations.

Assuming a target return of 3% for the quarterly returns in Exhibit 1, the number of observations with a return below 3% is 33 for the Treasury Index and 28 for the High Yield Index. Thus, the shortfall risk is 60% (33/55) for the Treasury Index and 51% (28/55) for the High Yield Index. Notice that this risk measure suggests that there is less risk for the High Yield Index than the Treasury Index. One problem with this risk measure is that the *magnitude* of the losses below the target return is ignored.

When the target return is zero, the shortfall risk measure is commonly called the *risk of loss*. Again, it is calculated from historical data by dividing the number of observations with a return less than zero by the total number of observations. The risk of loss for both the Treasury Index and the High Yield Index is 18% since 10 of the 55 observations had a return that is less than zero.

As Ronald Kahn notes, when using shortfall risk the same problems are encountered as noted for target semivariance, namely, "ambiguity, poor statistical understanding, difficulty of forecasting."[5]

Value at Risk

In shortfall risk, the portfolio manager specifies a target return and then computes the percentage of returns less than the target return. A similar approach is for the portfolio manager to specify a target probability; the return will not fall below a yet-to-be determined value the percentage of time represented by the target probability.

For example, suppose that the portfolio manager specifies a target probability of 95%. The portfolio manager then determines the return for which the area in the left hand tail would have a 5% probability. The target return computed is commonly called the *value at risk* (VaR).

While we have expressed VaR in terms of return, it is more commonly used to measure dollar exposure. For example, suppose that a manager wants to make the following statement: "There is a *Y*% probability that the loss in value from a position will be less than \$*A* in the next *T* days." The \$*A* in this statement is the value at risk. The VaR can be determined from probability theory assuming a normal distribution, the expected value and standard deviation of the distribution, the target probability (*Y*%), and the number of days (*T*).

The VaR can be exhibited graphically. Exhibit 8 shows a normal distribution for the change in the value of a position over the next *T* days. The VaR is the loss of \$*A* where the probability to the right of that value is *Y*%. Or equivalently, the VaR is where the probability to the left of that value (i.e., the probability in the tail) is equal to 1−*Y*%.

Let's see how we obtain the VaR using a numerical example. Suppose that the probability distribution for the change in value of a bond over the next four days is normally distributed with an expected value of zero and a standard deviation of $20,000. Assume

---

[5] Kahn, "Fixed Income Risk," p.3.

also that the target probability specified by the manager is 95%. From the normal distribution table (Exhibit 5), the standardized value that will give a probability in the tail of 5% can be found. This is done by searching the table for where the probability is 5%. From Exhibit 5, this is where the standardized value is about 1.65.

The standardized value indicates the number of standard deviations above or below the expected value. The VaR is the value which is 1.65 standard deviations *below* the expected value. Since the expected value of the change in value of the bond over the next four days is zero and the standard deviation is $20,000, then the VaR is $33,000. Therefore, there is a 95% probability that the loss in value from the bond will be less than $33,000 in the next four days.

Alternatively, the VaR can be expressed as follows: "There is a 1−*Y*% probability that the loss in value over the next *T* days will be greater than $*A*." In our example, there is a 5% probability that the loss in value over the next four days will be greater than $33,000.

Daily Earnings at Risk

VaR begins with measuring the *daily earnings at risk* (DEaR). This is simply the value at risk for a day. For a single position in a bond, DEaR is measured as follows:

DEaR = Market value of position
× Sensitivity of the value of position to a 1 basis point adverse change in yield
× Adverse yield movement per day (in basis points)

Exhibit 8: Graphical Depiction of VaR

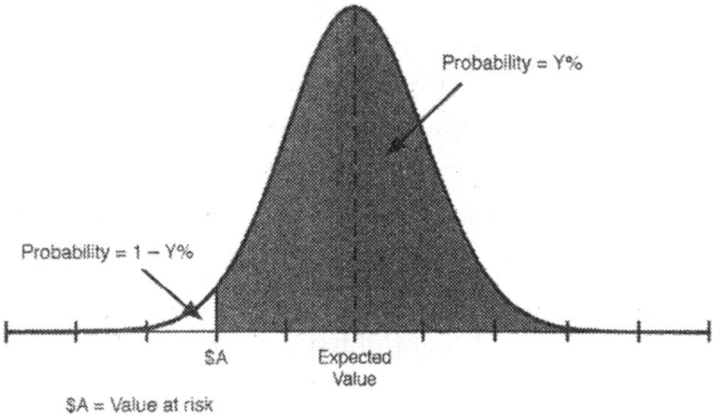

Since the duration of a position is the approximate percentage change for a 100 basis point change in yield, dividing the duration by 100 gives the percentage change in value for a 100 basis point change in yield. That is,

Percentage change in value for a 100 basis point change in yield
= Duration/100

Dividing by 100 gives the percentage change in value for a 1 basis point change in yield. That is,

Percentage change in value for a 1 basis point change in yield
= Duration/10,000

DEaR can then be restated as follows:

DEaR = Market value of position × Duration/10,000
× Adverse yield movement per day (in basis points)

The adverse yield movement per day is based on the daily yield volatility, the yield level, and the target probability specified. In the next chapter, we will see how daily yield volatility can be estimated. It is the forecasted daily standard deviation of yield changes. Also in the next chapter it will be shown that the product of the yield level and the daily standard deviation of yield changes gives the change in yield. The adverse yield movement per day is the product of the forecasted daily standard deviation of yield changes, the yield level, and the standardized value from the normal distribution. That is,

Adverse yield movement per day
= Forecasted daily standard deviation × Yield level
× Standardized value from normal distribution

For example, suppose that the forecasted daily standard deviation for the yield change of the 30-year Treasury zero-coupon bond is 0.63% and the yield is 8%. Assuming a normal distribution, then the standardized value is 1.65 if the target probability is 95% for the VaR. Therefore, the adverse yield movement per day is:

$$\text{Adverse yield movement per day} = 0.0063 \times 0.08 \times 1.65$$
$$= 0.00083$$

In basis points, the adverse yield movement per day is 8.3.

If the market value of a position of 30-year Treasury zero-coupon bonds is \$5 million and its duration is 4, then the DEaR is:

$$\text{DEaR} = \$5{,}000{,}000 \times (4/10{,}000) \times 8.3 = \$16{,}600$$

Relationship Between DEaR and VaR

Given the DEaR, the VaR is calculated as follows:

$$\text{VaR} = \text{DEaR}\sqrt{\text{Days expected until position can be neutralized}}$$

where "Days expected until position can be neutralized" is the number of days that it is expected it will take to neutralize the risk of the position.

Limitations of VaR

There are several criticisms that have been levied against the VaR framework. First, VaR depends on good estimates for both the sensitivity of a position to rate changes and for daily volatility of yield changes as measured by the daily standard deviation. As explained in previous chapters, for a complex security, estimating the effective duration is not simple. Moreover, as demonstrated in the next chapter, there could be substantial variations in the forecasted daily standard deviation. In one study, Tanya Beder found that there is a wide variation in the VaR for a given position based on different assumptions about the required inputs.[6]

A second limitation of the VaR framework is that it assumes yield changes are normally distributed. Finally, multiplying the DEaR by the square root of the number of days expected until the position can be neutralized assumes that the distribution for the daily percentage change in yield is not serially correlated.

Confidence Intervals

When a range for the possible values of a random variable and a probability associated with that range are calculated, the range is

[6] See Tanya Styblo Beder, "VAR: Seductive but Dangerous," *Financial Analysts Journal* (September-October 1995), pp. 12-24.

referred to as a *confidence interval*. In general, for a normal distribution, the confidence interval is calculated as follows:

(Expected value − Standardized value × Standard deviation) to
(Expected value + Standardized value × Standard deviation)

The standardized value indicates the number of standard deviations away from the expected value and corresponds to a particular probability. For example, suppose a manager wants a confidence interval of 95%. This means that there will be 2.5% in each tail. From Exhibit 5, we see that a standardized value with a 2.5% probability is 1.96. Thus, a 95% confidence interval is:

(Expected value − 1.96 × Standard deviation) to
(Expected value + 1.96 × Standard deviation)

For example, suppose that a manager wants to construct a confidence interval for the change in the value of a bond over the next four days. Assuming that the change in value is normally distributed with an expected value of zero and a standard deviation of $20,000, then a 95% confidence interval would be:

($0 − 1.96 × $20,000) to ($0 + 1.96 × $20,000)
or −$39,200 to $39,200

PORTFOLIO RISK

Thus far, we have dealt with the measurement of risk for an individual bond (although some of our numerical illustrations used an index). One of the advantages of the standard deviation or variance as a measure of risk is the ability to move from the risk of an individual bond position to the risk of a bond portfolio.

For a bond portfolio, the expected return for the portfolio is the weighted average of the expected returns for the individual bonds. The weight assigned to each bond in the portfolio is simply the percentage of the market value of the bond to the market value of the portfolio. No surprises here. However, the variance of a portfolio's return is not simply a weighted average of the variances of the returns of the bonds comprising the portfolio. The basic principle of modern portfolio theory is that the variance of a portfolio's return depends not only on the variance of the returns of the assets, but also their covariances or correlations.[7] We'll explain what is meant by the covariance and correlation below.

The Risk for a 2-Bond Portfolio

Let's first illustrate the calculation of the variance of a return for a bond portfolio consisting of just two bonds, identified as bond 1 and bond 2. The variance of the return of this portfolio is equal to

$$\mathrm{Var}(r_{\mathrm{Port}}) = w_1^2 \mathrm{var}(r_1) + w_2^2 \mathrm{var}(r_2) + 2w_1 w_2 \mathrm{cov}(r_1, r_2) \quad (5)$$

where

$\mathrm{Var}(r_{\mathrm{Port}})$	=	variance of the return of a portfolio comprised of bond 1 and bond 2
$\mathrm{Var}(r_1)$	=	variance of the return of bond 1
$\mathrm{Var}(r_2)$	=	variance of the return of bond 2
$\mathrm{Cov}(r_1, r_2)$	=	covariance between the return on bond 1 and bond 2
w_1	=	percentage of the portfolio in bond 1
w_2	=	percentage of the portfolio in bond 2

In words, equation (5) says that the variance of the portfolio return is the sum of the weighted variances of the two bonds plus the weighted covariance between the two bonds.

The key in the risk of a bond portfolio as measured by the standard deviation or variance is the covariance of the returns between the two bonds. The covariance is related to a more commonly understood statistical measure called the correlation coefficient.

Correlation Coefficient

The *correlation coefficient* measures the association between two random variables. No cause and effect relationship is assumed when a correlation coefficient is computed. The correlation can have a value between −1 and 1.

---

[7] Markowitz, "Portfolio Selection."

For example, if the random variable is the return on a bond, then a positive value for the correlation between the returns on two particular bonds means that the returns for both bonds tend to move together. In such cases, the two random variables are said to be *positively correlated.* A negative value means that the two returns tend to move in the opposite direction. Two random variables that exhibit this characteristic are said to be *negatively correlated.* A correlation close to zero means that the returns for the two bonds tend not to track each other.

The correlation between the quarterly returns for the Lehman Brothers Treasury Index and the Lehman Brothers High Yield Index based on the first quarter of 1984 through the third quarter of 1997 is 0.456. This means that Treasury returns (as measured by the Treasury index) and high yield returns are positively correlated.

Covariance

The *covariance* also measures how two random variables vary together. The covariance is related to the correlation coefficient as follows:

$$\text{Cov}(r_1,r_2) = \text{Std}(r_1)\ \text{Std}(r_2)\ \text{Cor}(r_1,r_2)$$

where $\text{Cor}(r_1,r_2)$ is the correlation between the returns on bond 1 and bond 2.

Since the standard deviations will always be a positive value, the covariance will have the same sign as the correlation coefficient. Thus, if two random variables are positively correlated they will have a positive covariance. Similarly, the covariance will be negative if the two random variables are negatively correlated.

The covariance between the quarterly returns for the Treasury Index and the High Yield Index is found as follows. The standard deviation for the return of the Treasury Index is 2.99%. For the High Yield Index it is 4.17%. The correlation is 0.456. Therefore, the covariance is

$$\text{Cov}(r_1, r_2) = 2.99 \times 4.17 \times 0.456 = 5.69$$

Portfolio Risk for Different Allocations

Notice from Exhibit 2 that the expected return for the Treasury Index is less than for the High Yield Index. However, as expected, the risk, as measured by the standard deviation, is greater for the High Yield Index than for the Treasury Index.

Exhibit 9 shows the portfolio standard deviation for different allocations to the Treasury Index and the High Yield Index. To see the importance of the correlation/covariance on the portfolio's standard deviation of returns, Exhibit 10 shows the portfolio standard deviation for different assumed correlations for the returns between the two indexes. Note that the expected value is unchanged from that shown in Exhibit 9 since it is unaffected by the correlation. The four correlations assumed are −1, −0.5, 0, and 1, as well as the estimated correlation of 0.456. For a given allocation between the two bond indexes in the portfolio, the more negatively correlated the returns, the lower the portfolio standard deviation. The minimum variance (for a given allocation) occurs when the correlation is −1.

Exhibit 9: Portfolio Risk and Expected Quarterly Return for Different Allocations between the Treasury Index and the High Yield Index (Based on Quarterly Returns from First Quarter of 1984 to the Third Quarter of 1997)

	Lehman Brothers Treasury Index	Lehman Brothers High Yield Index
Expected value	2.45%	3.14%
Variance	8.9268	17.3930
Standard dev.	2.99%	4.17%
Covariance	5.69	
Correlation	0.456	

	Weight (Allocation) in Treasury Index						
	20%	30%	40%	50%	60%	70%	80%
Expected value (%)	3.00	2.93	2.86	2.79	2.72	2.65	2.59
Standard deviation	3.64	3.42	3.22	3.06	2.95	2.88	2.86

Exhibit 10: Portfolio Standard Deviation for Different Correlations and Weights for the Treasury Index and the High Yield Index

Assumed	Weight (Allocation) in Treasury Index						
Corr	20%	30%	40%	50%	60%	70%	80%
−1.000	2.74	2.02	1.31	0.59	0.12	0.84	1.56
−0.500	3.08	2.59	2.17	1.86	1.73	1.82	2.10
0	3.39	3.05	2.77	2.57	2.45	2.44	2.53
0.456	3.64	3.42	3.22	3.06	2.95	2.88	2.86
1.000	3.93	3.82	3.70	3.58	3.46	3.34	3.22

Measuring the Variance of a Portfolio with More than Two Bonds

Thus far we have looked at the variance and standard deviation for a portfolio consisting of two bonds. The extension to three bonds is as follows:

$$\begin{aligned}\mathrm{Var}(r_{\mathrm{Port}}) &= w_1^2\mathrm{Var}(r_1) + w_2^2\mathrm{Var}(r_2) + w_3^2\mathrm{Var}(r_3)\\ &\quad + 2w_1w_2\mathrm{Cov}(r_1, r_2) + 2w_1w_3\mathrm{Cov}(r_1, r_3)\\ &\quad + 2w_2w_3\mathrm{Cov}(r_2, r_3)\end{aligned}$$

In words, the portfolio's variance is the sum of the weighted variances of the individual bonds plus the sum of the weighted covariances of the bonds.

The formula for the portfolio variance and standard deviation can be generalized to any number of bonds. The computation of a portfolio of J bonds requires the computation of all pairwise covariances. Typically, the formula for the portfolio's variance is presented using mathematical notation from matrix algebra. While we will not use that notation here, the key input is the variance-covariance matrix. This is nothing more than a table that has variances of each bond in the diagonal of the table and the covariance between each pair of bonds as the off-diagonal terms. For a portfolio of J bonds, there will be J variances that must be computed plus all of the covariances. The number of covariances will be $J(J + 1)/2 - J$. Thus, for a portfolio of J bonds, the number of inputs (variances plus covariances) that must be estimated is equal to

$$\text{Number of variances and covariances} = \frac{J(J+1)}{2}$$

Implementation Problems

If the standard deviation is accepted as the measure of risk, this means that the variance and covariance for each bond must be estimated to compute the portfolio's standard deviation. Let's look at two major problems with this approach. After we discuss these problems, we will see how to handle them.

The first problem with this approach is that the number of estimated inputs increases dramatically as the number of bonds in the portfolio or the number of bonds being considered for inclusion in the portfolio increases. For example, consider a manager who wants to construct a portfolio in which there are 5,000 bonds that are candidates for inclusion in the portfolio. (If this number sounds large, consider that the broad-based bond market indexes include more than this number of bonds.) Then the number of variances and covariances that must be estimated is

$$\text{Number of variances and covariances} = \frac{5{,}000(5{,}000 + 1)}{2}$$

$$= 12{,}502{,}500$$

That is a good size matrix that requires calculation and manipulation to estimate a portfolio's standard deviation or risk.

The second problem is that whether it is 55 variances and covariances for a 10-bond portfolio or 12,502,500 for a 5,000-bond portfolio, these values must still be estimated. Where does the portfolio manager obtain these values? They must be estimated from historical data. While equity portfolio managers have the luxury of working with a long time series of returns on stocks, bond portfolio managers do not have good sources of historical bond data. In addition, even with time series data on the return of a particular bond, a portfolio manager must question what the returns mean. The reason is that the characteristics of a bond change over time.

For example, consider a 10-year Treasury note issued 8 years ago and for which quarterly returns have been calculated. The first quarterly return is the return on a 10-year Treasury note. However, the second quarterly return is the return on a 9¾-year Treasury note. The third quarterly return is the return on a 9.5-year Treasury note, etc. If that original 10-year Treasury note is in the current portfolio and the manager wants to estimate the standard deviation for that security, looking at its historical standard deviation will not be meaningful. This security is now a 2-year Treasury note since it was purchased 8 years ago and will not necessarily share the return volatility characteristics of the earlier maturities it had. It is not only the changing time to maturity that will affect the historical data and render it of limited use, but there are some securities whose characteristics change dramatically over time because of call provisions. For example, CMO support bonds have average lives that change dramatically due to prepayments which will affect the historical return pattern.

Now, if we couple the problem of a large number of estimates required and the lack of good data, we can see another major problem. Consider a 100-bond portfolio. There are 5,050 inputs that must be estimated. Suppose that just 10% are misestimated because of a lack of good historical or meaningful data. This means that there will be 505 misestimated numbers which could have a material impact on the estimated portfolio risk.

FACTOR MODELS

Because of the problems with using historical data to estimate the standard deviation of a portfolio, bond portfolio managers have turned to factor models. Factor models seek to analyze historical data and identify the key risk factors that drive bond returns. The risk of a bond portfolio is then gauged in terms of the exposure of a portfolio to these risk factors.

Evidence from the Treasury Market

Empirical studies have investigated the factors that affect the historical returns on Treasury portfolios. Studies by Robert Litterman and José Scheinkman[8] and Frank Jones[9] identified three factors. The first factor is changes in the level of rates, the second factor is changes in the slope of the yield curve, and the third factor is changes in the curvature of the yield curve.

Litterman and Scheinkman use regression analysis to determine the relative contribution of these three factors in explaining the returns on zero-coupon Treasury securities of different maturities. Exhibit 11 summarizes their results. The second column of the exhibit shows the coefficient of determination, popularly referred to as the "R-squared," for each zero-coupon maturity. In general, the R-squared measures the percentage of the variance in the dependent

---

[8] Robert Litterman and José Scheinkman, "Common Factors Affecting Bond Returns," *The Journal of Fixed Income* (June 1991), pp. 54-61.

[9] Frank J. Jones, "Yield Curve Strategies," *Journal of Fixed Income* (September 1991), pp. 43-51.

variable explained by the independent variables. The R-squared will have a value between 0% and 100%. In terms of the study conducted by Litterman and Scheinkman, the R-squared measures the percentage of the variance of historical returns explained by the three factors (i.e., the independent variables). As can be seen in the second column, the R-squared was very high for all maturities, indicating that the three factors had a very strong predictive or explanatory effect.

The last three columns show the relative contribution of each of the three factors in explaining the return on the zero-coupon bond. Consider the 18-year zero. The second column indicates that 95% of the variance of the return in the 18-year zero is explained by the three factors. The first factor, changes in the level of rates, holding the other two factors constant, contributes about 81% of the explanatory power. This factor has the greatest explanatory power for all the maturities, averaging about 90%. The implication is that a portfolio manager should control for exposure to changes in interest rates by adjusting the effective duration (sensitivity to rate levels) of the portfolio. Hence, this is the reason for devoting so much coverage to the measurement of duration in this book.

Exhibit 11: Factors Explaining Treasury Returns

Factor 1: Changes in the level of interest rates
Factor 2: Changes in the yield curve slope
Factor 3: Curvature of the yield curve

Zero Coupon Maturity (years)	Variance of Total Returns Explained (%)	Proportion of Total Explained Variance Accounted for by (%)		
		Factor 1	Factor 2	Factor 3
0.5	99.5	79.5	17.2	3.3
1.0	99.4	89.7	10.1	0.2
2.0	98.2	93.4	2.4	4.2
5.0	98.8	98.2	1.1	0.7
8.0	98.7	95.4	4.6	0.0
10.0	98.8	92.9	6.9	0.2
14.0	98.4	86.2	11.5	2.2
18.0	95.3	80.5	14.3	5.2
Average	98.4	89.5	8.5	2.0

Source: Table 2 in Robert Litterman and José Scheinkman, "Common Factors Affecting Bond Returns," *The Journal of Fixed Income* (June 1991), p. 58.

The second factor shown, changes in the yield curve slope, is the second largest contributing factor. For the 18-year zero-coupon bond, the relative contribution is about 14.3%. The average relative contribution is 8.5%. Thus, changes in the yield curve slope are, on average, about one-tenth as significant as changes in the level of rates (8.5%/89.5%). While this may not seem very significant, remember that Litterman and Scheinkman examined a portfolio containing a series of zero-coupon Treasury bonds, which typically have much less yield curve slope risk than mortgage-backed securities (discussed below). Moreover, while the relative contribution is only 8.5%, this can still have a significant impact on a portfolio's return and a portfolio manager must control for this risk.

Notice that the third factor, changes in the curvature of the yield curve, contributes relatively little to explaining historical returns. This is why we have ignored this factor in the book.

Evidence from the MBS Market

A study by Schumacher, Dektar, and Fabozzi replicated the Litterman-Scheinkman study for mortgage-backed securities.[10] Only two factors are considered instead of three. The two factors are the level of interest rates and changes in the yield curve slope.

Exhibit 12 reports the regression results for current coupon fixed-rate passthroughs, 1-year CMT adjustable-rate passthroughs, a principal-only strip, a high coupon interest-only strip, and four CMO bonds (a 7-year PAC, a 10-year Very Accurately Defined Maturity (VADM), a short average life floater, and a long average life floater). The dependent variable in the regression is the return on the particular mortgage-backed security. The independent variables are the level of rates and changes in the yield curve slope. The time period studied was December 1983 to December 1992.

The second column shows the R-squared. The third and fourth columns report the estimated regression coefficients for the two factors, with the corresponding T-statistics in the last two columns. The results are quite interesting. With the exception of the

---

[10] Michael P. Schumacher, Daniel C. Dektar, and Frank J. Fabozzi, "Yield Curve Risk of CMO Bonds," Chapter 16 in Frank J. Fabozzi (ed.), *Advances in the Valuation and Management of Mortgage-Backed Securities* (New Hope, PA: Frank J. Fabozzi Associates, 1999).

floater, the ARM, and the high-coupon IO strip, the R-squareds are reasonably high. While not reported here, R-squareds for the floating-rate securities have been much higher in other periods. The level and slope variables explained a very high percentage of the variance of PAC and VADM returns.

The R-squared gives the explanatory power of the two factors collectively. The T-statistics shown in the last two columns indicate the statistical significance of each factor separately. Generally, a T-statistic with an absolute value greater than two is considered statistically significant at the 5% level of significance. The T-statistics reported for changes in the level of interest rates are statistically significant for all but the short and long average life floater. The T-statistics reported for changes in the yield curve slope are statistically significant for the PO strip, the PAC, the VADM, and the current coupon mortgage. The only instruments for which changes in the yield curve slope were not statistically significant are the floaters, the ARM, and the IO strip. These results further support the importance of yield curve risk as a risk factor.

Exhibit 12: CMO Bond Returns versus Changes in Level and Slope of the Yield Curve: Regression Results 12/83 through 12/92

Dependent Variable	R^2 (%)	Coefficients		T-Statistics	
		Level	Slope	Level	Slope
Current Coupon Fixed-Rate Mortgage	79	−4.01	−1.20	−18.50	−5.70
1-Year CMT Adjustable-Rate Mortgage	30	−1.30	0.03	−4.90	0.10
Principal-Only Strip	64	−11.43	−2.66	−10.20	−2.40
High-Coupon Interest-Only Strip	32	12.47	1.13	5.00	0.50
7-Year PAC	86	−6.70	−1.15	−14.00	−2.80
10-Year VADM	95	−8.00	−2.31	−9.60	−2.90
Short Average Life Floater	11	−0.43	−0.22	−1.90	−1.10
Long Average Life Floater	13	−0.64	−0.51	−1.10	−0.90

Source: Exhibit 5 in Michael P. Schumacher, Daniel C. Dektar, and Frank J. Fabozzi, "Yield Curve Risk of CMO Bonds," Chapter 16 in Frank J. Fabozzi (ed.), *Advances in the Valuation and Management of Mortgage-Backed Securities* (New Hope, PA: Frank J. Fabozzi Associates, 1999), p. 237

SUMMARY

The variance of a probability distribution is a measure of the dispersion of the outcomes of a random variable around its expected value. The standard deviation is the square root of the variance. The standard deviation of the return of a bond is commonly used as a measure of a bond's risk.

The standard deviation is a misleading measure of risk if the probability distribution for bond returns is not symmetric (i.e, if the distribution is skewed). When using standard deviation as a measure of the risk for bond returns it is assumed that the underlying probability distribution is a normal distribution. This probability distribution is symmetric around the expected value and the only information needed to make probability statements about outcomes is the expected value and the standard deviation.

Downside risk measures focus on only that portion of the return from an investment that is below a specified level. Downside risk measures include target semivariance and shortfall probability. For the different downside risk measures, the portfolio manager must define the target return so that returns less than the target return represent adverse consequences.

The target semivariance is a measure of the dispersion of the outcomes below the target return specified by the portfolio manager. The semivariance is a special case of the target semivariance where the target return is the expected value. When a probability distribution is symmetric around the expected value, using the semivariance as a risk measure will give the same ranking of risk as using the variance or standard deviation. While theoretically the target semivariance is superior to the variance (standard deviation) as a risk measure, it is not used in bond portfolio management to any significant extent because of the ambiguity in its use, the poor statistical understanding of these measures, and the difficulty of forecasting the necessary required data.

In a value-at-risk measure the portfolio manager specifies a target probability and then computes the return that the outcomes will not fall below that return that percentage of times. When applied to a bond position, value-at-risk uses the duration of the bond to measure the potential change in value when interest rates change.

Shortfall risk is the probability that the outcome will have a value less than the target return. A special case of shortfall risk is the risk of loss which is based on a target return of zero.

A portfolio's variance is not simply the weighted average of the variance of the return of the component bonds. A portfolio's variance depends not only on the variance of the returns of the component bonds but also the covariances (correlations) between each pair of bonds. The lower the covariance (correlation) between the returns of bonds in the portfolio, the greater the reduction in the portfolio's variance.

The two problems in computing a portfolio's variance are (1) the number of estimated inputs increases dramatically as the number of bonds in the portfolio or the number of bonds being considered for inclusion in the portfolio increases and (2) the difficulty of obtaining meaningful historical return data for bonds. Factor models can be used to overcome the problems associated with using historical standard deviations to compute the risk of a bond portfolio. The three factors that have been found to drive bond returns are changes in the (1) level of interest rates (the most important factor explaining historical returns), (2) slope of the yield curve, and (3) curvature of the yield curve (the least important of the three factors in explaining historical returns).

Chapter 10

Measuring Yield Volatility

There are two critical components to measuring the risk exposure of an individual position and a bond portfolio to changes in interest rates. The first component is an estimate of the price sensitivity to changes in interest rates. As explained in earlier chapters, this estimate is typically obtained by shocking interest rates and calculating based on a valuation model how the price changes. The result is an effective duration measure. If the valuation model employed is poor, the resulting duration measure will not be a good measure of the price sensitivity of an instrument to rate changes. A critical input to valuation models for cash market instruments with embedded options and option-like derivatives is the estimated yield volatility. The second component is the estimated yield volatility, which is used to assess the potential change in yield in the value-at-risk framework described in the previous chapter.

In this chapter, we look at how to measure yield volatility and discuss some techniques used to estimate it. Volatility is measured in terms of the standard deviation or variance. We begin this chapter with a review of historical volatility for Treasury yields. We then explain how yield volatility as measured by the daily percentage change in yields is calculated from historical yields. We will see that there are several issues confronting an investor in measuring historical yield volatility. Next we turn to modeling and forecasting yield volatility, looking at the state-of-the-art statistical techniques that can be employed.

HISTORICAL VOLATILITY

A study by Ryan Labs, Inc. documented the history of interest rate volatility for the on-the-run Treasury issues since the inception of the auction for each maturity series through December 31, 1995. Exhibit 1 shows this history in terms of the basis point change in yield for the rolling 12-month periods for the 2-year and 30-year maturity series. Reported in the exhibit are the percentages of times that the number of basis points in the interval were observed. The auction of the 2-year maturity series began in August 1974 and there were 257 observations; for the 30-year maturity series which began in May 1973, there were 260 observations.

Exhibit 1: The History of 2-Year and 30-Year Treasury Interest Rate Volatility in Terms of Basis Point Changes
(Rolling 12-Month Periods from Inception of Auction to December 31, 1995)

Basis point change in yield	Percentage of time observed for	
	2-Year (257 obs)	30-Year (260 obs)
−550 to −500	0.8%	0.0%
−500 to −450	2.3	0.0
−450 to −400	1.2	0.8
−400 to −350	1.2	0.4
−350 to −300	1.6	3.5
−300 to −250	1.2	2.7
−250 to −200	7.0	2.7
−200 to −150	6.6	3.8
−150 to −100	9.3	5.8
−100 to −50	10.9	11.5
−50 to 0	12.1	17.7
0 to 50	7.0	13.5
50 to 100	8.2	18.1
100 to 150	8.6	7.3
150 to 200	8.9	4.6
200 to 250	5.8	3.5
250 to 300	3.1	1.9
300 to 350	1.2	2.3
350 to 400	0.0	0.0
400 to 450	0.4	0.0
450 to 500	1.2	0.0
500 to 650	1.6	0.0

Source: Ryan Labs, Inc.

Exhibit 2: Summary Statistics for The History of 2-Year and 30-Year Treasury Interest Rate Volatility in Terms of Basis Point Changes

(Rolling 12-Month Periods from Inception of Auction to December 31, 1995)

	2-Year	30-Year
Average change (bp)	−7.21	−2.82
One standard deviation (bp)	−209 to 194	−149 to 144
Two standard deviations (bp)	−411 to 396	−296 to 290
Maximum positive change (bp)	611	350
(beginning date - ending date)	7/80 - 7/81	9/80 - 9/81
(beginning yield - ending yield)	9.69% - 15.8%	11.69% - 15.18%
Maximum negative change (bp)	−546	−415
(beginning date - ending date)	9/81 - 9/82	3/85 - 3/86
(beginning yield - ending yield)	16.72% - 11.27%	11.63% - 7.48%

Source: Ryan Labs, Inc.

Exhibit 2 provides summary statistics regarding the historical basis point movements. Note that while the average basis point change of −7 and −3 basis points for the 2-year and 30-year, respectively, was small, this masks the volatility because of the averaging of significant upward and downward movements of yields. What is apparent from all the summary statistics reported is that interest rate volatility is greater for the 2-year yield than the 30-year yield. That is, interest rate volatility is greater at the short end of the yield curve. While not reported in the exhibit, this relationship holds for the 3-year, 5-year, and 10-year Treasury maturity series — that is, the longer the maturity, the lower the interest rate volatility. The maximum basis point change occurred consistently at high yield levels.

Exhibit 3 reports the history of interest rate volatility in terms of the percentage change in yield for the same period for the 2-year and 30-year issues. Exhibit 4 provides summary statistics. Again, the average change has little meaning and it can be seen that the longer maturity series exhibited less interest rate volatility than the shorter maturity series. The magnitude of the percentage change depends on the level of yields. It was found that the maximum percentage positive yield change occurred at low yield levels while the maximum percentage negative yield change occurred at high yield levels.

Exhibit 3: History of 2-Year and 30-Year Treasury Interest Rate Volatility in Terms of Percentage Yield Changes
(Rolling 12-Month Periods from Inception of Auction to December 31, 1995)

Percentage change in yield	Percentage of time observed for	
	2-Year (257 obs)	30-Year (260 obs)
−40 to −35	1.17%	0.38%
−35 to −30	5.84	1.92
−30 to −25	7.78	1.15
−25 to −20	5.84	5.77
−20 to −15	7.00	5.00
−15 to −10	9.73	10.38
−10 to −5	7.39	9.23
−5 to 0	9.34	15.00
0 to 5	5.06	12.31
5 to 10	7.39	12.31
10 to 15	6.61	11.92
15 to 20	5.84	4.62
20 to 25	3.11	4.23
25 to 30	4.67	3.46
30 to 35	4.67	1.92
35 to 40	1.95	0.38
40 to 45	0.78	0.00
45 to 50	1.17	0.00
50 to 55	1.17	0.00
55 to 60	0.78	0.00
60 to 65	0.78	0.00
65 to 70	0.00	0.00
70 to 75	0.78	0.00
75 to 80	0.78	0.00
80 to 85	0.39	0.00

Source: Ryan Labs, Inc.

MEASURING HISTORICAL YIELD VOLATILITY

Market participants seek a measure of yield volatility. As explained in the previous chapter, the measure used is the standard deviation or variance. Here we will see how to compute yield volatility using historical data. The variance of a random variable using historical data is calculated using the following formula:

Exhibit 4: Summary of the History of 2-Year and 30-Year Treasury Interest Rate Volatility in Terms of Percentage Yield Changes

(Rolling 12-Month Periods from Inception of Auction to December 31, 1995)

	2-Year	30-Year
Average change (%)	1.72	0.70
One standard deviation (%)	−23 to 26	−14 to 15
Two standard deviations (%)	−47 to 51	−29 to 30
Maximum positive change (%)	81	37
(beginning date - ending date)	12/93 - 12/94	3/80 - 3/81
(beginning yield - ending yield)	4.25% - 7.69%	9.02% - 12.32%
Maximum negative change (%)	−37	−36
(beginning date - ending date)	9/91 - 9/92	3/85 - 3/86
(beginning yield - ending yield)	6.03% - 3.82%	11.63% - 7.48%

Source: Ryan Labs, Inc.

$$\text{Variance} = \frac{1}{T-1}\sum_{t=1}^{T}(X_t - \bar{X})^2 \tag{1}$$

and then

$$\text{Standard deviation} = \sqrt{\text{Variance}}$$

where

X_t = observation t on variable X
$\bar{X}$ = the sample mean for variable X
T = the number of observations in the sample

Our focus is on yield volatility. More specifically, we are interested in the percentage change in daily yields. So, X_t will denote the percentage change in yield from day t and the prior day, t−1. If we let y_t denote the yield on day t and y_{t-1} denote the yield on day t−1, then X_t, the percentage change in yield, can be expressed as the natural logarithm of the ratio of the two yields. That is,

$$X_t = 100[\text{Ln}(y_t/y_{t-1})]$$

For example, on 10/18/95 the Treasury 30-year zero-coupon rate was 6.555% and on 10/19/95 it was 6.593%. Therefore, the value of X for 10/19/95 is:

$$X = 100[\text{Ln}(6.593/6.555)] = 0.57804$$

To illustrate how to calculate a daily standard deviation from historical data, consider the data in Exhibit 5 which show the yield on Treasury 30-year zeros from 10/8/95 to 11/12/95 in Column (3). From the 26 observations, 25 days of percentage yield changes are calculated in Column (4). The last column shows the square of the deviations of the observations from the mean. The bottom of Exhibit 5 shows the calculation of the daily mean for the 25 observations, the variance, and the standard deviation. The daily standard deviation is 0.6360%.

The daily standard deviation will vary depending on the 25 days selected. For example, when the daily yields from 8/20/95 to 9/24/95 were used to generate 25 daily percentage yield changes, the computed daily standard deviation was 0.8453%.

Determining the Number of Observations

In our illustration, we used 25 observations for the daily percentage change in yield. The appropriate number of observations depends on the situation at hand. For example, traders concerned with overnight positions might use the 10 most recent days (i.e., two weeks). A bond portfolio manager who is concerned with longer term volatility might use 25 days (about one month).

The selection of the number of observations can have a significant effect on the calculated daily standard deviation. This can be seen in Exhibit 6 which shows the daily standard deviation for the Treasury 30-year zero, Treasury 10-year zero, and Treasury 5-year zero using 60 days, 25 days, 10 days, and 683 days ending 11/12/95.

Annualizing the Standard Deviation

The daily standard deviation can be annualized by multiplying it by the square root of the number of days in a year.[1] That is,

---

[1] For any probability distribution, it is important to assess whether the value of a random variable in one period is affected by the value that the random variable took on in a prior period. Casting this in terms of yield changes, it is important to know whether the yield today is affected by the yield in a prior period. The term *serial correlation* is used to describe the correlation between the yield in different periods. Annualizing the daily yield by multiplying the daily standard deviation by the square root of the number of days in a year assumes that serial correlation is not significant.

Exhibit 5: Calculation of Daily Standard Deviation Based on 25 Daily Observations for 30-Year Treasury Zeros (October 9, 1995 to November 12, 1995)

(1) t	(2) Date	(3) y_t	(4) $X_t = 100[\text{Ln}(y_t/y_{t-1})]$	(5) $(X_t - \bar{X})^2$
0	08-Oct-95	6.694		
1	09-Oct-95	6.699	0.06720	0.02599
2	10-Oct-95	6.710	0.16407	0.06660
3	11-Oct-95	6.675	−0.52297	0.18401
4	12-Oct-95	6.555	−1.81411	2.95875
5	15-Oct-95	6.583	0.42625	0.27066
6	16-Oct-95	6.569	−0.21290	0.01413
7	17-Oct-95	6.583	0.21290	0.09419
8	18-Oct-95	6.555	−0.42625	0.11038
9	19-Oct-95	6.593	0.57804	0.45164
10	22-Oct-95	6.620	0.40869	0.25270
11	23-Oct-95	6.568	−0.78860	0.48246
12	24-Oct-95	6.575	0.10652	0.04021
13	25-Oct-95	6.646	1.07406	1.36438
14	26-Oct-95	6.607	−0.58855	0.24457
15	29-Oct-95	6.612	0.07565	0.02878
16	30-Oct-95	6.575	−0.56116	0.21823
17	31-Oct-95	6.552	−0.35042	0.06575
18	01-Nov-95	6.515	−0.56631	0.22307
19	02-Nov-95	6.533	0.27590	0.13684
20	05-Nov-95	6.543	0.15295	0.06099
21	06-Nov-95	6.559	0.24424	0.11441
22	07-Nov-95	6.500	−0.90360	0.65543
23	08-Nov-95	6.546	0.70520	0.63873
24	09-Nov-95	6.589	0.65474	0.56063
25	12-Nov-95	6.539	−0.76173	0.44586
		Total	−2.35020	9.7094094

$$\text{Sample mean} = \bar{X} = \frac{-2.35025}{25} = -0.09401\%$$

$$\text{Variance} = \frac{9.7094094}{25 - 1} = 0.4045587$$

$$\text{Std} = \sqrt{0.4045587} = 0.6360493\%$$

Exhibit 6: Comparison of Daily and Annual Volatility for a Different Number of Observations (Ending Date November 12, 1995) for Various Treasury Zeros

Number of observations	Daily standard deviation (%)	Annualized standard deviation (%)		
		250 days	260 days	365 days
Treasury 30-Year Zero				
683	0.4901505	7.75	7.90	9.36
60	0.6282858	9.93	10.13	12.00
25	0.6360493	10.06	10.26	12.15
10	0.6242041	9.87	10.06	11.93
Treasury 10-Year Zero				
683	0.7497844	11.86	12.09	14.32
60	0.7408469	11.71	11.95	14.15
25	0.7091771	11.21	11.44	13.55
10	0.7458877	11.79	12.03	14.25
Treasury 5-Year Zero				
683	1.0413025	16.46	16.79	19.89
60	0.8267317	13.07	13.33	15.79
25	0.7224093	11.42	11.65	13.80
10	0.8345784	13.20	13.46	15.94

$$\text{Daily standard deviation} \times \sqrt{\text{Number of days in a year}}$$

Market practice varies with respect to the number of days in the year that should be used in the annualizing formula above. Typically, either 250 days, 260 days, or 365 days are used.

Thus, in calculating an annual standard deviation, the investor must decide on:

1. the number of daily observations to use
2. the number of days in the year to use to annualize the daily standard deviation.

Exhibit 6 shows the difference in the annual standard deviation for the daily standard deviation based on a different number of observations and using 250 days, 260 days, and 365 days to annualize. Exhibit 7 compares the 25-day annual standard deviation for two different time periods for the 30-year zero, 10-year zero, and 5-year zero.

Exhibit 7: Comparison of Daily Standard Deviation Calculated for Two 25-Day Periods

Dates		Daily standard deviation(%)	Annualized standard deviation(%)		
From	To		250 days	260 days	365 days
Treasury 30-Year Zero					
10/8/95	11/12/95	0.6360493	10.06	10.26	12.15
8/20/95	9/24/95	0.8452714	13.36	13.63	16.15
Treasury 10-Year Zero					
10/8/95	11/12/95	0.7091771	11.21	11.44	13.55
8/20/95	9/24/95	0.9044855	14.30	14.58	17.28
Treasury 5-Year Zero					
10/8/95	11/12/95	0.7224093	11.42	11.65	13.80
8/20/95	9/24/95	0.8145416	12.88	13.13	15.56

Interpreting the Standard Deviation

What does it mean if the annual standard deviation for the 30-year zero is 12%? It means that if the prevailing yield is 8%, then the annual standard deviation is 96 basis points (12% times 8%).

Assuming that the yield volatility is approximately normally distributed, we can use the normal distribution to construct an interval or range for what the future yield will be. For example, we know that there is a 68.3% probability that the yield will be between one standard deviation below and above the expected value. The expected value is the prevailing yield. If the annual standard deviation is 96 basis points and the prevailing yield is 8%, then there is a 68.3% probability that the yield next year will be between 7.04% (8% minus 96 basis points) and 8.96% (8% plus 96 basis points). For three standard deviations below and above the prevailing yield, there is a 99.7% probability that the yield next year will be in this interval. Using the numbers above, three standard deviations is 288 basis points (3 times 96 basis points). The interval is then 5.12% (8% minus 288 basis points) and 10.88% (8% plus 288 basis points).

As explained in the previous chapter, the interval or range constructed is called a confidence interval. Our first interval of 7.04%-8.96% is a 68.3% confidence interval. Our second interval of 5.22%-10.88% is a 99.7% confidence interval. A confidence interval with any probability can be constructed.

HISTORICAL VERSUS IMPLIED VOLATILITY

Market participants estimate yield volatility in one of two ways. The first way is by estimating historical yield volatility. This is the method that we have thus far described in this chapter. The resulting volatility is called *historical volatility.* The second way is to estimate yield volatility based on the observed prices of interest rate options and caps. Yield volatility calculated using this approach is called *implied volatility.*

The implied volatility is based on some option pricing model. One of the inputs to any option pricing model in which the underlying is a Treasury security or Treasury futures contract is expected yield volatility. If the observed price of an option is assumed to be the fair price and the option pricing model is assumed to be the model that would generate that fair price, then the implied yield volatility is the yield volatility that when used as an input into the option pricing model would produce the observed option price.

There are several problems with using implied volatility. First, it is assumed the option pricing model is correct. Second, option pricing models typically assume that volatility is constant over the life of the option. Therefore, interpreting an implied volatility becomes difficult.[2]

FORECASTING YIELD VOLATILITY

As can be seen, the yield volatility as measured by the standard deviation can vary based on the time period selected and the number of observations. Now we turn to the issue of forecasting yield volatility. There are several methods. Before describing these methods, let's address the question of what mean should be used in the calculation of the forecasted standard deviation.

Suppose at the end of 10/24/95 a trader was interested in a forecast for volatility using the 10 most recent days of trading and

---

[2] For a further discussion, see Frank J. Fabozzi and Wai Lee, "Measuring and Forecasting Yield Volatility," Chapter 16 in Frank J. Fabozzi (ed.), *Perspectives on Interest Rate Risk Management for Money Managers and Traders* (New Hope, PA: Frank J. Fabozzi Associates, 1998).

updating that forecast at the end of each trading day. What mean value should be used?

The trader can calculate a 10-day moving average of the daily percentage yield change. Exhibit 5 shows the daily percentage change in yield for the Treasury 30-year zero from 10/9/95 to 11/12/95. To calculate a moving average of the daily percentage yield change on 10/24/95, the trader would use the 10 trading days from 10/11/95 to 10/24/95. At the end of 10/25/95, the trader will calculate the 10-day average by using the percentage yield change on 10/25/95 and would exclude the percentage yield change on 10/11/95. That is, the trader will use the 10 trading days from 10/12/95 to 10/25/95.

Exhibit 8 shows the 10-day moving average calculated from 10/24/95 to 11/12/95. Notice the considerable variation over this period. The 10-day moving average ranged from –0.20324% to 0.07902%. For the period from 4/15/93 to 11/12/95, the 10-day moving average ranged from –0.61705% to 0.60298%.

Rather than using a moving average, it is more appropriate to use an expectation of the average. It has been argued that it would be more appropriate to use a mean value of zero.[3] In that case, the variance as given by equation (1) simplifies to:

$$\text{Variance} = \frac{1}{T-1}\sum_{t=1}^{T} X_t^2 \qquad (2)$$

Now let's look at the various methods for forecasting daily volatility.

Equally-Weighted Average Method

The daily standard deviation given by equation (2) assigns an equal weight to all observations.[4] So, if a trader is calculating volatility based on the most recent 10 days of trading, each day is given a weight of 10%.

---

[3] Jacques Longerstacey and Peter Zangari, *Five Questions about RiskMetrics™*, JP Morgan Research Publication 1995.

[4] In April 1995, the Basel Committee on Banking Supervision at the Bank for International Settlements proposed that volatility (as measured by the standard deviation) be calculated based on an equal weighting of daily historical observations using one year of observations. Moreover, the committee proposed that volatility estimates should be updated at least quarterly.

Exhibit 8: 10-Day Moving Daily Average for Treasury 30-Year Zero

10-Trading Days Ending	Daily Average (%)
24-Oct-95	–0.20324
25-Oct-95	–0.04354
26-Oct-95	0.07902
29-Oct-95	0.04396
30-Oct-95	0.00913
31-Oct-95	–0.04720
01-Nov-95	–0.06121
02-Nov-95	–0.09142
05-Nov-95	–0.11700
06-Nov-95	–0.01371
07-Nov-95	–0.11472
08-Nov-95	–0.15161
09-Nov-95	–0.02728
12-Nov-95	–0.11102

Exhibit 9: Moving Daily Standard Deviation Based on 10-Days of Observations

10-Trading Days Ending	Daily Standard Deviation (%)
24-Oct-95	0.75667
25-Oct-95	0.81874
26-Oct-95	0.58579
29-Oct-95	0.56886
30-Oct-95	0.59461
31-Oct-95	0.60180
01-Nov-95	0.61450
02-Nov-95	0.59072
05-Nov-95	0.57705
06-Nov-95	0.52011
07-Nov-95	0.59998
08-Nov-95	0.53577
09-Nov-95	0.54424
12-Nov-95	0.60003

For example, suppose that a trader is interested in the daily volatility of the Treasury 30-year zero yield and decides to use the 10 most recent trading days. Exhibit 9 reports the 10-day volatility for various days using the data in Exhibit 5 and the formula for the variance given by equation (2). For the period 4/15/93 to 11/12/95, the 10-day volatility ranged from 0.16370% to 1.33006%.

Weighted Average Method

There is reason to suspect that market participants give greater weight to recent movements in yield or price when determining volatility. To give greater importance to more recent information, observations further in the past should be given less weight. This can be done by revising the variance as given by equation (2) as follows:

$$\text{Variance} = \frac{1}{T-1}\sum_{t=1}^{T} W_t X_t^2 \tag{3}$$

where W_t is the weight assigned to observation t such that the sum of the weights is equal to 1 (i.e., $\sum W_t = 1$) and the further the observation from today, the lower the weight.

The weights should be assigned so that the forecasted volatility reacts faster to a recent major market movement and declines gradually as we move away from any major market movement. One approach is to use an *exponential moving average*.[5] The formula for the weight W_t in an exponential moving average is:

$$W_t = (1-\beta)\beta^t$$

where β is a value between 0 and 1. The observations are arrayed so that the closest observation is $t = 1$, the second closest is $t = 2$, etc.

For example, if β is 0.90, then the weight for the closest observation ($t = 1$) is:

$$W_1 = (1-0.90)\,(0.90)^1 = 0.09$$

For $t = 5$ and β equal to 0.90, the weight is:

$$W_5 = (1-0.90)\,(0.90)^5 = 0.05905.$$

The smaller the value of β, the lower the relative weight assigned to further observations. For example, for β equal to 0.80, the weight assigned to the first observation is 16%. For the 16th observation, a weight of only 0.6% is assigned. In contrast, for β

---

[5] This approach is suggested by JP Morgan *RiskMetrics*™.

equal to 0.95, the corresponding values for the first and 16th observations are 4.8% and 2.2%, respectively.

The parameter β is measuring how quickly the information contained in past observations is "decaying" and hence is referred to as the "decay factor." The smaller the β, the faster the decay. What decay factor to use depends on how fast the mean value for the random variable X changes over time. A random variable whose mean value changes slowly over time will have a decay factor close to 1. A discussion of how the decay factor should be selected is beyond the scope of this book.[6]

ARCH Method and Variants

A times series characteristic of financial assets suggests that a period of high volatility is followed by a period of high volatility. Furthermore, a period of relative stability in returns appears to be followed by a period that can be characterized in the same way. This suggests that volatility today may depend upon recent prior volatility. This can be modeled and used to forecast volatility.

The statistical model used to estimate this time series property of volatility is called an *a*uto*r*egressive *c*onditional *h*eteroskedasticity (ARCH) model.[7] The term "conditional" means that the value of the variance depends on or is conditional on the value of the random variable. The term heteroskedasticity means that the variance is not equal for all values of the random variable.

The simplest ARCH model is

$$\sigma_t^2 = a + b(X_{t-1} - \bar{X})^2 \tag{4}$$

where

σ_t^2 = variance on day t

$X_{t-1} - \bar{X}$ = deviation from the mean on day $t-1$

and a and b are parameters. The parameters must be estimated statistically. The statistical technique of regression analysis is used to estimate the parameters.

---

[6] A technical description is provided in *RiskMetrics*[TM]*—Technical Document*, pp. 77-79.

[7] See Robert F. Engle, "Autoregressive Conditional Heteroskedasticity with Estimates of Variance of U.K. Inflation," *Econometrica* 50 (1982), pp. 987-1008.

Equation (4) states that the estimate of the variance on day t depends on how much the observation on day $t-1$ deviates from the mean. Thus, the variance on day t is "conditional" on the deviation from day $t-1$. The reason for squaring the deviation is that it is the magnitude, not the direction of the deviation, that is important for forecasting volatility.[8] By using the deviation on day $t-1$, recent information (as measured by the deviation) is being considered when forecasting volatility.

The ARCH model can be generalized in two ways. First, information for days prior to $t-1$ can be included into the model by using the squared deviations for several prior days. For example, suppose that four prior days are used. Then equation (4) can be generalized to:

$$\begin{aligned}\sigma_t^2 &= a + b_1(X_{t-1} - \bar{X})^2 + b_2(X_{t-2} - \bar{X})^2 \\ &\quad + b_3(X_{t-3} - \bar{X})^2 + b_4(X_{t-4} - \bar{X})^2\end{aligned} \tag{5}$$

where a, b_1, b_2, b_3, and b_4 are parameters to be estimated statistically.

A second way to generalize the ARCH model is to include not only squared deviations from prior days as a random variable that the variance is conditional on, but also the estimated variance for prior days. For example, the following equation generalizes equation (4) for the case where the variance at time t is conditional on the deviation squared at time $t-1$ and the variance at time $t-1$:

$$\sigma_t^2 = a + b(X_{t-1} - \bar{X})^2 + c\sigma_{t-1}^2 \tag{6}$$

where a, b, and c are parameters to be estimated statistically.

Suppose that the variance at time t is assumed to be conditional on four prior periods of squared deviations and three prior variances, then equation (4) can be generalized as follows:

$$\begin{aligned}\sigma_t^2 &= a + b_1(X_{t-1} - \bar{X})^2 + b_2(X_{t-2} - \bar{X})^2 + b_3(X_{t-3} - \bar{X})^2 \\ &\quad + b_4(X_{t-4} - \bar{X})^2 + c_1\sigma_{t-1}^2 + c_2\sigma_{t-2}^2 + c_3\sigma_{t-3}^2\end{aligned} \tag{7}$$

---

[8] The variance for the unconditional variance (i.e., a variance that does not depend on the prior day's deviation) is $\sigma_t^2 = a/(1-b)$.

where the parameters to be estimated are a, the b_i's (i=1,2,3,4), and c_j's (j=1,2,3).

Equations (5), (6), and (7) are referred to as *generalized* ARCH or GARCH models. GARCH models are conventionally denoted as follows: GARCH(i,j) where i indicates the number of prior squared deviations included in the model and j the number of prior variances in the model. Equations (5), (6), and (7) would be denoted GARCH(4,0), GARCH(1,1), and GARCH(4,3), respectively.

There have been further extensions of ARCH models but these extensions are beyond the scope of this chapter.[9]

SUMMARY

Yield (interest rate) volatility estimates play a critical role in the both the valuation of bonds with an embedded option and the measurement of risk exposure. In this chapter we have reviewed historical yield volatility, how yield volatility is calculated based on historical volatility, and the issues associated with its estimate.

The standard deviation is commonly used as a measure of volatility. Yield volatility can be estimated from daily yield observations. The observation used in the calculation of the standard deviation is the natural logarithm of the percentage change in yield between two days. Yield volatility is greater at the short end of the yield curve than at the long end. The magnitude of the percentage change in yield depends on the level of yields.

The issues associated with calculating yield volatility using historical data include the number of observations and the time period to be used, the number of days that should be used to annualize the daily standard deviation, the expected value that should be used, and the weighting of observations. The selection of the number of observations and the time period can have a significant effect on the calculated daily standard deviation. A daily standard deviation is annualized by multiplying it by the square root of the number

---

[9] For an excellent overview of these extensions as well as the GARCH models, see Robert F. Engle, "Statistical Models for Financial Volatility," *Financial Analysts Journal* (January-February 1993), pp. 72-78.

of days in a year. Typically, either 250 days, 260 days, or 365 days are used to annualize the daily standard deviation. Assuming that the yield volatility is approximately normally distributed, the annual standard deviation can be used to construct a confidence interval for the yield one year from now.

Implied volatility can also be used to estimate yield volatility. Implied volatility depends on the option pricing model employed. There is not a liquid option market for all yields whose underlying depends on the yield of interest.

In forecasting yield volatility, it is more appropriate to use an expectation of zero for the mean value. The simplest method for forecasting yield volatility is weighting all observations equally. A forecasted yield volatility can be obtained by assigning greater weight to more recent observations such that the forecasted yield volatility reacts faster to a recent major market movement and declines gradually as we move away from any major market movement. Generalized autoregressive conditional heteroskedasticity (GARCH) models can be used to capture the times series characteristic of yield volatility in which a period of high volatility is followed by a period of high volatility and a period of relative stability appears to be followed by a period that can be characterized in the same way.

Index

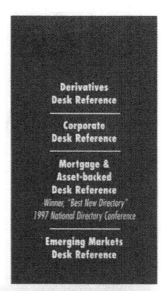

SIZE DOESN'T MATTER...

Why tie yourself down to old-fashioned, hard-wired, calculation behemoths?

Printed and bound by CPI Group (UK) Ltd, Croydon, CR0 4YY
16/04/2023
03210838-0004